Destined for Failure

DESTINED FOR FAILURE

American Prosperity
in the Age of Bailouts

Nicolás Sánchez,
Christopher Kopp,
and Francis Sanzari

 PRAEGER

AN IMPRINT OF ABC-CLIO, LLC
Santa Barbara, California • Denver, Colorado • Oxford, England

Library of Congress Cataloging-in-Publication Data

Sanchez, Nicolas.
  Destined for failure : American prosperity in the age of bailouts / Nicolas Sanchez, Christopher Kopp, Francis Sanzari.
    p. cm.
  Includes bibliographical references and index.
  ISBN 978–0–313–39263–4 (hard copy : alk. paper) — ISBN 978–0–313–39264–1 (ebook)
  1. United States—Economic policy—2009–   2. Government spending policy—United States.   3. Fiscal policy—United States.   4. Keynesian economics.   I. Kopp, Christopher.   II. Sanzari, Francis.   III. Title.
  HC106.84.S36   2010
  330.973—dc22   2010022048

ISBN: 978–0–313–39263–4
EISBN: 978–0–313–39264–1

14 13 12 11 10   1 2 3 4 5

This book is also available on the World Wide Web as an eBook.
Visit www.abc-clio.com for details.

Praeger
An Imprint of ABC-CLIO, LLC

ABC-CLIO, LLC
130 Cremona Drive, P.O. Box 1911
Santa Barbara, California 93116-1911

This book is printed on acid-free paper ∞

Manufactured in the United States of America

Sánchez   *To those who taught me the most*
My mentor, Professor Jeffrey B. Nugent
My aunt, Carmencita San Miguel Pagés[†]
My uncle, José Calle Ripoll[†]
My teacher at Colegio Trelles, Prudencia Díaz[†]
[†]In memoriam

Kopp   *To my parents*
Christopher Kopp, M.D., and Karen Kopp, and all of my
family and friends who encouraged me to complete this
project, especially Gerald A. Buchheit Jr.

Sanzari   *To my parents and twin brother*
Anna, Michael, and Philip Sanzari

CONTENTS

CONTENTS

LIST OF ILLUSTRATIONS

FIGURES

TABLES

FOREWORD

This book is written for a general audience, but especially for those individuals who have doubts that the Bush administration first and now the Obama administration have conducted effective economic policies— but find it difficult to articulate their own concerns. It hopes to attract readers who are surprised that anyone could question the wisdom of recent policies. Is it not the case that all economists agree with what our two most recent presidents have done?

The answer is No. We argue in this book that bailouts, first begun by Bush and then continued by Obama, fail because they do not address productivity growth, which is the main factor driving our economy. The United States faces a serious recession not because there has been a lack of demand for goods and services but rather because there are structural problems that have made the country less competitive relative to other nations. During President George W. Bush's term huge budget deficits arose, and these have expanded during President Barack Obama's tenure. The demand for goods has been so great that it has had to be satisfied with enormous quantities of imports. We will show that most of our problems are our own doing.

The senior author of the book, and writer of this foreword, was telling his students since 2007 that the economy was in serious trouble. He was especially concerned that the United States was rapidly accumulating foreign debts and nothing was being done to bring the international accounts into balance. Both the federal government and consumers were spending as if they faced no budget constraints, and Congress was pressing financial institutions to lend money to people who had little chance of repaying their mortgages. The nation seemed to be experiencing very good times indeed, but its debts were skyrocketing.

Escalating debts have to be repaid, and to do so people need not just high-paying jobs, but jobs that become more productive as time marches on. This has become problematic, as people have imposed more and more constraints on themselves. The auto unions of Detroit, like unions everywhere, demand much for their own members and are not receptive to technological innovations. Teachers' unions want their members to teach fewer students in the classroom (which decreases their members' productivity) and fight vigorously the new technologies that could make teachers more productive. State and municipal budgets grow in size, and unfunded liabilities are not taken into account. These are but a few of the problems that are now familiar to the reader and that illustrate our concerns.

For years, this writer has taught a macroeconomic course that makes little use of Keynesian economics; instead it is based on the work of Harvard professor Robert J. Barro. This distinguished professor emphasizes the factors that enhance productivity and bring about growth in an economy, and to him government spending is no free lunch.[1] While this writer conveyed Barro's theoretical ideas to his students in the fall of 2008, it occurred to him that it would be worthwhile to write a book explaining why U.S. policies and institutions are making the country less and less productive, or at the very least, how they discourage the adoption of new technologies.

However, this writer wanted to make sure that he could reach a broad audience, and as a result invited two of his brightest students to help him produce this work. It has taken us several months to do so, but the experience has been wonderful. We have had the opportunity to present the work-in-progress in four different venues across the United States and even on TV programs. People who have heard these students have been in awe of their intelligence, knowledge, and poise.

The book can be read from start to finish and it will present a coherent argument. However, if the reader wants a summary of this work, we urge him or her to read Chapter 13, which explains the logical structure of the book. For those who believe in the relevance of Keynesian economics, they should first read Chapter 12, which tries to demonstrate that Keynesian economics does not address the problems that we face now.

The reader, however, may want to be more eclectic, and choose topics of special interest. There are many that we offer: the role of information in decision making, why many regulations are counterproductive, an analysis of the health care sector (which is followed by an analysis of health and education proper), the impact of labor unions, housing and financial disasters, the negative role of wars on the economy, our thoughts on the environment and taxation, and the general problem of what is known as moral hazard. We even discuss crony capitalism.

The first two chapters provide the theoretical anchor for all the others (except the one on Keynesian economics). Let me emphasize that this is not a book against John Maynard Keynes, who was a great economist— it is against the facile belief that Keynesian economics has a significant role to play in the current economic environment. Many people still think that we got out of the Great Depression because of the Second World War, failing to understand that wars are like hurricanes; namely, great catastrophes. Sometimes we need to engage in war, but we should do the utmost to avoid them, for they are engines of growth only when they have a major impact on technological progress—that usually affects the economy years after the wars are over.

Neither the Bush nor the Obama administration has faced up to the economic problems; they have both enlarged the size of government bureaucracies and enabled greater union power. Ask yourself, Can a country of bureaucrats and union members generate technological know-how? If you think that the answer is Yes, then ask yourself another question: What will happen to us when we exercise our political power to determine our own salaries, benefits, and incomes? We are only human, and we will use that power to enhance our personal finances. The good news is that the electorate appears to be, as reflected by the Scott Brown Senate election in Massachusetts, weary of more government expenditures and the special interests that drive them.

As of the first quarter of 2010, the stock indexes were recovering some ground from the lows that they reached in March 2009, and many people are interpreting these changes as signs that the economic problems are almost over. We strongly disagree with this perspective. Many factors have to be taken into account. People forget that if an index falls 50 percent of its value (say from 14,000 to 7,000), it needs later to increase 100 percent of its value (from 7,000 to 14,000) to get back to where it began! Furthermore, indexes such as the Dow are biased to reflect success, because they eliminate from their component those companies that have failed or encountered serious difficulties—most recently General Motors, Citigroup, American International Group, the Altria Group, and Honeywell (all within the last two years).

It is regrettable when press and television reporters become partisan supporters of the administration in power, either ignoring the economic problems (during the Bush years) or trying to convince people that our economic problems are almost over (during the Obama administration). At the end of summer 2009, when the monthly unemployment rate went down from 9.5 percent to 9.4 percent, the news was treated with elation by reporters—failing to point out that an additional 247,000 jobs had been lost and that the statistics reflected people dropping out of the labor force. Bob Herbert sadly pointed out that only 65 of every 100 men aged 20 to 24 were working and that just 81 of 100 men were employed in the prime age group of 25 to 34 years. Because this information was printed in an op-ed article, most readers were likely to miss it.[2] As of April 2010, the percentage of people unemployed is close to 10 percent, and the Congressional Budget Office predicted in early 2010 that a 5 percent unemployment rate will not be reached until 2015.[3]

For us, the current recession will not be over until serious structural changes are made in the economy. It may be the case that a gigantic infusion of money into the economy may improve asset values and may even improve the employment situation. However, without structural changes productivity (measured at previous employment levels) will not increase[4] and prices will not reflect true scarcities. The economy will not be working either efficiently or close to its full potential. The Great Depression had periods of weak economic expansions, and the current recession is turning out to be a Great Recession, with similar periods of weak economic expansions.

The most troubling development in the last two years has been that the monetary base has more than doubled and the money supply has grown rapidly. This has allowed the government to bail out favored enterprises, making it harder to achieve the necessary adjustments.

We hope to hear from you and get feedback on the book! Also, we want to thank all of those who made this project possible, including my student Katherine Tedesco, who helped with some of the graphs, and my colleague in the Economics Department, Dr. David Schap, who checked some statistical assertions. Others deserving recognition for their assistance are: Sethu Baskaran, Herbert Brito, Kristyn Dyer, Chip Faulkner, Kristine Maloney, Ken Mandile, Sandi Martinez, John Nolan, Jack Prindiville, Brian Romer, María Elena Sánchez, and Drew Tillman. I used the first draft of this book in my introductory college course *Speculation, Bubbles and Collapse* (Fall 2009), and the students made useful comments that have been incorporated into the book. This writer also thanks his wife, Roxana Sánchez, for her kind support and understanding.

Nicolás Sánchez, Ph.D.
Professor of Economics
College of the Holy Cross
Worcester, MA 01610-2395

NOTES

1. Robert J. Barro, "Government Spending is No Free Lunch," *Wall Street Journal,* January 22, 2009, sec. A.

2. Bob Herbert, "A Scary Reality," *New York Times,* August 11, 2009, sec. A.

3. John D. McKinnon, "A 'Bleak' Budget But Slightly Better," *Wall Street Journal*, February 27, 2010, sec. A.

4. Productivity *naturally* rises as employment falls because the economy is moving along its production function. The productivity improvements that promote growth are those which occur at previous employment levels—in other words, when the production function is shifting up. This technical note is only a warning to those who read the news and might interpret current "productivity gains" as good news.

Chapter 1

INTRODUCTION AND THEORY

The U.S. economy has been in a recession since December 2007, as determined by the National Bureau of Economic Research (NBER), a private organization founded in 1920 which has published information on business cycles since 1929. Contrary to popular belief, a recession is not necessarily announced by the NBER when two consecutive quarters show declines in real (adjusted for inflation) domestic income or output, even though such declines play important roles in the determination of the business cycle. Rather, the NBER declares a recession when "a significant decline in economic activity spreads across the economy, lasting more than a few months, normally visible in production, employment, real income, and other indicators."[1]

Most people erroneously believe that unemployment (which refers to the number of people in the labor force looking for jobs at prevailing wages) rather than employment (which refers to the number of people who actually have jobs) signals the start of recessions. In reality, unemployment lags behind the decline in output and economic activity by several months. The NBER announced the start of the current recession because employment in the economy reached a peak near December 2007, while at the same time production had been flat from September 2007 to June 2008.

Since the 1950s, the United States has faced several recessions, but most have been short. If we go back half a century, a peak in economic activity was reached in 1957 and, from that time to the present, short recessions took place in the following periods: 1957–1958, 1960–1961, 1969–1970, 1973–1975, during 1980, 1981–1982, 1990–1991, and during 2001. In the past quarter century, as detailed in Figure 1.1, the United States has been blessed with three consecutive periods of long-lasting expansions of 92, 120, and 73 months. In contrast, the Great Depression consisted of two periods of recession; the first one lasting from 1929 to 1933 and the second one from 1937 to 1938. The Great Depression was remarkable because the 1929 level of production was not reached again until late in 1940. Most observers believe that this 11-year period of either contracting or weak economic activity and severe unemployment defines the Great Depression.

The current recession that officially began in December 2007 (despite real gross domestic product [GDP] growth in the second quarter of 2008) is unusual because of the confluence of various events: the burst in housing prices, the crash in stock values, the actual and potential insolvency of financial institutions, the large negative balance in international accounts, and extremely low interest rates. The severity of these events has taken people by surprise partly because of the mild business cycles in the recent past.

From July 1990 to December 2007, the economy experienced 16 months of contraction and 193 months of expansion; in other words, only 7.7 percent of the months in this period involved recessions. In contrast, if we go back from August 1957 (a peak in economic activity) to December 2007 (the most recent peak in economic activity), there were 73 months of contraction and 521 months of expansion, giving us recessions in more than 12 percent of the months in the period. But even this larger figure compares favorably to the recessions involving more than 25 percent of the months from August 1929 to August 1957. People wonder, then, how long will the current recession last?

As of the first quarter of 2010, the NBER has yet to declare that the current recession has ended. After four consecutive quarters of declining real GDP, the third quarter of 2009 showed weak growth of 2.2 percent, the fourth quarter showed a stronger expansion of 5.7 percent, and the first quarter of 2010 returned to a weaker expansion of 3.2 percent. According to the April 30, 2010 news release of the Bureau of Economic Analysis, GDP minus change in private inventories "increased 1.6 percent in the first quarter, compared with an increase of 1.7 percent in the fourth."[2] These figures demonstrate the weakness of the current economic expansion. There has not yet been robust expansion in economic activity throughout the country, and it is unlikely that the recession will be over soon. In fact, the U.S. Bureau of Labor Statistics reported employment of the civilian labor force just above 146 million people at the end of 2007, while it was 137 million persons in the first quarter of 2010. The U.S. long-term economic experience up to the start of the recession is shown in Figure 1.1.

The U.S. economy performed rather well from the last quarter of 1957 to the last quarter of 2007, a period of 50 years. The GDP of the United States

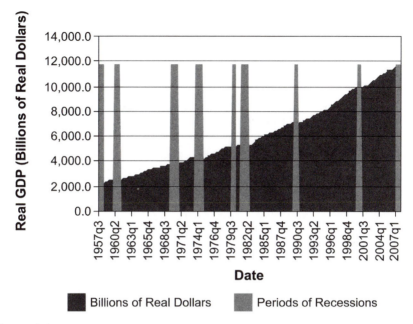

Figure 1.1
U.S. Long Run Economic Growth. Columns are Periods of Recession;
Rising Line Gives Levels of Real GDP in 2000 $s.
Source: U.S. Department of Commerce, Bureau of Economic Analysis

expressed in real terms (adjusted for inflation) has increased by a factor of five, or at the rate of 3.3 percent per year. This happened while the population grew by a factor of 1.75, at the rate of 1.13 percent per year. Neither the Vietnam War (1964–1975) nor the terrorist attacks of September 2001 destroyed the viability of the U.S. economy. Except for the Jimmy Carter presidency (for reasons that will be discussed in Chapter 2) the U.S. economy performed well or at least satisfactorily until 2007.

Regrettably, the George W. Bush presidency came to an end with 13 months of recession and the widespread fear that the recession would turn into a depression. Now, many people are hurting and are fearful about their economic prospects. Most people realize that a bubble in the housing market burst, the stock market collapsed rapidly (even if it now appears to be in a recovery phase), and financial institutions lack the means to recover the loans that they made. These loans appeared as assets in the balance sheets (financial statements that report assets, liabilities, and equity or net worth for households and firms) of financial institutions. Businesses continue to dismiss workers in significant numbers, and the count of unemployed people far surpasses 14 million. Hence the public has good reasons to be hurting, to fear for their economic future, and even to believe that another Great Depression will engulf them. The international trade figures, which are regularly reported by the press, are equally discouraging.

In the shadow of a deep recession and in the midst of public fear, anger, and disappointments, it makes sense to look back to the Great Depression; historians and economists agree that some lessons were learned from that terrible economic experience. The presidency of Franklin D. Roosevelt brought back hope to the people and it is believed that the presidency of Barack Obama has been making every effort to restore the people's confidence. On the economic front, it is widely accepted that reductions in liquidity (the availability of money and credit) and restrictions to international trade via increases in tariffs should not be allowed to happen, for such policies exacerbated and prolonged the Great Depression.

However, knowing what *not* to do is a lot simpler than knowing *what* to do. The counterproductive policies and reactions that followed the 1929 stock market crash and the ensuing depression could be attributed to the lack of good economic theories and poor economic logic. It is for this reason that a new theoretical consensus emerged after 1945, based on the work of the English economist John Maynard Keynes, stipulating that the federal government should have taken forceful actions in getting the United States out of the depression. Yet that Keynesian consensus (reached after the Great Depression) did not face a situation that compared in magnitude to the events after the 1929 stock market crash—with one possible exception, namely those that drove the Japanese economy to crash starting in the 1990s.

There, the financial sector collapsed, a housing market bubble burst, the stock market crashed, and interest rates literally reached zero. Since then the Japanese economy has experienced a prolonged recession that has persisted on and off for almost 20 years. All of this took place despite the Keynesian consensus that sufficient liquidity and massive government expenditures and bailouts had the power to lift a country out of a deep recession. Is it possible, then, to apply successfully to the United States the Keynesian policy tools that have proven unsuccessful in modern day Japan?

Before we proceed to argue in favor of economic reforms rather than the traditional Keynesian tools of excessive liquidity and massive government expenditures and deficits, let us compare and contrast the U.S. and Japanese economies. We begin by emphasizing that the U.S. economy has many positive characteristics. For 50 years prior to the current recession, unemployment rates in the United States have been rather low by international standards. The economy had a long record of steady growth. The population is not just well educated but has demonstrated in international tests that it has achieved high cognitive abilities. Life expectancy has risen. Innovation continues to occur and the United States still generates and files the most patents. Discriminatory barriers have fallen. People from all over the world still try to migrate to the United States. The dollar has been the anchor of international transactions. Most important of all, the United States has retained a democratic process that allows for changes in how the economy is run. However, we must note that the Japanese economy prior to 1990 performed equally well or even better than the U.S. economy. Hence, we must look for differences rather than similarities.

JAPAN GIVES US A CLUE

In many ways, the United States and Japan are very different countries indeed. Their differences are reflected in their cultures, politics, and even economic structures. But because Japan has been, until recently, second only to the United States in economic prowess, we should be able to learn something from Japan's more recent economic experience. The work ethic of the average Japanese is similar to or even better than that of U.S. workers: average workers in both Japan and the United States put up with long hours of work. Both peoples have attained their wealth through hard work and innovation.

However, Japan's political structure is different from that of the United States, because long ago Japan opted for a welfare state. From 1949 on, "the welfare state would cover people against all the vagaries of modern life. If they were born sick, the state would pay. If they could not afford education, the state would pay. If they could not find work, the state would pay. If they were too ill to work, the state would pay. When they retired, the state would pay. And when they finally died, the state would pay their dependents."[3] "By the late 1970s a Japanese politician, Nakagama Yatsuhiro, could boast that Japan had become 'The Welfare Super-Power,' precisely because its system was different from (and superior to) Western models."[4] The difference, which has been pointed out by historian Niall Ferguson, was the willingness of the Japanese to play substantial supporting roles in the welfare system. The Japanese people did not try to game or undermine the system. Japan has had an effective safety net for its people, and yet it has endured a severe and prolonged recession.

The Japanese and U.S. economies are different in another important respect: whereas Japan accumulated assets from abroad almost as rapidly as China, the United States has become indebted to Japan, China, and several oil-producing nations at a speed that is truly unprecedented. And yet despite Japan's prevailing work ethic, despite having a safety net for its people and a consistent effective demand for its output (derived from export markets), and despite its people's willingness to save extraordinary percentages of their income, the country has faced a severe and long-lasting recession since the early 1990s. The one advantage the United States has over Japan is that the U.S. population has continued to expand and is aging at a slower rate. What, then, has gone wrong in Japan since the 1990s?

The Japanese recession has been characterized as a "balance sheet" recession.[5] Japan experienced a housing bubble, a crash in the stock market, and a collapse of financial institutions—which were unable to recover the loans that they had made. Interest rates reached the value of zero. The clue we get from Japan is that its "balance sheet" recession mirrors the events that have led to the current economic contraction in the United States. And it is our opinion that massive government expenditures, bailouts, and excessive liquidity will only prolong U.S. economic distress. The United States is in need of economic reforms, for reasons that will be explained throughout this work.

While this is not the time to explain the reasons behind a balance sheet recession—for that is, in fact, the contribution that this book will make—a few comments are in order. When interest rates reach zero or are close to zero, one would expect that asset prices would be reaching unprecedented heights—and yet they have not! This suggests that for some reason the income potential of those assets has collapsed. Why? That is precisely what needs to be explained.

It has been argued that when asset prices collapse, the goal of firms ceases to be the maximization of profits but rather the minimization of debts.[6] To the extent that firms still make some money and have some positive cash flows, the funds are used to retire debt rather than to engage in new productive activities. The circular flow of funds in the economy is broken and something needs to be done to repair it. The question that remains, and the question that we address in this work, is whether this circular flow can be repaired from the demand side *or* the supply side of the market.

Some readers might find that the last three paragraphs use abstract notions that may be beyond their comprehension at this point. However, we urge these readers to be patient and follow the arguments that we are about to set forth. We will begin by explaining the role of balance sheets in capturing the concept of wealth.

BALANCE SHEETS CAPTURE HOUSEHOLDS' WEALTH

All households start out with some assets; by this we mean that households are made up of people with basic labor skills who may also possess land, property, and financial instruments (such as bonds) which are capable of generating income in the future. It is correct to assert that for most households *people* are the most important asset, because individuals generate the largest share of household income. Regrettably, people in the modern world have relatively short productive lives, being dependent on others for approximately the first 20 years of their lives and, if they live long enough, dependent on others for another 20 years or more after retirement. It is unusual for people to earn income from their own labor for more than 40 years. Most often, people either depend on transfers from others or they accumulate physical and financial assets that they use up as their lives come to an end.

Land, which is a technical term commonly used not only for land itself but also for natural resources, can serve to provide income throughout a lifetime. The same is true of physical capital, either in the form of housing, buildings, or business enterprises—some of which is held in the form of stocks in companies. Finally, financial instruments, in the form of bonds, 401Ks, or rights over pension funds (of one type or another, including government pensions) also generate income. However, ultimately, people get income from their own labor, from natural resources, from physical capital that is endowed with productive potential, or from transfers of income from other individuals. (As a first approximation, which will be modified later, financial instruments are not productive in their own right—they simply assign the income that is generated by land, labor, and capital to different economic players.)

The three inputs of labor, land, and capital constitute the main factors of production that go into the production of commodities; their productivity is helped by technological know-how, which is difficult but not impossible to measure. Another factor affecting production is the type of environment in which all inputs come together to generate output; more on this point later.

People also acquire liabilities during the course of their lives. Although it is common to think of these liabilities in terms of the debts that one individual or firm owes others, we want the reader to think of liabilities in two different senses. First, there are the monetary debts that occur when people borrow funds to purchase education, or to purchase automobiles, houses, and businesses. The reason for incurring these debts is to make individuals more productive. When they do, people repay their debts. These debts or liabilities are formally included in balance sheets. Second, there are liabilities of a different type; namely events or circumstances that make people or other assets less productive. These other liabilities are *drawbacks* which decrease the earning potential of people, natural resources, physical capital, or even technology. These other liabilities (or drawbacks) diminish the value of assets that appear in balance sheets.

Several examples will help convey the full importance of these drawbacks. A worker who suffers a temporary or permanent physical disability has a lower earning potential. Physical capital that is in the path of a hurricane will be damaged and will produce fewer services—thereby also reducing its earning potential. Natural resources that are displaced in the production process by alternative resources, because of a technological change, also fall in value. Land values depend on the demographic circumstances that make them more or less productive. Old technologies become obsolete as new technologies are developed.

Using the concept of "liability as drawback" allows us to understand that the wealth of households—which is the combined net worth of individuals in the household—corresponds not simply to the difference between all assets (human and non-human) that they possess and all of their financial liabilities in the strict sense of debts, but to the productive potential of individual assets. A well-trained professional with a high income potential will suffer a tremendous drawback if he or she becomes a paraplegic after an accident. The general idea can be extended to firms and even to countries. Firms and countries do not become disabled, of course, but they suffer significant drawbacks that reduce the value of their assets. The 2010 earthquakes in Haiti and Chile demonstrate this point. In many ways, this work is about the drawbacks that sometimes households, firms, governments, and even countries face—or even that they impose on themselves, thereby reducing their own wealth.

BALANCE SHEETS REFLECT THE HEALTH OF FIRMS

Let us now turn to the success or failure of firms. Firms are similar to households, but with one important difference: they are created with the intention of lasting forever. They combine human and non-human resources to generate income for their owners, and when these owners die, the firms can be sold and resold to successive generations. To be successful, firms must produce goods and services that satisfy the needs of consumers and governments, for otherwise their productive potential is destroyed. Firms try to generate profits. Profits are the bottom line which capture the health of firms, for without them the firms are absorbed by others, go bankrupt, or get liquidated—returning the value of the existing assets to the current owners of the firm. As profits accumulate, more assets can be bought and debts get paid off. Therefore, the net worth entry on balance sheets reflects the economic health of firms.

Firms, too, engage in borrowing activities that allow them to acquire productive assets. These are their financial liabilities. But firms, like individuals, also experience drawbacks that affect their value. The product that firms sell may go out of style; or the environment in which they operate may become more risky in the presence of events with negative consequences for profits. Production costs can also rise, reducing the difference between revenues and costs, thereby diminishing profits. Taxes can reduce the profits that are left for the owners of the firm and hence reduce the equity of the firm. Competition from newcomers reduces the prices that firms charge and hence also their revenues. The list of drawbacks is endless but some are more important than others, as we will observe in the rest of this work.

BALANCE SHEETS OF GOVERNMENTS ARE MOST IMPORTANT

While firms are created with the hope that they have a long duration—though in fact they may not—national governments do have, for all practical purposes, an indefinite (but not infinite) life span. It does not matter that households disappear and that firms pass on: national governments stay, from the viewpoint of all participants in the economic process. National governments set the rules for economic processes within a confined physical space that is changed only as the result of conquest or war. This reality makes governments far from efficient entities. While households are created, expand, contract, and ultimately disappear, and while firms are created with a specific purpose or goal in mind, evolve over time, and ultimately vanish, national governments are unwilling to let go of the things they control. Their ability to endure depends on their coercive power to tax and their constitutional power to create funds out of thin air. Sometimes they need to use force to guarantee their existence. Yet their success or failure also depends on their balance sheets. Let us explain.

The assets of national governments are not simply the buildings, roads, jails, ships, planes, and natural resources that they own, but also their power to tax the income of households and firms. To the extent that governments provide an environment where households and firms prosper, the wealth of national governments can also increase.

Governments, of course, must provide services to people in order to gain legitimacy and justify their existence. These services are in effect their liabilities, for the public expects services that contribute to its general welfare and prosperity. To provide these services, governments must acquire physical assets and natural resources that, in conjunction with labor, can be used to serve the needs of people. In this sense, national governments are no different from households or firms, for all three entities require the production of goods and services. To understand the unique role and importance of government, let us consider one type of government service: national and local security.

The national government must acquire physical capital to provide national security: It needs military bases, ships, planes, embassies abroad, satellites, and so on, to give everyone security; similarly, it must hire people to run these assets and make them productive. Regrettably, the economic efficiency of these productive units is difficult to measure, and their benefits are not acknowledged until something goes wrong. When it comes to national security, the government is in the business of reducing risks—namely, limiting the number of events that can generate deaths, fear, and mayhem in the population that it protects. Governments, too, must prevent other governments from taking away the assets of their own citizens.

When governments fail to provide security, whether national or local security (which is provided in the United States by federal, state, and local police forces), the value of assets held by the population must fall for at least two reasons. People will demand the reestablishment of prior security levels, and people will take into their own hands the provision of their own security. Because resources must come from somewhere, either the population will be taxed more heavily to get better security or people will have to use their own private resources to provide for safer environments. In other words, when we talk about government activities, society as a whole faces a budget or resource constraint which depends upon every person's and every asset's productive capacity. Simply, as the saying goes, there is no free lunch.

When we look at security in general we gain additional insights. Technical changes, such as the deployment of satellites or surveillance cameras in the streets, increase security—making asset prices for households and firms increase because the productivity of these assets has in fact increased. Waste in government, on the other hand, makes us all poorer, as would happen if security measures were in fact useless or even counter-productive (increasing potential conflicts, for example). The problem with government expenditures is that there is no bottom line (profits) that serves as a guidepost to evaluate whether the expenditures are worth the benefits that they provide. We must never forget that those expenditures draw on resources that could be used elsewhere, even when those expenditures are supported not from taxes but by the creation of money out of thin air.

It is regrettable that governments do not issue balance sheets; instead they produce budgets that reflect income and expenditures over limited periods of time. These budgets reflect the income potential of households and firms, but only imperfectly. The economic health of nations is affected by the promises that governments make to their citizens, for these promises depend upon future tax burdens that the governments must impose on those same citizens. The promises may be unrealistic or even counterproductive, if citizens realize that future tax burdens impair their own ability to generate net income.

Also, the failure to provide balance sheets allows government officials to hide how well or poorly assets are being managed. It is ironic that governments force firms to disclose the market value of their assets, yet governments make no effort to estimate the value of their own assets, which are vast in number and complexity. (The reader may think of the vast land holdings of federal, state, and local governments to appreciate this point.) Equally important, governments do not publicly measure the value of the promises that they have made to their citizens—this is equivalent to failing to reveal the tax burden that citizens will face in future years. Unfunded liabilities of governments, regrettably, have become widespread.

VALUE OF INFRASTRUCTURE AND SOCIAL CAPITAL IN GENERATING WEALTH

The bottom line (savings and profits) is easy to observe for households and for firms. In the former case, when accumulated savings vanish and net worth becomes negative, households break up or require the assistance of third parties (private or public charities) to survive. In the latter case, firms without profits and with negative equity dissolve, are absorbed by other firms, or literally go bankrupt. And yet, this simple analysis fails to capture all the factors that affect the productive capacity of households and firms. We must also understand the environment in which these entities operate.

Let us first consider simple economic activities that are carried out between households and firms. These activities require an infrastructure of roads and government services that are generally taken for granted. Security is assumed; the enforcement of contracts is also assumed; clean water and sewer services are taken for granted. Weather forecasts are provided by government agencies, and insurance against national disasters is dealt with by state and national governments. In effect, government services generate environments that make households and firms more productive. (The reason for government intervention resides in the "public goods" nature of the services provided and in the existence of natural monopolies that require governmental provision or supervision—these topics are discussed in various chapters.) Governments are, then, in the business of providing many intermediate goods—namely, those goods that facilitate the production of other goods that are directly consumed by households and firms (consumption and investment goods). When these intermediate government goods are missing, the country is worse off, and this will be reflected in the balance sheets of households and firms. Let us go back to security to illustrate this point.

The catastrophe referred to as "9/11" affected the productivity of airlines, as they had to devote more resources to the screening of luggage and passengers, and they had to reconfigure the internal layout of planes. Households, too, were affected as the national government undertook a war to root out terrorism—which had to be funded by an increase in taxes. The reallocation of resources toward security was inevitable and, due to the ever-present budget or resource constraint, the output of labor and physical assets in the private sector had to decrease.

This last sentence needs further elaboration, for it is at the heart of what this work is all about. A skeptic could argue that the switching of resources from one type of activity (e.g., vacations) to another (e.g., security) has in no way altered the country's productive capacity or wealth. The GDP, which measures the current value of newly produced goods and services, should not necessarily fall. The skeptic could even argue that some asset values (e.g., resorts) would fall while other asset values (e.g., those of firms engaged in the provision of security) would rise. But there are two problems with these assertions.

First, even if gross domestic output, as measured in official statistics, remained unchanged, it is the case that the well-being of the population decreases as security initially falls and is then restored. Security is both a final good (because people derive a feeling of safety from it) and an intermediate good (because in its absence households and firms are forced to use precautionary measures, and hence resources, to protect the productivity of their assets). Hence a decrease in security makes people worse off. Even after security is restored, people remain worse off as long as potential threats remain and resources are tied up in maintaining appropriate security levels.

Second, security is provided mainly by government agencies, and there is no market for shares in government. We grant that some firms will be selling some additional security-related goods and services to governments and that the value of these few firms will rise; but the bulk of security is provided by government, and therefore the equity of most other firms will fall in value as resources are transferred to governments. Security is, in large measure, an intermediate good. Therefore, gross domestic output should fall as more resources are used up in security measures.

One additional elaboration is necessary. It is well known that GDP is *not* a measure of our well-being, a point that is made clear by a vast literature on the use of natural resources. When we deplete our natural resources, our national income may stay constant but our national wealth, which measures the income potential of our country over time, has to decrease. This is reflected in the asset values of that country. A satisfactory level of security is equivalent to a capital resource that is maintained. When the security level in a country falls, the national wealth of that country also falls.

For lack of a better term, we should think of security as part of our social capital. The concept of social capital is normally defined in terms of the trust that facilitates exchange among people. When people fear one another as a result of terrorism in particular, or lack of security in general, the cost of producing commodities has to increase, and the level of final goods and services that the economy is able to produce must fall. This means that asset values, and the value of equity and net worth in balance sheets, are a better measure of how well an economy is performing than GDP, as we will demonstrate below with a simple thought experiment.

THOUGHT EXPERIMENT

Suppose that there are two countries (A and B) with similar populations and similar amounts of land resources and physical capital. In one of the countries distrust and fear prevail, while this is not the case in the other country. Twins come up with a technological discovery that will reduce production costs for an identical and important production process in each country. Twin A develops the discovery in country A where fear and distrust prevail, while twin B develops it in country B. The increase in asset values in the country lacking trust will be less than in the country where

trust prevails—for the simple reason that in the former the costs of implementing and maintaining the technology will be much higher than in the
latter. And yet, because government expenditures are counted as part of
gross domestic output, the two countries will *appear* as if their outputs
were the same. However, asset values in country B (which produces a
greater output of final goods because fewer resources are used for security) should be higher than asset values in country A—and hence asset
values turn out to be better measures of welfare in each country.

This argument can be generalized to any type of social capital—meaning
more generally any type of institutional arrangement (both formal and
informal) that facilitates trade, because social capital increases the productivity of human or physical capital, or even natural resources. While the
consequences of greater or lesser social capital (in this case, greater or
lesser amounts of security) are easier to see when national, state, and local
governments are involved, it must be clearly stated that cultural norms of
behavior and institutional arrangements that contribute to social capital
can originate at the household, firm, or government levels.

Let us take up some examples. A government that promotes market
exchange is providing social capital that is more productive than a
government that promotes central decision making, at least under normal
circumstances, because the market provides signals about supply and
demand that lead to better resource allocations. A government of laws is
more efficient than a government of men, for the former has consistent
rules while the latter has arbitrary mandates. A government that prevents
discrimination allows for an efficient allocation of human resources.

Similarly, a firm or even an industry that is in the business of providing
public information generates more or less social capital to the extent that
the information is accurate and easy to evaluate. A firm that promotes
innovation and takes into account the evolving nature of the environment
will last longer, will facilitate trade, and will increase output at a lower
cost. A household that builds up the human capital of its members,
making them honest, truthful, and hardworking, helps to create a social
environment that promotes trust and hence productivity in the economy.

One final but important analysis follows. It was previously stated that
financial instruments are not productive in their own right. Yet these financial instruments serve to reallocate resources among productive units,
deploying them where they can yield the greatest return. Financial assets,
then, are an essential part of the social capital that facilitates trade. Financial
markets, when they are well structured and people have confidence in them,

both direct the assignment of income streams and embody the trust that is needed to carry out impersonal transactions. Labor, land, and capital without government-provided infrastructure and privately provided financial instruments would cease to be highly productive resources.

OUR APPROACH

In this introductory chapter we have identified the factors that generate output and wealth. These are land, labor, physical capital, and social capital. To these we must add technology, which is embodied in the various factors of production. While most of these factors can be measured, some of them cannot be bought and sold. We have pointed out that social capital, in the form of trust, can be a part of the culture that pervades the environment where economic transactions take place. Financial instruments embody trust and information, but they are fragile instruments that lose their worth once people engage in deception and malfeasance. Having truthful and dependable information is so important that it will be discussed in Chapter 2.

For some readers, our discussion will appear far removed from the policy prescriptions that would get the economy moving away from a severe recession or possibly a second Great Depression; however, we all must try to understand the environment the United States faces. We have argued that the U.S. situation is similar to that of Japan in the last two decades, with drastic falls in asset prices, large drops in the net worth of firms, decreases in the wealth of households, and most importantly, interest rates that are close to zero. Japan has taken up a Keynesian approach to its economic problems, bailing out firms, extending liquidity to the financial sector, and engaging in dramatic expenditures in infrastructure projects. Yet Japan is not yet out of its recession.

Our approach agrees with the idea that the balance sheets of firms, households, and governments are crucial in understanding the U.S. situation, and we will go as far as to claim that the United States faces, too, what has been described for Japan as a "balance sheet" recession. Yet our use of the concept of a "balance sheet" recession is more didactic than analytical: it is intended to show how the economic problem *confronts* households, firms, and governments, but it does not explain *why* the problems arise in the first place.

We find it incredible that, after the second Bush administration expanded the size of government and ran huge government deficits, some people argue that the nature of the problem is based on the lack of demand for goods and services. Households, firms, and governments are broke not because someone lacked the ability to purchase their goods but because they produced costly goods or acquired the wrong goods—in the sense that these goods did not enhance the productive capacity of the economy.

We want, on the contrary, to emphasize the productive side of economic activities; this approach is commonly associated with explanations for the real business cycle and growth theory. However, we are not trying to predict the business cycle, but rather the systemic failure of the U.S. economy—for the damage that has been done to the U.S. economy is so profound that a long-term recession (similar to Japan's) is on the horizon.

The two most recent administrations have increased the money supply by large amounts, trying to restore the status quo ante prior to the meltdown of the economy. This solution may be effective within the span of two or three years, after which the probability of high inflation increases; but this solution does not address the structural problems which we will describe in detail. The government's dangerous approach may turn out to be politically viable: it may even increase asset values, employment, and economic activity, prompting the NBER to declare that the current recession is over. Such finding, however, without the needed structural changes that we propose, will turn out to be short lasting and misleading.

Let us recall that the Great Depression was made up of two recessions, lasting from 1929 to 1933 and from 1937 to 1938, and that the 1929 level of production was not reached until 1940, when the Great Depression was considered to be over. Given the current deep and long-lasting recession, we will not be content to declare this extraordinary period finished until a real GDP level of $13.4 trillion (in chained 2005 dollars) is reached— the level of real output that occurred the second quarter of 2008—and employment goes back to the 146 million people who were working at the start of the recession. We will be willing to call this long period of either contracting or weak economic activity the Great Recession, using the terminology of Bob Herbert in his 2009 op-ed piece in the *New York Times*.[7]

NOTES

1. National Bureau of Economic Research, Business Cycle Dating Committee, "The NBER's Recession Dating Procedure," January 7, 2008, http://www.nber.org/cycles/jan08bcdc_memo.html.

2. Bureau of Economic Analysis, "Gross Domestic Product: First Quarter 2010 (Advance Estimate)," April 30, 2010.

3. Niall Ferguson, *The Ascent of Money: A Financial History of the World* (New York: Penguin, 2008), 207.

4. Ibid., 208.

5. Richard C. Koo, *The Holy Grail of Macro Economics: Lessons from Japan's Great Recession* (Singapore: Wiley, 2008).

6. Ibid., 14–16.

7. Bob Herbert, "A Scary Reality," *New York Times*, August 11, 2009, sec. A.

Chapter 2

SURVIVING THE MEDIA AGE
OF MISINFORMATION

The main role of markets is to provide economic information, by which we mean signals that allow participants in the economy to make decisions that promote their goals. These signals are embedded in the prices that markets generate. Both consumers and producers have to be aware of the *relative prices* of goods and services (including the going wage rates); consumers and policy makers have to be aware of the *real prices* that determine the purchasing power of income; and everyone has to know the *value of time*, as it is reflected in interest rates. Importers and exporters must determine both the relative and real price of foreign currencies.

While the list of relevant prices is endless (though the most important will be explained below), the importance of accurate information cannot be underestimated. A country may possess an abundance of land, labor, physical capital, and useful technology, and yet, if the signals that determine the allocation of resources are not consistently in accord with the truth or facts, then the economy will not be productive. That is why the U.S.S.R. and China failed when they used a system of commands to direct their economies.

We do not deny that successful economies require an ample supply of factors of production and social capital (which involves institutional structures that promote trust and the rule of law) but here we argue that the lack of accurate information can be very damaging to the success of an economy. Surprisingly and often, the information is available but is inaccurately reported or improperly conveyed; that is the topic of this chapter. The reader who fully understands the distinction between nominal and relative prices, and that between nominal and real prices, may skip this chapter; however, the reader should also be cognizant of how often the media convey misinformation.

One of the first lessons that students of economics learn is that decisions must be made using relative and real prices rather than *nominal* prices. This distinction is crucial to understanding economics. Economics stresses that nominal prices—namely those that simply carry a dollar sign—are generally misleading. Whether an apple costs $1 or $100 is not of much relevance; the problem is deciding two things: how much apples cost relative to goods that could substitute for apples (known as the *relative price* of a good) and how much apples cost relative to the cost of all other goods (known as the *real price* of a good).

The importance of determining the price of goods relative to other economic variables cannot be underestimated. If apples cost $1 and oranges cost 5¢, then apples are expensive items. If apples cost $20 but substitute goods cost more than $25, then apples are relatively cheap—the relative price of apples is low. If apples cost $20 but the average income of people is $1 million as a result of inflation, then the purchase of apples is not a problem for consumers.

Real variables refer to nominal variables (stated simply in dollar terms) divided by the price level (which captures the average of all prices or the average price of a large bundle of commodities). Real variables, then, are similar to relative variables but make comparisons that are broader in scope. When we can talk about the real income of consumers we divide the nominal income by the price level, being aware that the consumer can purchase a broad range of goods and services. The real interest rate is found by adjusting the interest rate listed in newspapers for inflation. Relative commodity prices are important because they signal to producers how scarce various commodities are, thereby allowing producers to make appropriate production decisions.

We will now discuss four variables of extreme importance to the economy: real interest rates, the real price of goods and services, the real quantity of money, and the real price of foreign exchange.

REAL INTEREST RATES

Anyone who has dealt with people in the business world knows that their attention is consumed by interest rates. This requires an explanation, for there is little doubt that no other prices in the economy can match their importance. At any one period of time, goods and services are exchanged at specific relative prices. But it must be recognized that at different times the same goods and services can exchange for different relative prices. Here is where interest rates play a role: they serve as links that chain together prices across time periods—even when there is no inflation! As the saying goes, time is money, and one way of thinking of interest rates is as the price that links the value of goods across time periods.

Let us begin by assuming that there is no inflation, to simplify the analysis. If you pay for a car, it makes a big difference whether you pay for it now, later, or over several time periods. Suppose the car now costs $20,000. If somehow the seller accepted payment 10 years from now, the seller would demand later a lot more than $20,000; for if he had $20,000 and banks were paying 10 percent on deposits, he could take the money now and deposit it in a bank, and 10 years later have the sum of $51,874.85. Notice that if the interest rate on deposits were 5 percent, then the $20,000 now would convert to $32,577.89 later. In other words, interest rates affect the relative price of commodities across time. Imagine that! *One single price affects the relative price of all goods and services across time*. It is for this simple reason that interest rates are so important for business and economic decisions, because failure to take into account the relevant interest rate will lead to losses and the misallocation of economic resources.

We must now tackle two important complications. The first one is inflation. If a farmer lends out a ton of wheat, he or she will expect to be paid back later a ton of wheat plus interest on that ton of wheat. As it happens, of course, people do not generally borrow and lend commodities—they borrow and lend money. But the purchasing power of money is affected by inflation. Hence, if a ton of wheat were worth $4,000 and the borrower repaid the farmer $8,000 a year later, we remain uncertain as to whether the farmer gained or lost income. If the rate of inflation were 100 percent, then the farmer gained nothing. The farmer literally lost income, for he or she should have received $4,000 plus an interest return that exceeded 100 percent. In other words, interest rates have to be adjusted for inflation. The common formula, which works well enough when inflation is low, is simply that the nominal rate of interest (which is quoted in the newspapers) should equal the real rate of interest (that reflects the value of time) plus the inflation rate. Regrettably, nominal interest rates reflect at best expected rather than actual inflation, and so the actual real returns that individuals get can easily diverge from the real returns that they want to receive.

The important thing to remember is that economic decisions should be made using real variables, not nominal variables. Hence, if the interest rate quoted in the media is 7 percent, but the actual and expected rate of inflation is 6 percent, then the lender is paying only 1 percent for the value of time. Yet here is where the media go wrong, for the media report nominal interest rates without consideration for the expected or the actual rate of inflation. Hence a 20 percent interest rate may be quite low, in fact, if the expected and actual rate of inflation is 19 percent; on the other hand, an interest rate of 2 percent may in fact be quite high, if the expected and actual rate of inflation turns out to be negative 5 percent (meaning that the economy is facing conditions of deflation). In that case the value of time is 7 percent, which would be extremely high by historical standards.

There is one other important complication. Interest rates are also affected by a risk factor. The U.S. government is supposed to borrow money at no risk to the lender. Other businesses, however, borrow money that might not be repaid. Hence nominal interest rates must also take into consideration what is called a risk premium, in addition to an inflation premium. Determining these risk premiums is quite difficult, and there are agencies that attempt to determine the risk associated with financial instruments. Regrettably, rating agencies have recently failed to be well informed and have systematically understated the risk that lenders faced vis-à-vis borrowers.

These are the conclusions that we must draw when the media report interest rates. First, they report nominal rates, giving most people the false impression that nominal rates are the important variables for making economic decisions; this represents misinformation. Second, the media make no attempt to report expected rates of inflation, even though some sources for this information are available. Third, if and when the media report expectations of inflation, they have the responsibility to report the actual rates of inflation at a later date—allowing readers to evaluate the credibility of the media reports for these expectations. Fourth, the media must report the actual real rates of interest, which should take into account the nominal interest rates, the actual rates of inflation, and, if at all possible, the risk premium reported by credit agencies. Finally, the media ought to evaluate the reports of credit agencies by reporting on the accuracy of their past predictions.

Because none of the above is generally done, it is not surprising that some economists and financial analysts earn their living by filtering out raw data and converting it into useful information. Most citizens do not have the luxury of obtaining the assistance of experts in the field, but they should still be educated and constantly reminded of what constitutes valuable economic news. When the media reports, and insists on reporting, that interest rates are rising—when the expected and the actual real interest rates are in fact falling—it becomes impossible for experts in the field to convince the general public that markets are informing everyone that the value of time is falling, rather than rising.

If the United States is misinformed regarding its most basic economic price, how is it then possible for the population to undertake personal decisions that make economic sense or, even more importantly, to vote for policy proposals that make economic sense? The presidency of Jimmy Carter, who (though otherwise well intentioned) was either totally ignorant of economic analysis or totally misinformed about the consequences of his policies, illustrates well the danger of misinformation. By almost any measure of expected inflation, expected real interest rates during his presidency were in negative territory, and the same was true for actual real rates of interest. The four years of Carter's presidency undermined the health of the financial sector—which is crucial for the efficient allocation of resources—and that could have led to the total destruction or ineffectiveness of this industry. Somehow, though, the media failed to report that the Carter administration was slowly but surely leading the United States toward economic collapse.

THE REAL PRICE OF COMMODITIES AND SERVICES

Most businesses have to know the real price of the goods and services they produce and sell—and in fact they do, for otherwise they could not survive the marketplace. When a producer of shirts is selling them for a price that is rising over time by 2 percent per year, but inflation is rising at an average rate of 5 percent per year, the producer knows that the relative value of shirts is falling and that he or she must consider moving on to produce some other commodity or, at the very least, install different production processes that would decrease production costs.

Producers, of course, also pay wages, and they must determine whether these wages are rising, falling, or remaining constant in real terms. The workers themselves have to attend to the real value of those wages (wages divided by an index of inflation), for if they do not then they will have no clue as to whether their economic situation is improving, worsening, or staying the same. Because labor markets are quite dynamic, employees must determine whether they should stay in their jobs or move on to improve their economic situation. These location changes occur by the movement of individuals from job to job and by the moving of families from one part of the nation to another.

However, the information problems that employees face are particularly severe. On the one hand, different jobs require different skills, which may take time to acquire and in some cases may be impossible to obtain. Then there is the problem of judging correctly the total compensation packages that are available in the labor market. The tax code is such that it pays employers to hide the total compensation that employees receive—which includes not just the nominal salaries, but also perquisites, health insurance, retirement benefits, and bonuses that may be available.

If the media had the goal of improving labor markets and hence assisting in the workings of the macro economy, it would make every effort to report regularly the full compensation packages that are available to workers across all levels of skills and across all local and regional markets. Yet, this is rarely done, despite the ease of access to such information.

First we note that the government sector is a very important part of the economy, making up at least 35 percent of all economic activity in the United States. The media have the right to obtain information about government employees, which is in fact readily available but hardly ever published in newspapers or other media. Such information includes the salaries of public school teachers and public officials. While there is no need to reveal what individuals actually make in government jobs, it would be appropriate to reveal the average salaries of school teachers (taking into account grade levels and experience), administrative staff positions, clerks in municipalities, police officers and firefighters, toll takers, social service workers, and medical personnel in public hospitals. These salaries can be compared both with national salaries published by the census and with the average income of workers in the communities where the media are located.[1]

Regrettably, even this information may not be enough to provide an accurate measure of the *total* compensation for services rendered, which would include the actual number of hours worked, vacation time and sick leave, workers' contribution to health insurance, and, possibly most important, the retirement packages that have been promised. While it is more difficult to determine this information, one should not underestimate the impact that this could have on labor markets, because efficiency requires that all human resources be allocated to their highest value in use. In addition, minorities will be especially helped by the public availability of such information, given that they face discrimination and often language barriers that make it difficult to conduct the appropriate search.

Now, the argument could be made that it is not fair to divulge the full compensation packages of only public employees, and this is a valid criticism. But we must remember the packages for other sectors of the population are equally accessible, even if a greater effort is required to uncover such information. Besides public employees, we have industries that are regulated and industries that are part of the non-profit sector. Most of these industries also have full reporting requirements, which are generally available upon inquiry. Universities (most of which are non-profit institutions) provide documents with details about salaries and full compensation of employees. These documents, in summary form, should be retrieved by the media and published and broadcast on a regular basis—once again with comparisons of the salaries of people with comparable skills. Similar documents are prepared by non-profit social service agencies and non-profit medical entities. Again, summaries of these documents ought to be made public.

It now seems well established, too, that organizations receiving subsidies from the state (in the form of bailouts or for other reasons) should provide information that is demanded of them. A large number of such organizations, from farmers to car manufacturers to the highest-paid bankers, fall under this umbrella. All the organizations receiving taxpayer subsidies should be required by legislation to provide public information about salaries and packages earned by their employees.

Finally, then, we have those economic entities that are nongovernmental, for profit, and not receiving subsidies by the state. It should be no surprise that they represent less than half of all economic entities—but even these entities report compensation to federal agencies, and the information gets published as part of labor statistics or other federal censuses. As previously mentioned, this information can be used to make comparisons with the specific data that has been obtained from other sectors of the economy. There is much to be gained by this. Beginning, for example, with the average income of communities (which is readily available in census figures) one can then compare how well government employees are compensated, how well the non-profit sector is paid, and how much the workers in subsidized industries are earning. This would facilitate the allocation of resources in the short run, allow individuals to make better decisions about their long-run human capital investments, and even help businesses better target their potential customers. Without doubt, this information will surprise people who are not familiar with the data.

While most of this section has been devoted to the labor market, one type of commodity that has become crucial to the well-being of society deserves special attention: energy. It comes in various guises: as electricity, natural gas, home-heating oil, and petrol-related products such as gasoline

and diesel fuel. The media periodically report the prices of these commodities, but improperly, because they fail to correct nominal prices for
inflation.

The above correction is extremely important because people live under
the false impression that the cost of energy has consistently skyrocketed
over many years, when in fact this is far from the truth. The real costs of
oil and other types of energy have had long periods of decline, with only
short-lived and abrupt increases in real costs, mainly because of political
factors. While the nominal prices of oil and other types of energy have
dramatically increased over time, so have the prices of all other basic
commodities as a result of inflation. Once inflation is factored in, the
results are surprising indeed. First, let us look at the price of natural gas
delivered to consumers, in real terms with the CPI = 100 in 1983 and the
data ending in October 2009. The data in Figure 2.1 come from the U.S.
Energy Information Administration.

This graph is remarkable because it shows that the real price of natural
gas delivered to consumers at the start of 1983 was a bit higher than the
price in October 2009. In nominal terms, of course, the story is quite
different, because prices went from $5.86 to $11.65 over the time period.

A similar story can be told with gasoline prices, using the same time
period (see Figure 2.2). The nominal price of gasoline in January 1983

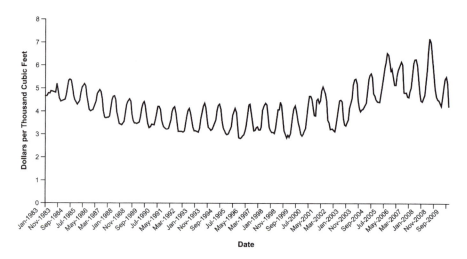

Figure 2.1
U.S. Real Price of Natural Gas.
Source: U.S. Energy Information Administration

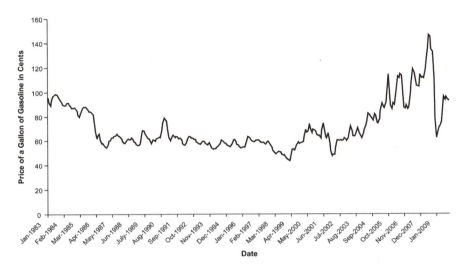

Figure 2.2
U.S. Real Price of Gasoline.
Source: U.S. Energy Information Administration

was $1.23, and in October 2009 it was $2.56. In real terms, though, the price of gasoline actually decreased over most of this time period.

THE REAL QUANTITY OF MONEY AND THE REAL VALUE OF OTHER ASSETS

Most people know that money has various definitions, but few people have heard of the concept known as the "real quantity of money." This concept is simply the money supply divided by the price level.

Money serves three functions: a unit of account, a medium of exchange, and a store of value. Everyone understands that coins, currency, and the funds in checking accounts can be used as money to purchase other commodities; but the concept of money can be extended to anything else that is highly liquid, meaning that it can be converted quickly into coins, currency, or checking account funds. The two most common definitions of money are M1 and M2. M1 includes coins, currency, checking account funds, and traveler's checks; M2 includes M1 plus other assets that have check-writing features, such as money market deposit accounts, money market mutual fund shares, and other small-denomination time deposits, savings deposits, overnight repurchase agreements, and overnight

Eurodollars. M1 and M2 are the only two measures of money that we will be using in the book when we make reference to the money supply.

The concept of the real quantity of money (M1 or M2 divided by the price level) is important for two reasons. First, real money is an asset that adds to our store of wealth, and it will generally rise as the real income of people rises. Real money, then, reflects the rising wealth and well-being of the individual or community that holds it. Second, the real quantity of money is a barometer of how well the financial sector is performing in a particular community. The reason for this is as follows: If too much nominal money is introduced in a community or country, inflation accelerates and people desire to flee from nominal money holdings, thereby decreasing the real quantity of money that they hold. Inflation, therefore, is generally destructive of wealth; when the real quantity of money falls, people and communities are worse off.

The long-run relationship between nominal money and prices is well known, and it will be illustrated with one of the few equations that will appear in this text:

$$(1)\ M \times V = P \times Y$$

This equation says that the quantity of money M times its velocity V (how quickly money changes hands) is equal to the price level P times Y, the real value of goods and services produced in an economy over a given period of time. When velocity (V) and output (Y) remain constant, changes in the money supply will be followed by similar changes in the price level; in other words, inflation in the long run can be explained by increases in the money supply. If production is rising over time, as is usually the case under normal economic conditions, then the money supply can rise faster than prices and, as previously stated, the ratio of M to P will increase and the wealth of the people in an economy will also increase. The relationship between money and prices, then, makes it important to have the media report two variables: changes in the nominal money supply M (which augurs changes in the price level) and changes in the real quantity of money (M/P).

In the view of most economists, inflation is bad news for the average citizen of a country. First, rogue executive branches of government tend to resort to the printing of money when legislators do not give them the power to tax people for the provision of government services; an upsurge in inflation is a good indication that the political process is breaking down, for the executive power is using the printing press to engage in policies that do not have widespread appeal to the population. Second, inflation tends to create difficult information problems for both producers and workers, because it will not be clear to them whether the changes in the observed prices and wages reflect changes in relative values or changes in absolute values for all goods and services. Third, inflation complicates the determination of the real interest rate, as people will have to form inflationary expectations that may or may not turn out to be correct. Fourth, inflation leads to a redistribution of wealth that has not been approved by the political process. Finally, and possibly most important, inflation leads people to engage in economic activities that are not productive from a social point of view, as everyone tries to evade the consequences of inflation by accumulating unproductive assets such as gold or foreign currencies.

Surprisingly, the same that has been said for money applies to other financial assets that serve to accumulate wealth—especially the holding of stocks in equity markets. One might suspect that stocks (which represent the ownership of physical capital) may move in the same direction as inflation, but that is not necessarily true. Inflation disrupts economic activity and hence has the potential of diminishing the productivity of physical capital, as people pay more attention to finance than to production.

Stock markets can rise and fall independently of long-term inflationary spirals. This requires an explanation, and for this reason it would be useful to report stock prices in real rather than in nominal terms. After that reporting is done, people may gain an understanding of how other processes (e.g., changes in tax policies, restraints of trade, and the influence of stakeholders) affect the movement of stock prices. However, it should be noted that in periods of hyperinflation, stock markets can rise with inflation for several years, until the value of the domestic currency collapses relative to the value of other currencies.

Observers of stock prices believe that fundamental factors such as income, population, supply and demand for commodities, technological breakthroughs, and the growth of trade help drive the value of stocks in a rational manner. Yet no one has done enough research to have a full understanding of the real values of equity holdings under unusual circumstances.

THE REAL FOREIGN EXCHANGE

The nominal foreign exchange rate (e.g., the value of Euros in terms of U.S. dollars) is the most complex relative price, in the sense that it reflects not only the current value of one currency in terms of another, but also differences in interest rates and differences in inflation rates, variables that are determined by events across time. Yet converting the nominal exchange rate into a real variable yields a very surprising puzzle, which we will try to explain; one would expect (but does not find) that a basket of goods in one country would exchange exactly (or almost exactly) for a similar basket of goods in another country, after taking into account inflation.

In order to illustrate this puzzle, let's consider how the consumer price index is determined. The government first decides on the composition of a basket of goods that the average consumer would purchase. The total monetary value of the basket is determined and the composition of the basket is kept constant over time. As prices of individual items rise over time, the total value of the basket rises, and the consumer price index measures over time how the total value of the basket changes relative to the original basket value. If the original basket was worth $2,000 and the new (identical) basket has the new value of $2,200, then the price index will signal an inflation rate of 10 percent. Formally, the price index will change from 100 to 110.

Now, if two countries use *identical* baskets and we ignore transportation costs, competition in the marketplace should force the two baskets to have an identical price, once the nominal foreign exchange rate is taken into account. Hence, if one English pound (£1) sells for $2 in U.S. currency, the basket should sell for £1,000 in England and for $2,000 in the United States.

This ideal relationship is known in the economic literature as the absolute purchasing power parity condition.

The idea that exchange rates should also account for inflation is expressed by the concept of the real exchange rate, which is given by the following equation:

$$(2)\ (E_{\$/£} \times P_{uk})/\ P_{us} = \text{real exchange rate}$$

$E_{\$/£}$ stands for the nominal exchange rate between dollars and English pounds, and the Ps stand for the price indexes that capture the (generally rising) value of an identical bundle of goods in the United Kingdom and in the United States. When the nominal and real exchange rates diverge, this is an indication that the relative value of identical or similar bundles of goods in the two countries is changing, thereby hurting the competitiveness of one country relative to the other. Surprisingly, this happens all the time, even when the "bundle" consists of a single identical commodity. Somehow, markets fail to function well across international frontiers. Let us now explain why this failure is so important.

Most economists believe that trade improves the allocation of resources, guiding production for individual goods to places where the resources used in the production process are relatively more plentiful and cheaper. Yet in the real world, many barriers prevent production from taking place where comparative costs are lower. Ideally, then, when the ratio of the nominal to real exchange rates differ from 1, we know that a better allocation of resources is possible.

People are aware of the role that tariffs and quotas play in diverting production to the wrong place, and our society pretends that most of these barriers have been eliminated, which is not true. Despite major rounds of international trade negotiations, such as Kennedy, Tokyo, Uruguay, and Doha, a lot more needs to be accomplished.

It seems to us, however, that the problems go far deeper than those reported by the media, which report only tariffs and quotas. Every single subsidy to special interests, every single tax on commodities that we may deem unattractive, creates the problem of trade distortion. The public does not understand this basic idea and as a result fails to understand the importance of free markets in achieving economic efficiency. How many people would complain about government subsidies to the arts, for example, when they lack a full understanding that such subsidies affect the relative price of artistic products that are traded across international borders (e.g., movies and musical recordings)? Subsidies and taxes create trade distortions.

Can we really believe that we live in a free-trade world when the OPEC cartel is allowed to control the marketing of significant oil supplies? Diamonds are also sold under the umbrella of an international cartel. "Buy American" provisions are standard in purchases by the U.S. government, and similar nationalistic provisions are endorsed by most other countries around the world. There are also domestic content provisions normally incorporated into regional trade agreements; and when competition among countries gets really rough, countries demand "voluntary" export controls from other countries. The truth about free trade is that there is no such thing, for, if it existed, then the absolute purchasing power parity condition would—approximately—hold.

It is for the above reason that it is important to publish, on a regular basis, any and all deviations between the nominal and real exchange rates, and the costs of commodity bundles across international frontiers, to make the public aware of how far we are from free trade and economic efficiency. So far, this is done for a single commodity: the McDonald's hamburger. The Big Mac index (which is published yearly by the popular journal *The Economist*) began as a joke in the field of international trade, but the truth is that we need many more "similar jokes" in the media, to demonstrate to the average American how distorted international production and trade patterns truly are. There is no reason why the public should *not* know how distorted production and prices are across countries, in order to begin understanding how the gains from trade can potentially make everyone wealthier.

SUMMARY OF OUR ARGUMENT

Anyone who reads this chapter in its entirety must agree that not only does the general public lack full information about the real exchange rate, changes in the money supply that create inflation, and labor market opportunities, but everyone gets misinformation or partial information about extremely important variables in the economy. People cannot make the right decisions when provided misinformation, partial information, or no information at all. Democracy cannot function with a public that is illiterate in economic matters. The media have a clear responsibility to report whenever international prices are distorted, as the Big Mac index clearly reveals; when changes in the money supply lead to potential inflation and the diminishing value of our real cash balances (M/P); when there are wage disparities across employment opportunities for jobs with equal human capital needs; and most importantly of all, when interest rates fail to reflect the true value of time.

The public needs to understand that real interest rates and real exchange rates are, in many ways, the two most important prices that consumers face, for they reflect relative prices across time and across frontiers—and when these prices do not reflect underlying economic fundamentals, the economy is not working properly. In a similar vein, the rise of inflation and the misallocation of resources in labor markets hurt the economic potential of our economy. The media need to change their reporting ways; for only then will the public understand how best to address the current deep misallocation of resources.

It was argued in Chapter 1 that an industry that generates information generates social capital. This chapter demonstrates that if the media misinform people, then the productive potential is impaired. When we mention structural changes in the economy, the most basic and yet simplest structural change that we propose is giving people truthful and dependable information. To achieve this end, the media must reassess the quality of their economic news, and get someone knowledgeable in economic matters to assist them. Often (e.g., during the Carter years) the most dramatic news is what is not reported! Hence we have chosen literally to shock the reader with the following bit of economic news, which should be front page in every newspaper.

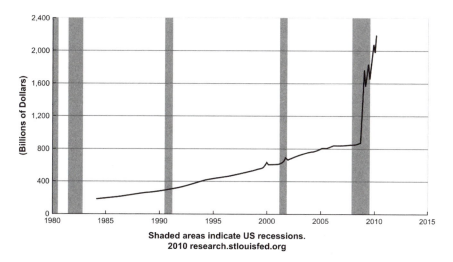

Figure 2.3
U.S. Adjusted Monetary Base.
Source: Federal Reserve Bank of St. Louis

While the concept of the monetary base is a bit esoteric and complex, all that the reader needs to know is that the monetary base *sustains* the level and growth of the money supply. What has happened to the monetary base illustrates the failure of the Bush and Obama administrations in controlling the debt that will affect the U.S. economy in the years to come, for the expansion of the base and the money supply have allowed the financial sector to absorb mountains of debt. While inflation has yet to occur, the graph in Figure 2.3 signals to us the greatest potential danger that the U.S. economy faces is—inflation. This view is shared by Professor Allan H. Meltzer of Carnegie Mellon University, in an article that we urge our readers to take in: "The Fed's Anti-Inflation Exit Strategy Will Fail."[2]

NOTES

1. U.S. Bureau of Labor Statistics, "National Compensation Survey—Wages," June 25, 2009, http://www.bls.gov/ncs/ocs/compub.htm.
2. Allan H. Meltzer, "The Fed's Anti-Inflation Exit Strategy Will Fail," *Wall Street Journal*, Jan. 28, 2010, sec. A.

Chapter 3

REGULATION: THE ACHILLES' HEEL OF THE U.S. ECONOMY

The economic theory stressed in Chapters 1 and 2 has laid the intellectual foundation for the case studies that follow. The case studies will demonstrate the significant role of both information and factors of production in the functioning of the real economy. By introducing the readers to real-world examples of nefarious policies that have adversely affected the productive potential of the U.S. economy, we hope to bring the economic theory to life.

We begin with a case study of government policy's impact on U.S. industry, whose products were once the envy of the world. An entrepreneurial spirit coupled with a business-friendly government embodied in the "American dream" helped produce the environment that played a critical role in the development, production, and diffusion of virtually every major technological revolution that has transformed the world over the last 150 years. The United States took center stage in the electrification of the world, the development of the telephone, the mass production of the automobile, the invention of the airplane, and the integration of the computer into everyday life. Many brilliant minds from diverse nationalities and backgrounds did contribute to this effort, but these transformations were initiated in the United States.

Today, U.S. quality in many industrial applications is synonymous with "second-rate." Anyone who has read a recent review of automobiles, computers, telephones, televisions, or home appliances has noticed that many of the top-ranking items are of foreign origin. In particular, several Asian nations have established themselves as the crème de la crème for many industrial and consumer products. Once mocked as substandard products made with inferior parts and an undereducated workforce, Asian goods are now in heavy demand by consumers. Japan is just one example of the many Asian countries that have embraced globalization and actively pursued trade with the Western world. Such industrial proficiency has allowed a plethora of Asian countries to increase dramatically their standard of living and maintain extensive periods of economic growth. The examples that follow highlight some of the industries that have suffered as a result of over-regulation, which has been a key contributing factor in bringing about the decline in U.S. industrial proficiency.

DETROIT'S FOLLY

Detroit was once the automobile capital of the world; U.S. automobile companies boasted an overwhelming share of the world's automobile market. Today, their former dominance is visible only in their rearview mirror. This spectacular fall from power occurred as a result of poor management, the clout of Detroit's labor unions, and ill-conceived government regulation. The role of management and labor unions is discussed elsewhere in this work; this chapter will focus primarily on government regulation as one of root causes of the present systemic failure.

In 1975, amid the chronic fuel shortages caused by the 1973 Arab oil embargo, Congress enacted Corporate Average Fuel Economy (CAFE) laws. These new laws placed binding fuel economy regulations on all automakers. According to the National Highway Traffic Safety Administration (NHTSA), these laws apply to "sales weighted average fuel economy, expressed in miles per gallon (mpg), of a manufacturer's fleet of passenger cars or light trucks with a gross vehicle weight rating (GVWR) of 8,500 lbs. or less, manufactured for sale in the United States, for any given model year."[1] Such measures were designed to reduce the consumption of oil in the United States amid a supply shock caused by OPEC. However, in today's increasingly competitive automobile industry in which dozens of both domestic and foreign auto companies produce a variety of car sizes and models, specialization has become important. Many companies have developed niches in the market, with a comparative advantage in the production of specific car sizes and models. The American automobile industry has gained a reputation for sport utility vehicles and trucks, vehicles with lower fuel economy; in contrast, their Japanese competitors have been recognized by consumers as producing superior compact and midsize sedans, vehicles with higher fuel economy. These regulations, therefore, have placed a heavy burden on the U.S. automobile industry, whose concentration and profitability lie in the production of vehicles that achieve a lower fuel economy. As a result of the strengthening of these regulations and very high labor costs, the U.S. automakers' market share has decreased while Asian automakers have taken the lead in the industry. This is evidenced by Toyota surpassing GM for the first time as the world's largest producer of automobiles.[2]

The CAFE laws are economically inefficient and decrease the demand for U.S. vehicles because they force U.S. automobile companies to produce vehicles in which they do not have a cost advantage. This misguided policy has led U.S. automakers to incur unsustainable losses as they struggle to produce compact cars at a higher cost than their competitors in order to satisfy the government-mandated average fuel economy regulations. The U.S. automobile manufacturers are then forced to charge a higher price for the vehicles that they are able to produce profitably, in order to compensate for the losses incurred on their production of compact cars. Because of those higher prices, a reduced quantity of vehicles that are highly popular in the market, such as SUVs, are demanded, and automakers suffer a reduction in sales. This adversely affects the value of the firms' assets and hence their balance sheets. A simple thought experiment reveals the problem with this approach.

Suppose two farmers produce apples and oranges. Farmer A specializes in the production of apples and Farmer B specializes in the production of oranges. The farmers then sell apples and oranges at a local farmers market for the price of $1 each. Now, suppose the government enacts a law that increases the cost of producing apples but not oranges. After the implementation of the law, Farmer A produces fewer apples while farmer B produces his usual harvest of oranges. Farmer A must charge a higher price that reflects his or her production costs; then apples cost $1.10, and oranges still cost $1. If consumers are somewhat indifferent between apples and oranges they purchase more oranges, which have become less expensive. We call this the substitution effect. As a result, the value of Farmer A's assets, which are suited to the production of apples, must decrease, and the value of Farmer B's assets, which are suited to the production of oranges, will increase, as the demand for oranges increases.

The thought experiment above proves an essential point: Government regulations impose real costs on firms that affect the value of their assets. The aforementioned auto case is just one example in which government regulations end up lowering the quantity demanded for a good; this happens when the price of the good is forced to rise as a result of the increased cost structure of firms burdened by government regulations.

The case of U.S. automobile companies is particularly relevant because in December 2008 the taxpayers bailed out Detroit for $17.4 billion.[3] The initial round of bailouts was subsequently augmented, and thus far the government has contributed nearly $58 billion to GM's bankruptcy reconstruction efforts.[4] These bailouts came with many stipulations that seek to increase the production of high fuel economy cars. We believe that such stipulations fail to address the fundamental problems in Detroit; Government requirements are not based on the capacities Detroit currently has at its disposal. Research and development for the new technologies will be necessary to achieve government goals, and reworking current plant capacities for the production of new types of vehicles will cost billions of dollars that Detroit simply does not have—even with the bailout funds. Immersed in a sea of liabilities, Detroit needs congressional help in allowing the market to dictate which cars consumers choose to drive. This assistance can be achieved by breaking down such government barriers as the CAFE laws that promote the government's social vision and not the demands of consumers in the marketplace. Such central planning is ineffective and detrimental to efficiency and progress. Simply building millions of cars that consumers do not want will in no way generate sustainable entities. In fact, it will probably result in Detroit returning to Washington, D.C., for another bailout. For these reasons, we believe that the deregulation of useless laws, coupled with comprehensive labor reforms based on market-clearing principles, will help generate an environment that is more conducive to competitive business.

The CAFE laws are an example of laws that do not make full use of the incentive principle. They do not give consumers an incentive to purchase more fuel-efficient vehicles; rather, they attempt to achieve this goal by making the manufacture of low fuel economy vehicles more expensive, effectively imposing a quota system. A market-based approach that gives consumers the incentive to purchase high fuel economy vehicles would likely achieve far better results and impose a smaller cost on both automakers and consumers.

NUCLEAR POWER

The ideology of the CAFE laws is further echoed in the regulatory structure of the nuclear power industry. The U.S. nuclear industry came under attack after the events at Three Mile Island in 1979 and Chernobyl in 1986 invoked public panic about the safety of nuclear energy. These public outcries led to the imposition of many needless and redundant regulatory measures that increased nuclear energy costs exponentially. As a result, the vision for a nuclear-powered United States was put on the back burner and numerous utility companies canceled plans for nuclear-plant construction. The Nuclear Regulatory Commission (NRC) revamped its safety requirements and virtually overnight the operating costs at existing nuclear facilities went through the roof.

The U.S. regulatory system has put the growth of nuclear energy on permanent hold. (It remains to be seen in the next few months whether President Obama's State of the Union promise to promote nuclear power is kept.) Since 1996 not a single nuclear power plant has been constructed in the United States, despite the increasing demand for energy during this time period. Today, 20 percent of U.S. electricity needs are met by its current nuclear capacity.[5] Meanwhile, foreign nations such as France and Japan have expanded their nuclear programs, providing them with a sustainable source of reliable energy output. Thus, many advanced countries have turned to nuclear power as the best source of energy output per dollar invested. The United States' path could not be more divergent from this reality. As a result of this policy, the U.S. remains critically dependent on risky oil exploration to fuel its energy needs. The negative consequences of this policy are evidenced by the April 2010 oil spill that occurred in the Gulf of Mexico. The spill has endangered wildlife and the livelihoods of those who reside on the Gulf Coast.

The U.S. reluctance to adopt nuclear energy stems from an event that occurred in the early morning of March 28, 1979. At this time the nuclear plant known as Three Mile Island began to experience abnormalities in its second reactor. The subsequent events led to the release of radiation into the atmosphere, fueling public panic about health concerns. However, these fears were later determined by a subsequent NRC investigation to be exaggerated: "Compared to the natural radioactive background dose of about 100–125 millirem per year for the area, the collective dose to the community from the accident was very small. The maximum dose to a person at the site boundary would have been less than 100 millirem."[6] Despite the fact that the worst nuclear incident in U.S. history produced little public danger, regulation efforts were disproportionately increased.

Prior to the mishap of Unit 2 at Three Mile Island, the usual construction phase of a nuclear power plant took about seven years. By 1990 the process took 12 years despite the technological advances in nuclear reactor technologies that occurred during this extended time period.[7] Given the massive scale involved in the building of a nuclear reactor, such time delays dramatically increase capital outlays required to finance such a project. Similarly, research prepared by the Electric Power Research Institute (EPRI) showed that, from 1981 to 1988, maintenance and operation costs increased by 80 percent (adjusted for inflation) and the average plant staff doubled. The EPRI study found that 30 to 60 percent of the increases in these costs were attributable to NRC requirements.[8] This evidence overwhelmingly demonstrates that NRC regulations have made nuclear reactors prohibitively expensive to build. Furthermore, increases in maintenance and operations costs imposed by the NRC regulations have undermined the ability of nuclear energy to compete with traditional fossil fuels.

The increased power and liberal political leanings of the judicial system further increased the decline of U.S. nuclear energy. Special interest groups ranging from fossil fuel competitors to environmental groups were strengthened by the increased support of the courts. Much of the credit for this movement goes to President Jimmy Carter, who appointed 35 new liberal-leaning appellate judges near the end of his term in office. The new tendencies of the courts coupled with the National Environmental Act of 1969 gave special interest groups the tools to drive the nail in the coffin on the nuclear energy debate. Between 1975 and 1983 more than 535 new regulations were put in place, demonstrating the effectiveness of this movement.[9]

The cost of constructing one new nuclear power plant in the United States exceeds $3 billion, which includes the safety and environmental safeguards imposed by the EPA and NRC.[10] This huge overhead makes competing with fossil fuels an impossible challenge. The empirical evidence clearly shows that these increases in overhead directly accompanied increases in regulations. Consequently, regulation has played a vital role in deterring investment in nuclear energy.

Some may object to our call for a systematic reform of these regulations, citing that in their absence the chance of a catastrophe like Chernobyl would be greatly augmented. The logic of such a claim seems reasonable, but under closer scrutiny the logic unravels. Consider France as an example. The French have actively embraced nuclear energy as a vital part of their energy policy. As a result, the French government has long been a crucial supporter of nuclear energy. This stance has resulted in the creation of 59 nuclear power plants operated by Electricité de France that generate 76 percent of the country's electricity demand.[11] This program is one of the largest energy programs ever instituted and the results have been productive. There have been no major incidents that have threatened the health or safety of the French people. Furthermore,

France is a net electricity exporter. This capacity results from the fact that it can produce energy and sell it for a cheaper price than its competitors. Such a comparative advantage is generated by a favorable regulatory structure that is comprehensive but flexible enough to ensure that the benefits of regulation more than match the costs associated with that regulation. This approach is sensible and we subscribe to it.

The highly toxic nature of nuclear waste warrants extreme caution, but many advances in engineering accompanied with better materials and a broader knowledge base have helped to lower substantially the risk of catastrophe. The plants are built with safety in mind and are far superior to the rudimentary reactor that exploded in Chernobyl. The incompetence of the Communist regime to keep that reactor up to international standards and the plant's total lack of safeguards are to blame for the disaster. For these reasons the incident should not be used as a deterrent in developed countries that possess the proper engineering skills and regulatory institutions to build and safely manage nuclear power plants.

Another issue with nuclear power is the permanence of the waste products. However, the amount of toxic waste produced by nuclear fission is relatively small, and when housed in the proper environment it poses no threat to human health or safety. In fact, the amount of the high-level waste generated is small when compared to the benefits: "[T]he contribution of a family of four using electricity for 20 years is a glass cylinder the size of a cigarette lighter."[12]

A comprehensive storage facility like the proposed Yucca Mountain storage center can provide a safe and long-term solution to housing these waste products until scientists figure out an even better way to take care of them. It should be noted that progress in this field has been strong and many countries have engaged in recycling the nuclear waste products to generate additional energy. Such practice is commonplace in France and allows for the maximum benefit to be achieved from this valuable resource. The United States should wisely follow suit by removing obstacles to the construction of a safe nuclear waste site and actively engage in the reprocessing of nuclear waste.

The U.S. government's regulatory structure is burdensome and undermines nuclear energy's competitiveness in the energy market. Current energy policy is predicated on many fears that science has conquered but, nonetheless, remain entrenched in the minds of many. This has been a major factor in crippling the expansion of an otherwise viable industry. Thus, the government regulation of nuclear energy has decreased the value of nuclear assets; it has favored a less efficient energy policy centered on fossil fuels. Failing to make full use of this scientific miracle is comparable to digging a hole with a shovel while an excavator stands idle. Ultimately, consumers are punished with higher energy prices and increased levels of fossil fuel pollutants.

The "energy independence" that politicians have long promised, while planning to spend billions of dollars in research, can be accomplished by allowing the nuclear energy industry to operate profitably. Nuclear energy's sustainability and efficiency should be the cornerstone of an effective energy policy. However, this can be achieved only by effective reform that overhauls the regulatory structure to ensure that redundancies and unnecessary provisions are terminated.

PRIVACY FALLACIES

Privacy rights are another area in which the government has imposed restrictions that inhibit the clearing of markets. It is important to note that although citizens now tend to think of such rights as fundamental, just like the freedom of speech and the right to a trial by jury, privacy rights have only recently become important policy issues in U.S. democracy. Debate over privacy rights stems not from the notion that they should in any capacity be rendered obsolete. Rather, the controversy focuses on exactly *how far* privacy should be extended in a society where information plays a vital role in the decision-making process of both consumers and firms. Owing to the many connotations associated with privacy, for the purposes of this section we will define privacy as the right that allows for "the concealment of information."[13]

A broad interpretation of privacy rights is costly to society. These costs arise because when relevant information is shielded from parties engaged in a transaction, asymmetries of information arise. These asymmetries of information distort prices (which are based on information) and thereby undermine the economic efficiency of transactions.

The effects of privacy have far-reaching consequences in both the workplace and in the market. Let us take the example of an employer who is engaged in searching for a new employee. Many of the qualities that this employer will try to discover about the individual he or she is hiring may not be readily observable. An employer must consider whether the person is honest, intelligent, industrious, and in the proper physical and mental condition to fill the position. The prospective employee, seeking to get hired, has every reason to conceal any deficiencies that would render him or her incapable of fulfilling the job description. Given the prospective employee's desire to hide shortcomings, he or she will use the notion of privacy as a shroud of secrecy that protects any deficiencies from being detected. This behavior has adverse consequences for any employer who is prevented by privacy statutes from examining relevant aspects of the potential employee's life. The massive volume of privacy legislation that such an employer would be forced to navigate while conducting a thorough background check is costly in time and money.

Similarly, a firm operating under excessively protective privacy laws would be inclined to hide deficiencies in the services that it provides and in the products that it sells. If they were prone to cause harm, the firm would seek to cover up potential dangers at great cost to the consumers. The results are clear: the market is undermined by one party's attempt to hide relevant information from the other party to the transaction. Privacy laws assist in blocking the transparency necessary for both the consumer and producer to engage in economically efficient exchanges by making information unavailable or costly to acquire. As a result, both are forced to incur extra transaction costs, and their well-being diminishes. Privacy laws have been pervasive in the recent history of the United States and they enjoy steadfast support from the majority of citizens—or so we are led to believe. A brief history of these laws helps demonstrate that privacy rights are relatively recent phenomena in the U.S. The 1965 case of *Griswold v. Connecticut* established the precedent of privacy rights by declaring that laws banning the sale and use of birth control were unconstitutional. "The court maintained that although *The Bill of Rights* does not mention privacy, its other guarantees established zones of privacy that must be respected."[14] The right to privacy was further strengthened by court cases such as *Eisenstadt v. Baird* and the abortion case of *Roe v. Wade*.[15] Thus, a fundamental shift in the Supreme Court's ruling on privacy helped to establish a precedent of privacy rights that was further strengthened by subsequent legislation.

A major push toward legislation favoring privacy occurred in 1974 when Congress passed the Privacy Act of 1974. The law regulated government records and placed restrictions on the ability of the government to collect, store, and disseminate information on the general public.[16] A variety of legislation affecting privacy rights has ensued, including the Right to Financial Privacy Act of 1978, the Privacy Protection Act of 1980, the Computer Fraud and Abuse Act of 1986, the Electronic Communications Privacy Act of 1986, the Computer Security Act of 1987, the Video Privacy Protection Act of 1988, the Americans with Disabilities Act of 1990, the Telephone Consumer Protection Act of 1991, the Electronic

Freedom of Information Act of 1996, the Health Insurance Portability and Accountability Act of 1996, the Fair Credit Reporting Act of 1999, and the Financial Modernization Act of 1999.[17] This extensive yet partial list serves to demonstrate the extent of privacy legislation that exists in U.S. society. It exhibits the degree of legislation that firms and consumers must search through in order to obtain relevant information on other parties to transactions. Certainly not all of this legislation is without purpose, but its volume makes the cost associated with complying and navigating it high and cumbersome. The list also demonstrates that the extension of privacy rights in the United States is a relatively recent phenomenon. Some will argue that the increased ability of technology to access information requires safeguards. An economist would agree with this statement up to a point, and that point would be where the socially optimal amount of privacy is provided. It is true that beyond a certain point, extra privacy can and does, in fact, make society worse off. Such is the case when an employer cannot be sure about the merits of his or her prospective employee. Thus, privacy delivers diminishing marginal benefits beyond some optimal point. This statement serves as a powerful argument against the notion that more privacy is always better. As a society we accept the idea that speed involves danger, but that danger is insufficient to warrant reducing vehicle speeds to zero. We search for an optimal level of speed by taking into accounts the marginal benefits and marginal costs of vehicular velocities.

A debate in modern society is whether schools should have the right to test students for drug use. Opponents of this measure argue that it undermines the student's right to privacy, fails to fight effectively drug use, and is a waste of taxpayer funding. Proponents argue that such a measure will help keep children drug-free during their crucial teenage development years and, thereby, help reduce educational failure. Proponents cite as evidence a three-year study showing a 17 percent decrease in drug use among teens since the 2002 Supreme Court decision of *Board of Education of Independent School District No. 92 v. Earls*, which enhanced the ability of school districts randomly to drug-test students engaged in extracurricular activities.[18] Another argument frequently favored by proponents of drug testing is that the military began similar drug testing of servicemen and women in the 1980s and has reported an astonishing decrease in drug use from 27 percent when the program started to about 2 percent today.[19]

This empirical evidence suggests that the above program is effective. Opponents argue that these studies do not represent the effects of only the Supreme Court decision, but rather that they are a continuation of a long-term trend of declining drug use. However, the empirical evidence demonstrates that when drug use became more transparent and abusers had to face the consequences of their actions, many stopped engaging in that behavior. This debate is relevant because a Supreme Court decision favoring less privacy has led to a reduction in drug use, a social liability. Drug use is detrimental to society not just because of its ability to cause harm to the user, but because in a much broader sense it generates externalities (e.g., crime and poverty) that reduce society's well-being. Consequently, more privacy does not always produce better results for society, and transparency helps eliminate detrimental consequences.

Privacy laws have also made many people afraid of writing letters of recommendation or serving as character references for people. Consider the case of a student applying to graduate school who is seeking a letter of recommendation from a faculty member at his current institution. The faculty member writes the letter for the student and mails it to the graduate school. The student is rejected and upon examination finds out that the faculty member wrote an unfavorable review. The faculty member wrote an honest opinion stating the strengths as well as the deficiencies of this particular student. Angered that certain negative traits about him or her were exposed, the student then sues the faculty member for defamation of character. There are instances where this has happened, and the reasoning behind legal actions is that the faculty member supposedly violated the student's right to privacy. As a result of privacy rights, many people write vague letters of recommendation fearing that truly honest letters may land them in the courts. Such practice makes it harder for graduate schools to identify whether or not to accept students.

This situation demonstrates that privacy laws can impose a type of social insurance. This insurance is based on the fact that persons have the ability to hide their undesirable traits under the guise of privacy while promoting their good traits. It is important to analyze who benefits from this policy and who loses. In this case, the student who has deficient traits is the one protected by privacy laws. The people who suffer the consequences are the faculty members who cannot violate the students' privacy rights by writing honest letters, the graduate schools that cannot gain a full understanding of prospective students' characters and abilities, and, most important of all, the other students who have nothing to hide. As economist Richard Posner candidly put it, "Concealment of adverse personal characteristics is surely an inefficient method of insurance; rather than spread the costs widely, it shifts them from one small group to another."[20]

CONCLUSIONS

The examples in this chapter highlight a few of the many obstacles that the legislative and judicial systems have imposed on U.S. firms. Consequently, it is not hard to understand the extent of the damage that has been done to our productive capacity. The damage is not irreversible, but it has become more difficult for domestic firms to compete against foreign firms that do not face such rigorous demands from their regulatory bodies. It should also be noted that the United States is not alone in its tendency to over-regulate; many European countries are in a similar rut. Other nations, though, especially Asian and emerging nations, have opted to impose a limited and much more flexible regulatory structure. Such a structure, coupled with lower wages, has provided them with a comparative advantage in the production of many consumer goods. As a result, the regulatory and legal structures have decreased the value of domestic productive assets by raising their operating costs; we need look no farther than Detroit to see this. Government regulation and taxation produce real cost effects on firms, which can lower their profitability and dull their competitive edge. The regulations also carry heavy human costs, as evidenced by the growing number of laid-off autoworkers.

The increasing desire to regulate, litigate, and tax for social and military programs is hindering U.S. economic efficiency and even threatening the country's long-term viability. U.S. companies are having an increasingly difficult time competing in the international economy. The current trade imbalances accentuate this point. In the recent past, U.S. technological progress fueled by innovative and entrepreneurial men and women has masked these problems, and the nation has been blessed with a long period of prosperity. The examples in this chapter show that a large and bulky bureaucracy that over-regulates and over-taxes can be destructive to economic progress.

Reducing the size, power, and influence of government will help the United States make better use of its scarce resources. Such actions, coupled with political reforms, will help dismantle the slow-moving behemoth of a bureaucracy that governs and regulates the nation today. By taking up the problems discussed in this chapter, the United States can ensure that its vital industries can continue to flourish and that its competitive edge remains for future generations. The future will be built on the entrepreneurial prowess and the inherent desire to reach beyond the horizon that characterizes the "American dream." Such qualities will surely provide the fuel for the next great invention or technological revolution. With that being said, the United States still has to pick up the pieces of the mess it is in right now. Extensive regulatory, legal, and legislative overhaul will be the cornerstone of success. The nation cannot allow past success to blind the obvious need for reform. Restructuring the U.S. economy will build a new foundation for a better future, which is a goal shared by all.

NOTES

1. U.S. National Highway Traffic Safety Administration, "CAFE Overview," January 25 2009, http://www.nhtsa.dot.gov/cars/rules/CAFE/overview.htm.

2. Nick Bunkley, "G.M. Says Toyota Has Lead in Global Sales Race," *New York Times*, April 24, 2008, http://www.nytimes.com/2008/04/24/business/worldbusiness/24auto.html.

3. *Wall Street Journal*, "Autos Bailout Fact Sheet," December 19, 2008, http://blogs.wsj.com/autoshow/2008/12/19/autos-bailout-fact-sheet/.

4. *Wall Street Journal*, "Politicians Butt In at Bailed-Out GM," October 30, 2009, http://online.wsj.com/article/SB125677552001414699.html

5. Thomas Murphy, "Nuclear Power: 12 percent of America's Generating Capacity, 20 percent of the Electricity," *Nuclear Power*, U.S. Energy Information Administration, http://www.eia.doe.gov/cneaf/nuclear/page/analysis/nuclearpower.html.

6. U.S. Nuclear Regulatory Commission, "Fact Sheet on the Three Mile Island Accident," January 22, 2009, http://www.nrc.gov/reading-rm/doc-collections/fact-sheets/3mile-isle.html.

7. Pietro S. Nivola, "The Political Economy of Nuclear Energy in the United States," September 9, 2004: Policy Brief #138, *Brookings Institute*, http://www.brookings.edu/~/media/Files/rc/papers/2004/09environment_nivola/pb138.pdf.

8. Magali Delmas and Bruce Heiman, "Government Credible Commitment to the French and American Nuclear Power Industries," *Journal of Policy Analysis and Management* 20, no. 3 (2001): 454.

9. Ibid., 446–447.

10. Nivola, "The Political Economy of Nuclear Energy in the United States."

11. The World Nuclear Association, "Nuclear Power in France," December 2008, http://www.world-nuclear.org/info/inf40.html.

12. Jon Palfreman, "Why the French Like Nuclear Energy," Public Broadcasting System, http://www.pbs.org/wgbh/pages/frontline/shows/reaction/readings/french.html.

13. Richard A. Posner, "The Economics of Privacy," *American Economic Review* 71, no. 2 (1981), 405.

14. Jamuna Carroll, ed., *Privacy: Opposing Viewpoints* (Farmington Hills, MI: Greenhaven, 2006), 14–15.

15. Ibid., 16.

16. Kai-Lung Hui and Ivan P. L. Png, "Economics of Privacy," *Handbook of Information Systems and Economics*, Terry Hendershott, ed. Elsevier, June 2005, http://ssrn.com/abstract= 786846.

17. *Information Shield*, "United States Privacy Laws," January 25, 2009, http://www.informationshield.com/usprivacylaws.html.

18. Carroll, *Privacy*, 176.

19. Ibid., 179.

20. Posner, "The Economics of Privacy," 406.

Chapter 4

CURING HEALTH CARE

Escalating costs, rising health insurance premiums, inconsistent quality, and trillions of dollars in unfunded liabilities have become recurrent themes in U.S. health care over the last decade. The overwhelming majority of professional literature on the subject affirms that U.S. health care is in a crisis of unprecedented proportions, and many are aware that an extensive overhaul of the nation's health care sector is vital to ensuring continued economic prosperity. Yet, efforts to correct that broken health care system have been consistently thwarted by an array of competing and often irreconcilable personal, political, economic, and moral interests. Some believe that a government-managed universal single-payer health care system would provide a uniform code of care, as well as a centralized compensation and regulatory framework that would simultaneously lower health care costs and improve quality. Others favor harnessing the power of free markets to reform health care by reorganizing institutional arrangements to foster value-based competition. The battle over health care is far from over, and the March 2010 legislation supported by the Obama administration incorporates elements from the two approaches that will be discussed below.

The authors of this work have failed to reach an agreement about whether it is possible to reform the American health care system within the range of policy choices that are normally discussed; however, we agree on the nature of the institutional changes that would be required under two very different structures. In the first structure, which is taken up in this chapter and reflects current arrangements in countries that are in the Organization for Economic Cooperation and Development (OECD), the changes that we propose are significant but not radical in nature; here our sympathies lie with what we call value-based competition. We try to demonstrate that competition helps both patients and the economy, and that a single-payer alternative run by government will lead to much inefficiency. This chapter provides the background on the current state of affairs and gives the pros and cons of two alternative approaches to health care.

The next chapter will take a much more radical approach, as we discuss investment in health rather than reforms to health care. We will suggest that medical practices, as currently run, could potentially disappear in an environment where there will be far fewer medical doctors and where patients may actually ingest far fewer drugs. If one were to accept this different structure to the provision of health care, then health care as currently understood would be far more restricted than it is anywhere in the world now. Surprisingly, this alternative structure would not only cost less and possibly improve economic productivity drastically, but people may find it more in tune with moral values and human limitations. Our disagreement as authors is based on deciding which of these two structures is more likely to prevail in the near future; for this reason we have devoted one chapter to health care and another to health.

INTERGENERATIONAL ACCOUNT DEFICITS

In 1970 health care comprised 7 percent of the U.S. gross domestic product (GDP). By 2007 that number had grown to 16 percent of GDP.[1] In fact, as a collective body the nation currently spends about $2 trillion per year on health care.[2] The growth of the health care sector as a percentage of the nation's GDP is alarming because these expenditures have done little to increase the aggregate productive potential of the economy. This is not to say that health care is necessarily unproductive. Rather, we are claiming that the current biotechnological revolution lacks the economic benefits that came along with the previous revolutions such as the telephone, mass production of the automobile, introduction of powered flight, and the computer. The biotechnological revolution is causing people to live longer, but it is not increasing their productivity. The consequence of this revolution is that people are living longer, but not working any more than they did in prior time periods. Consequently the productive potential of the economy is not expanding and the factors of production have not been altered in a manner that advances economic growth. Thus, just as the increased spending on security after 9/11, which is formally included in GDP calculations, did not make the economy more productive (as indicated in Chapter 1) rising expenditures on health care have provided few gains to output, although it has benefitted the people receiving more comprehensive care.

The escalating costs of health care are increasingly squeezing the budgets of households, firms, and government. This is reflected in the staggering fact that the number of uninsured persons now is 45.7 million or 15.3 percent of the population.[3] In 2007, 8.1 million children 18 years old or younger did not have health insurance, representing 11.0 percent of the 18 and younger population.[4] Similarly, firms have been under mounting financial pressures because of health care costs. In fact, health care adds $1,500 to every car the U.S. automakers sell.[5] These costs have been a major contributor to the recent bankruptcies of Chrysler and General Motors. Such enormous costs have proven to be a difficult financial obstacle for American companies competing in a global market. Perhaps the most disconcerting news is the projected future government expenditures on health care. If government expenditures remain relatively constant as a percentage of GDP, by the year 2020 rising Medicare expenditures will crowd out all other spending with the exception of defense.[6]

The government's official estimates for total Medicare liabilities outstanding, including Medicare Part A (hospital stays), Part B (doctor visits), and Part D (drug benefit plan instituted under the Bush administration), are an incredible $40.9 trillion in present value terms.[7] It should be noted that many economists hold this calculation to be severely understated. Richard W. Fisher, the president and CEO of the Federal Reserve Bank of Dallas, has estimated the unfunded liabilities of Medicare to be as high as $85.6 trillion in present value terms.[8] The current commitments that the U.S. government has made to future Medicare beneficiaries are illusory. In order to fund such commitments the government would have to engage in an unsustainable borrowing spree or substantially raise taxes.

The cause of the intergenerational imbalances that plague entitlement programs is largely due to that fact that they are financed on a *pay as you go* basis. The problem with the *pay as you go* system is that demographic trends show that the United States is aging rapidly. Currently the baby boomers are beginning to retire, and it is estimated that by the time they have all retired the United States will have doubled the size of its elderly population, while increasing its taxpaying base that funds the retiree's benefits by a paltry 15 percent.[9]

A study conducted by Federal Reserve economist Jagadeesh Gokhale and Kent Smetters demonstrates the extent to which the government has overstretched itself on promises to future entitlement recipients. In order to generate the present value of funds needed to finance the future liabilities and close the intergenerational gap, "income taxes would have to go up 74 percent." The majority of these future liabilities, 82 percent in fact, are attributable solely to Medicare.[10] Raising taxes by such a large margin would be politically impossible and economically inconceivable because those taxes would create a huge disincentive to work. Thus, a reduction in Medicare benefits must be part of a viable solution to ensuring that the U.S. government can cover its implicit liabilities over the long term. To fully comprehend the extent of the crisis in health care, one should consider that if the government were forced to report its present financial liabilities for current and future retirees on a balance sheet then almost every town and city in the United States would be bankrupt.[11]

The United States is distinct from other developed countries in that many people obtain medical insurance on the private market. However, as a result of The Patient Protection and Affordable Care Act of March of 2010, we expect that the government will begin to play an even larger role in the financing of health care. Although in the current system many people buy health care insurance on the private market, the rest of the population either pays medical costs directly out of pocket or is covered by a government health care program such as Medicaid or Medicare. Only 13 percent of total medical costs in the United States are paid directly out of pocket compared with 17 percent by Medicare and 35 percent by private insurers.[12] Furthermore, the government financed 45.4 percent of total expenditures on health care in 2007.[13] A criticism of this institutional arrangement is that it encourages individuals covered by insurance to seek out excessive amounts of health care because a third party pays the explicit costs. Because most individuals pay a small deductible relative to the costs of care, they choose care options without analyzing the relevant costs and benefits of the treatment. Thus, when given the option between multiple care options the consumer is likely to pick the one perceived to be the best, even if the costs of that treatment far outweigh the benefits. This incentive structure encourages the current trend of rising health care costs. By increasing the deductible, consumers would have an incentive to seek out care only when the benefits of doing so outweigh the costs. Encouraging patients to use health care efficiently must be a primary goal of any reform effort.

Others have attributed escalating health care costs to the monopoly power of prescription drug manufacturers, a revolution in health care technology, administration costs associated with private insurers, rising medical liability premiums, the lag in the implementation of information technology, and the fragmented structure of care created by fee-for-service reimbursements received by hospitals and health care providers.

Needless to say, many culprits have been identified. However, because many attempts to restructure have been narrowly focused, true reform remains elusive.

GOVERNMENT-RUN UNIVERSAL HEALTH CARE

The two ways in which health care is administered in OECD countries, by the government and the private sector, offer vastly different approaches to controlling ballooning health care costs. A government-run universal health care system could mirror existing institutions in developed countries such as Canada, the United Kingdom, and France or be a mixed public-private model like the health care system in Germany. The single-payer system offers the prospect of tremendously lowering per capita health care costs, but trade-offs in quality and accessibility are valid concerns. A move toward value-based competition involves restructuring health care by transforming the current zero-sum compensation that characterizes U.S. health care, in which one party's gain comes at the expense of another party, toward a system that is incentive driven on a *pay for performance* basis.[14]

Many advocates for universal health care argue that cross-country empirical data show that the United States spends more on health care than any other member of the OECD.[15] The OECD is an international organization that includes many of the world's wealthiest nations that accept free market principles. Despite the United States' significantly higher costs, other OECD countries maintain comparable or better statistics in key indicators of medical care. The United States has a higher than average infant and adult mortality rate, a lower than average life expectancy, and fewer physicians per capita than the average for OECD countries.[16] Furthermore, even when the uninsured are put aside, studies have been inconclusive as to whether the United States has better access to health care than other OECD countries.[17] In 2007, the per capita expenditures on health care in the United States were $7,290—which in the aggregate constituted 16.0 percent of total U.S. GDP.[18] Norway, the OECD country with the second highest per capita health care expenditures, spent $4,763 in 2007, which comprised 8.9 percent of GDP.[19] The average health care spending for all the OECD countries was $2,984 in 2007.[20] Thus, the United States exceeded the average OECD country by 244 percent.

Some claim that the United States has lofty expenditures because it has the highest incidence rate of AIDS, cancer, and obesity among the OECD countries.[21] In the United States, the obesity rate among adults was an astonishing 34.3 percent in 2006.[22] Obesity is often associated with an increased incidence of diabetes and cardiovascular disease, which are both costly and chronic in nature. Thus, differences in lifestyle offer a partial reason as to why health care costs are so much higher in the United States than any other OECD country.

Americans also have a hospital utilization rate that is well below the average of other OECD countries.[23] The United States experienced 121 hospital stays per 1,000 people in 2004, which was considerably fewer that the OECD average of 161.[24] One potential explanation for this is the increased availability and utilization of outpatient care in the United States.

A comparison of per capita doctor visits in OECD countries with per capita doctor visits in the United States reveals that the United States is the seventh lowest consumer of doctor visits. This is noteworthy because a statistically significant trend shows that as per capita doctor visits increase, the average spending on health care decreases.[25] The figures show that other OECD countries have more patient-doctor interaction than the United States.

Another area where the United States spends considerably more on health care than other OECD countries is on pharmaceuticals. According to the 2007 OECD data, the United States, with $878 per person, spent approximately double the $461 average OECD countries spent on prescription drugs.[26] Spending on pharmaceuticals accounted for 12.3 percent of U.S. health care expenditures.[27] The costs of pharmaceuticals has been a contentious issue because many fail to understand the high research and development costs that are required to bring pharmaceuticals to the consumer market successfully. It costs approximately $1 billion to bring a single drug to market.[28] In addition, the vast majority of pharmaceuticals researched by drug companies never pass the research and development phase. Thus, in order to remain financially viable and cover their tremendous fixed costs, pharmaceutical companies are forced to charge prices that exceed the cost of production for the products that are sold. Without earning significant net incomes, pharmaceutical companies would be unable to repay investors who financed the drugs' creation.

Many critics have commented about the "excesses" of the pharmaceutical industry, proclaiming that charging $2 for a pill that costs 50 cents to make is "unconscionable." Such critics argue that a single-payer system would drive down costs and increase the accessibility to pharmaceuticals. This argument fails to discount properly what such actions would do to long-term drug development. Under the critics' plan, research and development would all but cease and innovation would stagnate. Imagine if the government had controlled computer prices (which have fallen significantly on a quality-adjusted basis) in the 1980s. The result would have been that the profits that fueled the innovation of Intel, IBM, and Microsoft would not have been available, since competition would have been stifled. Hence consumers today would be unable to reap the tremendous benefits in productivity ushered in by the computer revolution had intervention occurred.

Another aspect that the media fails to mention in regard to pharmaceuticals is the fact that U.S. consumers and U.S. taxpayers subsidize the lion's share of the cost of developing new drugs. Single-payer systems frequently offer extremely low reimbursement rates to drug companies. This forces the drug companies to charge higher prices in geographical areas where price controls do not exist. Thus, the cost savings people attribute to the single-payer system are, in reality, cost-shifting practices. This explains why American drug consumers pay more than their OECD counterparts for identical products. It has been estimated that the U.S. taxpayers support 80 percent of the world's government-funded biomedical research.[29] Those who yearn for price controls need look no further than Europe to see the limited research and development of pharmaceutical drugs there.

In 1990 the United States and Europe each held approximately one-third of the world's drug market. In Europe the industry has contracted to 21 percent of global output, and in the United States the industry has expanded to 50 percent of the world's drug market. Also, European firms have moved a large volume of their research and development to the United States, which accounts for 60 percent of European drug manufacturers' profitability.[30]

The evidence clearly shows that the rest of the world is getting a free lunch and sticking the U.S. consumer and taxpayer with the cost. The refusal of European single-payer health systems to contribute to the research and development of medications has altered the dynamics of the industry and encouraged biomedical research to relocate to more business-friendly climates such as the United States. The short-term gains under price controls would come at a tremendous cost to long-term innovation. To follow in Europe's footsteps would curtail the funding that might lead to the next pharmaceutical breakthrough.

A sizable constituency has argued that conversion to a government-run health care system, or the introduction of a government alternative for the uninsured would help to alleviate the demonstrably high spending in the United States. A program aimed at providing "Medicare for All" has culminated in the passage of the Patient Protection and Affordable Care

Act after a failed attempt to create a similarly structured system failed in the 1990s under President Clinton. The theoretical framework of a single-payer system offers several advantages, including universal coverage for preventable treatment, elimination of excluding high-risk subscribers, simplified paperwork and a reduced management structure, and an end to price discrimination in the market. Furthermore, set reimbursement rates would make health care costs easier to predict and track. Currently, different health care plans offer different reimbursement rates, which makes the cost of care vary among people receiving identical treatments. This payment structure helps to explain why the tendencies to over-treat or under-treat certain conditions vary in different regions. Perhaps the most compelling aspect of a single payer is the incentive to provide better long-term care for patients because the government would be responsible for current as well as future costs, whereas under the current system future medical cost are borne by Medicare.

The benefits that could be attained from a single-payer system are high-lighted by the fact that spending on health administration and insurance in the United States was seven times that of the OECD median.[31] Furthermore, many studies have concluded that countries such as Canada and Germany pay lower quality-adjusted prices for medical care than the United States.[32] Also in terms of quality, a cross-country study that compared various statistics in the United States, Canada, the United Kingdom, Australia, and New Zealand was inconclusive in its findings. Each country performed extremely well in some categories but poorly in others.[33] Yet, despite the fact that differences in quality are difficult to detect, Canada only spends 51.9 percent of the amount the United States spends.[34]

However, the single-payer system has numerous shortcomings that challenge its effectiveness as an efficient model. One of the problems created by the single-payer system is the establishment of a monopoly run by the government that would have absolute bargaining power relative to the system's other participants.[35] Such a plan would eliminate the forces of competition that can, through extensive reform, better allocate resources using incentives and pricing.

The single payer would inevitably be subject to budget constraints that would force it to shift costs to suppliers and consumers and away from technological innovation. A common criticism of the single-payer system was captured by the British magazine *The Economist*, which proclaimed that "patients in other rich countries can get prompt medical treatment with state of the art medical technologies in clean rather than dirty wards."[36] Of course this problem is not captured in statistics, but it is a hidden cost of the price controls used by the government under single-payer system. It is a well-known fact in economics that price controls have a deleterious effect on quality in the long run.

The zeal with which many politicians and voters pursue price controls as a mechanism to control costs comes about because in the short term the costs are largely hidden. This reality makes price controls particularly attractive to politicians seeking reelections, because the adverse issues created by their actions take time to materialize; they can claim victory in the short run and force others to deal with the consequences in the future. The hidden costs arise because price controls distort the self-equilibrating process inherent in free markets. Lowering the cost below equilibrium level causes the quantity demanded to rise and the quantity supplied to decrease, leading to pervasive shortages. Hence, providers will supply fewer health care goods and services under a system that employs coercive price controls. The lack of competition under a single-payer system also reduces quality in the long run because under a monopoly the traditional profit-seeking behavior found in the free market, which drives innovation and improvements, is lessened. Another argument against a government-run single-payer health care system is the extensive waiting times endured by patients seeking elective or noncritical surgery. Waiting is a form of rationing, and it is an area in which the United States performs quite well compared to other OECD countries. A recent study reported that "a quarter to a third of respondents in Canada, the United Kingdom, and Australia reported waiting more than four months for a non-emergency procedure, compared with only 5 percent of Americans."[37] The *Wall Street Journal* reported that "an Ontario woman had a 40-pound fluid-filled tumor removed from her abdomen by an American surgeon in 2006. Her Michigan doctor estimated that she was within weeks of dying, but she was still on a wait list for a Canadian specialist."[38] In general, a study of OECD countries found that high waiting times were associated with physicians who received a salary instead of fee-for-service compensation.[39] The high waiting times associated with single-payer systems like those experienced in the Canadian model are particularly troubling because, for many ailments, a lag in treatment allows the underlying malady to worsen and therefore drives up the long-run cost of treating it. An example of this occurred in the United Kingdom where a women's cancer surgery was repeatedly delayed until finally her condition deteriorated to the point where it became inoperable.[40]

Technology is another area in which the average government-funded single-payer system lags behind the United States. In the United States there are 34.3 CT scanners per one million persons compared with 7.6 in the United Kingdom and 12.7 in Canada.[41] The numbers are similar for MRI units: 25.9 units per million persons in the United States compared to 8.2 in Britain and 6.7 in Canada.[42] The average number of units in all OECD countries is 11.0. The one notable exception and the only country with more MRI units than the United States is Japan, which has 40.1 MRI units per million persons and is a single-payer system.[43] However, the United States has the largest number of both MRI and CT exams per 1,000 persons.[44] The relative technological advantage the United States has over most OECD countries explains some variation in medical costs. Medical technologies such as CT scanners and MRI units are extremely expensive and contribute to a higher level of care, which drives up cost.

Rising concerns over extensive waiting times and restricted access to advanced procedures have led many to opt out of government-funded single-payer systems. Patients and doctors have pursued more efficient means to health care by abandoning the price controls instituted under government-run care. As the United States rushes to increase the government's involvement in health care, other countries including Canada, Sweden, and the United Kingdom are increasingly turning control over to the private sector to control costs and improve quality.[45] In Canada's British Columbia province nearly 50,000 patients are seen every year in private clinics, and the numbers are continuing to grow. Furthermore, private clinics continue to open at the rate of about one per week.[46] The movement has been empowered by a landmark case heard by the Canadian Supreme Court in 2005 that struck down key provisions that allowed for a government monopoly of health services in Quebec.[47] Claude Castonguay, one of the founders of the single-payer system in Canada has been cited by the *Wall Street Journal* as having regrets about the current Canadian health care system. "He declared the system in 'crisis' and suggested a massive expansion of private services—even advocating that public hospitals rent facilities to physicians in off-hours."[48] In the United States, many medical care providers have already opted out by refusing to treat patients with certain types of government-run insurance plans because they offer reimbursements that are lower than the cost of care.[49]

The empirical evidence demonstrates that single-payer systems tend to have lower per capita costs than the health care costs of the United States. In addition, differences in quality of care tend to vary but provide inconclusive evidence that either system has an absolute advantage over the other. The United States leads in research and development of new drugs. In terms of waiting, the U.S. model is superior, with significantly lower lag times for elective and noncritical operations than its OECD counterparts. Thus, trade-offs exist among costs, quality, medical innovation, accessibility, and waiting times.

The single-payer system reduces patients' explicit health care expenses but potentially increases their tax liability—especially if they expect to have innovations in the medical field. In addition, the assumption propagated by proponents of single-payer systems that a net reduction in health care expenditures is achieved by routing money through a government bureaucracy fails to account for the quantitative and qualitative consequences of price controls. Even if government leaders had the best of intentions, it is doubtful that a bulky command-style bureaucracy would consistently allocate resources in an efficient and effective manner. It strains credulity to assume that the government, void of competitive checks and balances, would eliminate inefficiencies, especially when one considers the conflicting pressures of budget constraints and the politicians' zeal to provide more goods and services to voters in an effort to get reelected.

VALUE-BASED COMPETITION

The alternative to the single-payer model is value-based competition. This model aims to reform the warped incentive structure that has stymied the market's competitive forces. Currently, medicine is a zero-sum game in which patients, providers, insurance companies, and the government expend tremendous resources to shift costs among various participants rather than concentrating on quality improvements. This structure has clearly failed to lower costs and provide consistent quality. Rather, it has driven up the cost of administrating medicine and possibly hindered innovation.

In a normal market, competition drives contending parties to continually improve the product they offer. Firms that innovate gain a relative advantage and prosper in the long run, while firms that fail to adapt must either reform or leave the market. Under such conditions the "invisible hand" leads to lower quality-adjusted prices and advances in the use and access to technological resources. The fact that prices have risen and gaps in quality persist is evidence that institutional arrangements have failed to structure incentives in a manner that promotes positive-sum competition.

The current system fosters competition on the administrative level, not on the care level. This has led inefficient and underperforming providers to endure rather than exit the market. Michael Porter, a professor at Harvard Business School, and Elizabeth Teisberg, an associate professor at the University of Virginia's Darden Graduate School of Business, proclaim that "the dysfunctional competition in health care results from misaligned incentives and a series of understandable but unfortunate strategic, organizational, and regulatory choices by each participant in the system that feed on and exacerbate each other."[50] As a cure for health care they have devised the idea of value-based competition that takes an integrated full care cycle perspective. This involves abandoning the standardized care approach and instituting a rigorous and mandatory measuring and reporting system.[51] Such a system would provide an incentive-based framework that would reward providers with good performance with a larger patient base and more lucrative reimbursements. The system would be indexed for initial patient risk and circumstance in order to provide meaningful comparisons across a diverse patient base.

Value-based competition ushers in a cycle in which providers must actively compete in order to remain in the game. This process would spur continuous innovation and improvements in efficiency by aligning compensation with results. In addition, care is driven by provider experience, scale, and treatment based on the full cycle of care as opposed to the delivery of health care through discrete services that characterizes the current care structure. Another advantage of value-based competition is that it strengthens the forces that drive competition by making providers and insurers accountable on a regional and national level, not only a local level.[52]

Competition must also focus on creating value, not just controlling costs. Increases in efficiencies will minimize costs in the long run far more than simply shifting costs from one party to another. Similarly, value cannot be linked simply to cost in the short run. If a patient is given low cost and less effective treatment that fail effectively to ward off the ailment then the cost savings are confined purely to the short run. Likewise, high-cost preventive care such as stroke intervention avoids the alternative costs of long-term assisted care that accompany a severe stroke.[53] The value perspective challenges the mantra of "cost cutting" propagated by the mass media and politicians. By focusing on the long term and full cycle of care we can make better use of our scarce medical resources and foster competitive innovation that will bring down long-term costs without necessarily reducing quality.

Providers that perform well will be rewarded with more patients and better compensation. Without competition based on results, inefficient providers that lack the skill and excellence to deliver health care effectively will continue to impose a burden on the system. In addition, competition will lead to fewer medical errors and fewer cases of under-treatment in patients. The use of ineffective tests, procedures, and prescriptions will be replaced with a streamlined process that encourages value-based care. Patients will experience better quality, and substandard approaches to care will no longer be financially viable. Thus, the goal is to maximize value, not merely to minimize costs. This approach is grounded in the belief that the latter will be an endogenous result of the former.

Competition will also create an incentive for health care providers to stay on the cutting edge and improve their skills in order to achieve consistent levels of high performance.[54] The new performance-based compensation system will lead providers to invest in the best equipment and staff. Such expenditures will be well covered by the gains in performance and compensation that result from their use.

Early intervention will be a key benefit of value-based competition because performance is tied to the full care cycle. Providers will have an incentive to provide a timely diagnosis and treatment. In addition, with early intervention many medical conditions can be controlled in a more efficient manner than if they had reached advanced stages. Informing the patient of healthy habits and providing appropriate cost-effective treatment will lead to fewer catastrophic illnesses that are costly in resources and far more damaging to the patient's well-being. Providers will focus more on detection and prevention than acute intervention.[55] Value-based competition will achieve an outcome that a single provider cannot—a simultaneous decrease in costs as well as an increase in quality; it will reproduce what happened in the United States with computers.

This model, which has microeconomic foundations, shows that igniting the largely dormant forces of competition will open up the possibility of achieving true health care reform. By providing insurers and medical providers with the incentive to maximize value or risk losing their patient or subscriber base, competition will achieve what regulation and command economics cannot—an integrated institutional arrangement that efficiently allocates the factors of production, and thus maximizes the well-being of both the consumer and the provider.

Criticism against value-based competition suggests that the evaluation framework may lead providers to *game* the system.[56] Since patient flows and compensation are tied to performance, providers and insurers may seek means to elevate their performance statistics to maximize revenue. This, critics fear, may lead providers and insurers to divert scarce resources away from care and toward unproductive activities. Others may resort to bribes or kickbacks to keep their performance figures high and avoid a reduction in compensation.

Another criticism levied against value-based competition is that creating a uniform and fair system of evaluation is impossible. Critics argue that inherent differences in patient bases (resulting from the higher incidence of certain illnesses in specific geographical areas, or among racial and ethnic groups, or because the genetic makeup of populations vary) make evaluating performance difficult. The counterargument to this is that by creating a relative health index that takes relevant factors into account, an accurate and statistically equitable foundation for performance is achievable.

Some argue that value-based competition will create a positional arms race among providers that will hinder the sharing of new information among providers. This means that people who compete will not share the know-how, which gives them a relative advantage. This view, however, fails to take into account the mutual benefit available to competing parties when they exchange information. Through exchange, parties can be made better off and maintain higher levels of efficiency. Even if exchange does not take place, competitors will copy the changes introduced by the most successful producers.

Many who have followed health care reform efforts over the last decade may ask, Can health care really be competitive? Even though numerous reforms have been attempted such as managed care and health savings accounts, prices have continued to rise and quality remains uneven across regions. This has led many to adopt the view that government is the only way to break the vicious trend of rising premiums, sluggish improvements in quality, and persistent rates of error.

THE PATIENT PROTECTION AND AFFORDABLE CARE ACT OF MARCH 2010

The nature of health care is unique in that it is one of the few industries where competition has so far not achieved a clear victory over single-payer health care systems. Debate rages over how competitive the practice of medicine can really be; needless to say, the competitive results we would expect have not been delivered. Such uncertainty is what makes reform so difficult. For the United States there is no clear winner or sound blueprint for reform. Both policy options that we have described offer insights and ideas for improving the current system and, in fact, ideas from both systems have been incorporated into the Patient Protection and Affordable Care Act.

The March 2010 health care legislation is unusual in a number of ways. While it attempts to provide health care for all U.S. citizens, it does not do so via the single-payer provisions that are common in OECD countries; rather, it mandates that people purchase health insurance (a mandate that has led to constitutional challenges by several states) and will establish, effective in 2014, state health exchanges for small businesses and individuals.

ObamaCare extends health coverage in several ways. Young adults will be able to remain on their parents' health plans until age 26. A temporary reinsurance program will be created for early retirees between the ages of 55 and 64. Small businesses will be given tax credits to start insurance programs. A larger portion of the population will be covered by Medicaid, as individuals below 133% of the federal poverty level will now qualify for coverage.

The program also encourages better services on the part of physicians. Doctors will be encouraged to form accountable health care organizations that improve efficiency of care. The Centers for Medicare and Medicaid Services will track hospital readmission rates to evaluate the quality of care. Effective in 2015, Medicare will create a physician payment program that will reward the quality of care rather than the volume of services.

ObamaCare is not very different from existing programs, except that it expands insurance coverage while, at the same time, it forces insurers to face greater restrictions than they face now. The cost of the program has been estimated to be just short of a trillion dollars, but we believe that such cost estimates are unrealistic.

Many critics of the bill argue that the government's vast resources and coercive ability to tax give it an unfair advantage over the private sector. Others argue that the new mixed system will create competitive forces while granting all citizens access to health care. Trade-offs in costs, accessibility, wait times, and quality will exist under any alternative. We hope that by showing the advantages and disadvantages of both competition and the single-payer system the reader will better understand the way policy changes will affect their long-term care.

CONCLUSION

Curing health care is not an option—it is a necessity. We have demonstrated that the current levels of spending and promises made by the government to future beneficiaries threaten to drown the federal budget. In our opinion, ObamaCare is not the solution to the problems we have raised. We are still creating overwhelming intergenerational deficits that will have a profoundly negative impact on future generations. We have discussed two vastly different alternatives and highlighted the respective merits and shortfalls of each. Our hope is that by doing so we have elevated the discussion on health care and provided a foundation for effective reform. However, if reform within the current political environment is not possible, then what is required is a dramatic change in our way of thinking about this problem. That is the topic of the next chapter.

NOTES

1. Clayton M. Christensen, Jerome H. Grossman, and Jason Hwang, *The Innovator's Prescription* (New York: McGraw-Hill, 2009), xv.

2. Michael E. Porter and Elizabeth Olmstead Teisberg, *Redefining Health Care: Creating Value-Based Competition on Results* (Boston, MA: Harvard Business School Press, 2006), 1.

3. U.S. Census Bureau, "Health Insurance Coverage: 2007—Highlights," http://www.census.gov/hhes/www/hlthins/hlthin07/hlth07asc.html.

4. Ibid.

5. Christensen, Grossman, Hwang, *The Innovator's Prescription*, xvi.

6. Ibid.

7. Michael Pakko, "Deficits, Debt and Looming Disaster," *Regional Economist*, January 2009.

8. Richard W. Fisher, "Storms on the Horizon," Richard Fisher Speeches, June 2009, Federal Reserve Bank of Dallas, http://www.dallasfed.org/news/speeches/fisher/2008/fs080528.cfm.

9. Niall Ferguson, *Colossus: The Rise and Fall of the American Empire* (New York: Penguin, 2005), 270.

10. Ibid., 273.

11. Christensen, Grossman, Hwang, *The Innovator's Prescription*, xvi.

12. Thomas Sowell, *Applied Economics: Thinking Beyond Stage One* (New York: Basic Books, 2008), 53.

13. Organization for Economics Cooperation and Development Online, *Health at a Glance 2009*, http://www.oecd.org/document/11/0,3343,en_2649 _33929_16502667_1_1_1_1,00.html, 80.

14. Porter and Teisberg, *Redefining Health Care*, 7.

15. Chris L. Peterson and Rachel Burton, "U.S. Health Care Spending: Comparison with Other OECD Countries," Congressional Research Service http://assets.opencrs.com/rpts/RL34175_20070917.pdf.

16. Ibid.

17. Ibid.

18. *Health at a Glance 2009*, 81.

19. Ibid., 80.

20. Ibid., 80.

21. Peterson and Burton, "U.S. Health Care Spending."

22. OECD Health Data 2009, "How Does the United States Compare?," http://www.oecd.org/dataoecd/46/2/38980580.pdf.

23. Peterson and Burton, "U.S. Health Care Spending."

24. Ibid.

25. Ibid.

26. *Health at a Glance 2009*, 83.

27. Ibid.

28. Ted Tuschka, *Wall Street Journal*, "Free Riders and Drug Development," July 2, 2008, sec. A.

29. Sowell, *Applied Economics*, 77.

30. Ibid., 78.

31. Peterson and Burton, "U.S. Health Care Spending," 34.

32. Ibid.

33. Ibid, 64.

34. Peterson and Burton, "U.S. Health Care Spending," 7.

35. Porter and Teisberg, *Redefining Health Care*, 89.

36. "Will Money Cure the NHS?" *The Economist*, 52, quoted in Sowell, *Applied Economics*, 56.

37. Peterson and Burton, "U.S. Health Care Spending," 52.

38. David Gratzer, "Canada's ObamaCare Precedent," *Wall Street Journal*, June 12, 2009, http://online.wsj.com/article/SB124451570546396929.html.

39. Peterson and Burton, "U.S. Health Care Spending," 52.

40. Sowell, *Applied Economics*, 61.

41. *Health at a Glance 2009*, 42.

42. Ibid.

43. Ibid.

44. Ibid.

45. David Gratzer, "Canada's ObamaCare Precedent"

46. Ibid.

47. Ibid.

48. Ibid.

49. Sowell, *Applied Economics*, 63.

50. Porter and Teisberg, *Redefining Health Care*, 4.

51. Ibid., 7.

52. Ibid., 98.

53. Ibid., 100.

54. Ibid., 104.

55. Ibid., 107.

56. Ibid., 104.

Chapter 5

INVESTING IN HEALTH AND EDUCATION

We warn the reader that this chapter is somewhat unusual, for it addresses deep flaws in the U.S. health and education sectors. The economic argument that there is widespread misallocation of resources in both sectors is quite simple. However, in order to reach this conclusion we need an analysis that requires an unusual conceptual framework. Hence we ask the reader for a bit of patience, for at times the discussion wanders away from economics into statistics, philosophy, and psychology. This may also be the most controversial chapter in the book because it challenges some deeply held beliefs. All we ask the reader is to give us the opportunity to make our case! We begin with simple economics.

The concept of "investment" as used in economics is quite different from the concept of investment that is used in business. Investment in economics means capital formation, or the acquisition and creation of resources that are to be used in further production. Households, firms, and governments make investments in the economic sense; for example, when they acquire houses, buildings, or roads. Please note that the acquisition of financial instruments does not constitute investment in the technical sense that will be used in this chapter.

In macroeconomics one has to be even more specific, for investment is the acquisition and creation of *newly produced* resources. Therefore, a new building will be counted as investment during a particular time period, but once the building is finished it no longer constitutes investment from the point of view of the national income and product accounts. Investment also includes changes in inventories, whether these are going to be used for further production (e.g., the parts of a car) or not (e.g., brand new cars that have not yet been sold to the general public).

Since investments give rise to resources or inputs that will be used in the production process, it turns out that what constitutes an investment is somewhat ambiguous, in some cases. When new automobiles are sold, they produce transportation services to consumers over future years, yet cars purchased by consumers are generally treated as consumption goods in official statistics. Households buy all sorts of small appliances that produce services over long periods of time, but they are also treated as consumption goods. Macroeconomic accounts even fail to differentiate between government expenditures for investment purposes (e.g., the building of a new airport) from those that are not (e.g., payments to police and firefighters for their services). This is a problem that distorts the public's understanding of the role of government in the economy, but it is relevant to this chapter, which deals with expenditures that improve the health and education of the population. Economists treat such expenditures as human capital investment.

The key to understanding investment is based on two central ideas. When an investment is made, it is expected to be productive (even if after the fact it is not); also, investments take time, and because they are unavailable when they are being produced (and yet the producers have to consume and survive) then someone else must be restricting his or her own consumption in order to fund production (which is what we call savings). Of course, it may turn out that the total savings that people find desirable may not match the amount of investment that households, firms, and government want to make, in which case there has to be a price that attempts to bring into equilibrium these two quantities of money; that price is the interest rate. If the interest rate is not able to equilibrate those two sums, then there may be more or less investment than is desirable; these show up as accumulated inventories beyond what firms desire or as a shortage of inventories desired by firms.

We stated in Chapter 2 that interest rates reflect the value of time. We now go on to state that the value of time depends on the use that can be made of that time, such as making investments that improve productivity and the economic efficiency of the economy. Our point at this juncture is that investment is made because it is perceived to be productive, and savings take place because they serve to transfer income streams from one period of time to another—because the improved productivity of the economy allows for increases in output and income in the future.

THE NATURE OF INVESTMENT (HOUSING)

Although this chapter does not deal with housing, we are about to make some assertions that may best be understood within the housing sector, for there they will not be controversial. We begin with the proposition that people are the most productive asset, and they require shelter in the form of housing. Furthermore, newly constructed housing is a type of investment—it both takes time to produce and provides services to people in the future. More importantly, no one would dispute a few additional assertions about housing:

1. Some housing may be defective;
2. The total amount of housing may be inadequate;
3. Some housing may be totally useless or even a burden on their owners;
4. Too much housing construction may end up with unoccupied houses; and
5. Some housing, built at the wrong time and place, may have a negative impact on those living in particular communities.

The general point of these important assertions is that there will always be an *optimal* amount of housing, which is not necessarily achieved by the *actual* amount of housing that is built.

Here are some examples of the above assertions. A house that is built and one year later crumbles is definitely defective. A community where one family lives in a palace and everyone else lives in hovels fails to provide sufficient housing services. A community made up of palaces will incur housing costs that are exorbitant to the occupants. A housing bubble that bursts will lead to unoccupied houses. A community that desires to keep open spaces and suddenly finds itself invaded by developers will resent that the nature of the community has changed. Hence, we cannot assume that the quality, type, and extent of housing will always be optimal. The same principle holds for medical care and education.

INVESTMENT IN HEALTH

Economists have always been adamant about the importance of health in the process of economic growth and development. A population that lives a short life will have to curtail its investment in productive assets, for the payoffs to those investments will not be recovered by them, and hence the incentives to make the investments disappear. This gives rise to a cycle of poverty: People are poor because they do not invest in themselves, and they do not invest in themselves because poverty does not provide them with lives that are long enough to recover their investments. Good health is paramount to achieving a successful level of economic well-being.

Then the question arises, How do we generate a population that lives long enough and that is sufficiently healthy to enjoy the fruits of its investments? Here, history is the best teacher. Personal cleanliness and public health policies that help to provide for community cleanliness are paramount. At the personal level, running water and the availability of soaps and other disinfectants are quite important; at the community level, water and sewer lines are vital—but also supervision and control over the food supply and, in particular, milk. Milk has a crucial impact on the health and survival of the young.

Then, of course, we have to consider the nutritional level of the population. Nutrition improves as better production methods in agriculture and animal husbandry are introduced. (Some of these investments have to be undertaken by the government, since technical knowledge, once acquired, can be easily copied and imparted to producers.) The body's best defense against illness is an immune system that is ready to fight foreign organisms because it is well supplied with food and nutrients.

Finally, we move on to formal medical treatments. Here, history reveals two things: Most medical treatment in antiquity actually made health worse, because treatments were not based on scientific tests; and modern medicine has found a plethora of ethical drugs, such as antibiotics, that have dramatically changed the outcomes of medical treatments. Regrettably, this is where our first problems with the acquisition of good health arise.

While the developers of modern medicines fully understand the science behind their methods, the general public does not. The public believes that if a medicine is taken, and that medicine has received government approval, then the medicine will cure the disease that the person has. This is generally false, especially as more and more medicines are introduced into the cabinet of the modern household.

This is how the approval of medicines works. Suppose a new medicine is developed to treat a particular disease, and a large number (e.g., 1,000) volunteers are willing to test its efficacy. The 1,000 volunteers are divided into two groups: 500 take a placebo (something known to have no medical effect, the equivalent of a sugar pill) and 500 take the drug. Let us suppose that 300 persons taking the medicine find a significant improvement in their condition, but only 250 do so in the placebo group. Statistical methods are then used to find whether the medical effect is "statistically significant," which in this case it would be,[1] in part because of the large number of volunteers. Then the medicine is approved for treatment, unless other significant side effects are discovered at the time that the medicine is being administered to volunteers.

Think about it. Half of the placebo group improved its condition with merely the equivalent of a sugar pill. (The immune system did its work!) However, 60 percent improved their condition as a result of taking the medicine—voilà, the medicine is ready for marketing! (This is a simplification because additional tests that confirm its efficacy may be required.) That means that there will be a large percentage of the patients taking the drug (40%) who cannot be expected to get better. Furthermore, a number of negative side effects are likely to be discovered as a wider number of people take the medicine over a longer time period.

When have you heard a doctor tell you about the percentage of people who actually improved as a result of a placebo, or tell you that the medicine had only a large (or small) differential effect relative to a placebo? One of the authors of this book is in his 60s, and he has *never* heard a doctor tell him or any of his relatives about the efficacy of medicines. The rationale for their behavior may lie simply in their practice of defensive medicine and the avoidance of lawsuits.

The situation in fact is much worse, for two reasons: The chances that the medicines are truly effective can be much, much lower than 60 percent (as in the example above) and often the doctors who prescribe the medicines do not understand the statistics that have been provided to them. Both of these themes have been extensively discussed in the writings of Gerd Gigerenzer, the director of the Center for Adaptive Behavior and Cognition at the Max Planck Institute for Development in Berlin, Germany. The following example is from one of his books:

> What is the benefit of a cholesterol-lowering drug on the risk of coronary heart disease? In 1995, the results of the West of Scotland Coronary Prevention Study were presented in a press release: "People with high cholesterol can rapidly reduce . . . the risk of death by 22 percent by taking a widely prescribed drug called pravastatin sodium. This is the conclusion of a landmark study presented today at the annual meeting of the American Heart Association." . . . What does "22 percent" mean? Studies indicate that a majority of people think that out of 1,000 people with high cholesterol, 220 of these people can be prevented from becoming heart attack victims.[2]

Dr. Gigerenzer, using the original study, demonstrates that this is not true. It turns out that deaths (per 1,000 people with high cholesterol) numbered 41 for people using the placebo, while deaths for those using the pravastatin treatment numbered only 32. In other words, the absolute risk reduction is 9 in 1,000 or 0.9 percent. The 22 percent figure is obtained by noting that 9 divided by 41 (in other words, the net benefit of the drug) was 22 percent *relative* to the placebo. This translates into another astonishing figure: just *one* life will be saved out of 111 who are taking the drug, because 9 in 1,000 deaths are supposedly prevented by the drug.[3] What, then, would the response of patients be (from a random sample of 111 individuals taking the drug) if they were asked about the effectiveness of the drug in preventing death?

Most patients will likely think that the drug is going to be responsible for their survival. Even if they thought carefully about the statistical result, they would still argue that a 22 percent chance of survival was worth the monetary cost of taking the drug (even if they are paying for it!) Regrettably, both the careless and the thoughtful response are wrong: the absolute risk reduction is only 0.9 percent, or the equivalent of 1 percent!

Critics may respond as follows: Can the authors demonstrate that medical drugs in general are in fact so ineffective? Here we need to give a nuanced response. First, some drugs (antibiotics) are highly effective, but even those are losing their effectiveness as they are abused. Second, medical treatments for different populations within the same country are widely different (e.g., medical treatments within states in the United States), yet neither are the morbidity (relative incidence of disease) and mortality regimes much different across states nor are medical treatments the main cause for differences in outcomes (public health and income being far more important factors).[4] Finally, comparing poor countries to rich countries, one finds that both morbidity and mortality in the former are approaching the levels of the latter, with minimal expenditures on health care—but with radical improvements in public health and in income levels.

HEALTH, HEALTH CARE, AND CHOICES

Earlier we proposed to compare investments in health to investments in housing. The United States has made great investments in health, yet its politicians insist that the health care system is broken. How could that possibly be the case? In what sense is our investment in health (not health care) defective?

First, people confuse health with health care, and these are two entirely different things. Second, some people do get more attention within the health care system than others, and somehow this is perceived to be unfair. Let's begin with a well-known example: Minorities, including blacks and Hispanics, receive less medical attention than the white population. Result? Adjusted for age, blacks have the highest mortality rate in the population, followed by whites, then Hispanics, and finally people of Asian descent.[5] However, please consider these results. We had said that Hispanics receive less attention than whites—how could it be possible, then, that their mortality is significantly lower than that of whites? Some people argue that we should concentrate on outcomes rather than opportunities; but in this case the outcomes indicate that Hispanics have a lower mortality rate, after adjusting for age!

Our health care system has succeeded in decreasing the mortality of low-weight infants; those weighing less than 1,500 grams. Between 1960 and 1990, the children who survived at these low weights decreased their chances of severe disabilities from two-thirds to one-third. In fact, studies seem to indicate that despite the tremendous cost involved in saving the lives of these babies, the rate of return to investment in medical procedures is not only high but incredibly high. These results are obtained by using standard economic measures related to the value of life, in dollar terms.

Let us give some numbers to illustrate the nature of the analysis.[6] In 1960, an infant born under 1,000 grams was expected to live 6.5 years; in 1990 the same infant would be expected to live 38.2 years. Even in 1990, two-thirds of these infants would suffer severe handicaps during their lifetimes. However, once one considers the cost of saving these babies relative to the benefits, then, as previously stated, the return to these extraordinary medical procedures yields a positive return to the investments. Why is this conclusion surprising?

Suppose that the medical profession agrees with it. If that is the case, the medical profession would have to believe that if the cost of saving these low-weight babies dropped to almost zero, then the positive return would be even greater, and that in fact almost all babies should be saved. What does this imply?

Well, millions of babies have been aborted, and the vast majority of them would have been born at normal weight. Hence, if the medical profession sees these low-weight babies as worth saving from an economic point of view, why does it not clamor to save the vast majority of babies who are aborted?

Our goal here is not to discuss the controversial topic of abortion, but to present the medical profession with what appears to be a clear contradiction. If the members of the profession truly believe that low-weight babies are worth saving, from an economic point of view, why would they not believe that most fetuses that are aborted should also be saved from abortion?

The argument is made stronger by the problems that we face in the Social Security system. Everyone agrees that there are not enough young people to make the system solvent. In fact, with long-term domestic fertility in the United States—and throughout Western Europe—below replacement levels, the need for additional births is a matter of extreme urgency. (Only recently, in 2008, the United States reached a fertility level that was above replacement, and this was due to black and Hispanic fertility rates). Yet the medical profession appears willing to justify saving low-weight babies with serious handicaps while at the same time appears willing to keep silent on abortion as a matter of principle, regardless of the demographic impact that it has on the country. The medical profession should explain its silence on this issue.

Next we move to the extraordinary procedures provided to the elderly, who in this chapter we will consider those people above the age of 85. First, let us agree that significant improvements in health care have been achieved in illnesses related to the heart and the circulation of the blood. These illnesses can affect people of any age, but they do become more severe and more common as people age. Second, let us also agree that the hard-working people of the United States deserve years of retirement, and that people in fact try to take advantage of these years by retiring earlier than in the past. But what happens next?

As individuals age, two other types of illnesses become much more important: dementias and cancers, and for these illnesses little has been found to improve the quality of life or the probabilities of survival (except in the case of some cancer preventions via changes in lifestyle, which have little to do with health care). Observed survival rates, which may appear to contradict this assertion, fail to take into account earlier cancer detection. Yet the medical profession, once again, fails to speak out against the amount of resources dedicated to prolonging the lives of people with terminal conditions. The economics profession also remains silent, and it accepts the idea that the care of these individuals should be counted as part of our gross domestic product, as if our change in circumstances from years past (namely, the increase in the dependency ratio within the population) was not an economic burden on the well-being of our nation.

We do not advocate euthanasia or stopping research on these two medical conditions; what we advocate is the awareness that the huge medical expenditures that commonly take place in the last year of life represent funds that are taken away from others who have many more years to live. People with terminal conditions should not have their lives prolonged when there is absolutely no hope of recovery; regrettably, many elderly patients find themselves in these circumstances because cancers and dementias are associated with the aging process.

Today people profess to be religious, but they appear willing to act against those same religious principles. If terminating the life of a fetus is wrong, then it should not be seen as a matter of personal choice, and abortions should not proceed unabated. Similarly, people see the deteriorating health of the elderly (in this case due to natural causes) but then demand that we spend all we can to prolong their lives when death is close at hand. Sometimes the benefit of drugs is measured in life-years saved, which seems at least a reasonable alternative to simple economic accounting; but then we must conclude that saving the unborn yields many more life-years than prolonging the lives of those who are near death.

What, then, is to be done? First, we support freedom of choice with regard to medical care. People should have access to insurance that will protect them while it is reasonable to protect them—in other words, when death is not imminent. This means, for practical purposes, that the health insurance should not cover medical treatments that have no hope of bringing about recovery; after that point, what people need is hospice insurance that would pay only for a peaceful way of ending their lives with dignity. The alternative to this approach consists of extraordinary expenditures that end up saving no lives, or what is already observed in several European countries—namely active euthanasia—which we condemn.

EXPLAINING OUR ALTERNATIVE VIEWPOINT

Investment in health (not health care) is similar to any other type of investment, such as housing. We must find the optimal level of investment, not only for us but for our country. This implies that we must recognize that in some cases our investment is misinformed—for investment in health is not the same as investment in health care. (The former improves the quality of milk; the latter treats those who drink spoiled milk.) We are failing to increase our numbers, by refusing to accept that children are assets rather than liabilities. We are failing to inform people about the effectiveness of drugs. Most important, we may be spending too much on elderly people who face imminent death—resources that can be used for the young.

If we are to make an informed choice among health care alternatives, we must think beyond the trade-offs that were discussed in Chapter 4 and keep in mind two things: that health is our goal, and that religious, moral, and philosophical values have to be brought explicitly or implicitly into the discussion. Yet we do not want to impose our values on anyone else. In fact, it may well be the case that the value systems held by people in the United States are so conflicting that it is impossible to reach a national health care compromise! If that is true, health care should be in the hands of regions or individual states, providing citizens with multiple policy choices and different tax burdens. Citizens might then choose to move to their preferred location, or at least avoid locations that offer choices they find objectionable.

When it comes to health care, people tend to hide, or put aside, the human values that dictate our preferences. Why don't we let competition among regions or states provide us with choices that would better reflect our own diversity of values? Until we do so, the economic cost of political conflict will continue to have a negative impact on our productive potential.

INVESTMENT IN EDUCATION

The broad expansion of educational services is a relatively new phenomenon, which dates back to the early twentieth century. Both Europe and the United States had a limited number of public schools at the start of that century and their universities were truly elite institutions that catered to individuals who had obtained the classical training that was traditional in European schools.

For the United States, school enrollment per 100 persons who were 5 to 19 years old was 54.3 in 1890 but 87.9 in 1970. There was also a large disparity in school attendance between secondary and elementary schools; the ratio between the two was 0.1624 in 1890 but 0.4341 in 1970. The percentage of persons who were 17 years old who graduated from high school was 3.5 percent in 1890 but 75.6 percent in 1970 (these years were used in order to report comparable figures). The total number of doctorates conferred in 1890 was only 149, yet 29,866 were conferred in 1970—this occurred while the resident population rose from 63 million to 205 million.[7]

The most important conclusion that can be drawn from this historical experience is that economic growth and economic well-being were able to proceed with a population that had only limited formal education. This experience also points out that education is not simply an investment good (which would give rise to improvements in productivity over the long run) but also a consumer good (which becomes desirable as the income and wealth of the population increases). The United States was able to grow rapidly in the nineteenth century despite limited formal schooling.

One can still argue that the modern world requires more knowledge on the part of its workers and citizens. This can be illustrated in conjunction with the previous discussion of this chapter. It was pointed out that people in this country do not have a good understanding of the efficacy of medical drugs. This lack of understanding allows politicians (who themselves may not understand the issues involved) to propose expenditures for prescription drugs that have only a limited impact on the health of the population. If the population is not well informed, then it is likely to accept policies that will have little health value but will make people feel good.

The importance of education with regard to medical decisions cannot be underestimated. A well-educated individual can keep track of the side effects that newly developed drugs can have. Furthermore, the Internet allows a person to search for the best-trained doctors and the best-performing hospitals—but doing so requires education.

We can go a step further. The process of obtaining medical attention is one in which the medical doctors ask questions and the patient responds to those questions (truthfully, one would hope). The doctor then prescribes blood tests and other procedures that ideally lead to the discovery of the patient's medical problem. However, please consider that computer programs themselves allow for such interactive questions and responses. In other words, a truly well-educated population may have limited use for traditional medical doctors, since their work can, to a great extent, be incorporated within the field of artificial intelligence.

Everyone agrees that we live in a very complex world; in fact, it is so complex that individuals know less and less of the complexity that ties together all of people's interactions—and that is the way it should be. Successful enterprises are not made of people who know all about the enterprises, but rather of people with deep knowledge about small aspects of each enterprise. This is called specialization (we are back to economics), which allows many minds with limited knowledge to create very large projects. To understand this, think of sending a man or woman to the Moon. The people working for such a project have to cover a vast number of fields—chemistry, physics, engineering, biology, mathematics, information systems, and many more; no individual could acquire deep knowledge of all or some of these fields simultaneously. It is specialization (often embedded in machines and devices) that allows us to concentrate on narrow aspects within joint projects.

Modern society confuses education with educational services. Education can be obtained and in fact should be obtained, in this day and age, with the help of machines, for these both simplify and amplify our educational experience. Consider the learning of a new language. There is no doubt that a teacher can stimulate the student to learn that language, but even that teacher will only be able to produce one accent in the new language—namely his or her own. A machine that records the speech of many people serves to amplify the experience of students. If one is learning Spanish, for example, after learning the "standard" language, which is what appears in radio and TV productions (to allow the vast majority of the population to understand the programs), the machine can reproduce dialogues from Spain, Mexico, Peru, Colombia, and Argentina—making the student aware of the complexity of sounds of a standard written language.

However, to acquire deep knowledge of a foreign language requires time, and time acts as a constraint on individuals. The person who tries to learn Spanish can have either a superficial understanding of the language or a deep knowledge of it. In practice, our educational services try to teach only the most superficial aspects of all that could be taught.

Why is this approach a failure? Schools begin with a large number of students whose talents are truly unknown. The teachers themselves have superficial knowledge of a broad range of subjects, and they attempt to pass on that superficial knowledge to students. It is rare when students show a deep interest in what is being taught; for some of them the education will be too difficult, for others too superficial, and for still others totally irrelevant. Some basic skills (e.g., reading and arithmetic) need to be acquired by all the students, but it is doubtful that the teachers can provide a wide range of experiences that serves to motivate the students to learn. In many cases we do not need teachers but rather machines that can adapt to the interests of *individual* students.

The obvious response to this criticism is that current educational practices represent the way education has been imparted for hundreds, if not thousands, of years. That is correct, but education long ago was imparted to a select group of students (most of whom were a minority of individuals whose families could afford education). It is not surprising that the educational systems of the past were looking for bright students who could assimilate the broad education of their teachers. Isaac Newton was such a child, and neither he nor his many brothers belonged to an elite family of his day, yet Newton was discovered by a system that looked for the brightest among all children.

The nation does need an educated polis that can understand the issues of the day. However, a political community has to discover first the hidden talents that lie within it—and teachers of the modern sort cannot do that, whereas machines can. Machines can offer students, millions of them, broad and deep experiences across alternative subjects.

Can this be done in the early grades? Probably not. The early grades constitute a period of psychological and emotional development where students need nurturing and personal understanding. The students need to be well fed and in good health, and under the supervision of a caring and compassionate person. Even then, though, teachers must familiarize students early on with machines of all types, for the students will have varied interests as they gain familiarity with the world that surrounds them.

After that, a diverse curriculum is needed. A musical genius would hate to have to learn world history or possibly the sciences—why should that child be placed in the constraints of a standard curriculum? In fact, there should be no standard curriculum at all, but rather standard curricula that will cater to the personal talents of many individuals. Regrettably, some students have no unique talent, and those students need to be taught trades and professions that will allow them to earn a living.

While this discussion may appear to be philosophical in nature, we want the reader to understand that this presentation has a much different purpose: to illustrate the idea that the *quality* of education, rather than the quantity of education, is what makes a difference in the educational process. While someone may disagree with the educational process that we propose, we will argue that such a process fits the acquisition of cognitive skills better than the current educational process. The importance of these skills will be made abundantly clear below.

We concentrate first, however, on the empirical evidence for the role of education in the achievement of economic growth and well-being. Much of what we state below depends on the most recent work of Hanushek and Woessmann, who summarized the very extensive literature on education and cognitive abilities in a journal article published in 2008.[8]

Hanushek and Woessmann point out that at least three mechanisms suggest that educational attainment increases economic growth. First, education increases the human capital of the labor force, thereby making it more productive; second, education has the potential for increasing the number of innovations in the economy, and since growth is highly dependent on innovation and technological change, education and growth could possibly be linked; and third, education helps facilitate the diffusion and transmission of knowledge, including that which is embedded in technological change. Using these basic ideas, the empirical evidence first suggests that education (measured via years of schooling) contributes to economic growth.

These results, however, do not stand up to scrutiny when they are combined with measures of cognitive skills, as demonstrated by the same two authors. The distinction between education and cognitive skills is hard to make. The authors begin their analysis with the intuition that is given by the following assertion: "Most people would, in casual conversation, acknowledge that a year of schooling in a school in a Brazilian Amazon village was not the same as a year of schooling in a school in Belgium."[9]

They also point out that while it is true that cognitive skills can be learned in schools, these skills can also be learned at the home, through peers, or even by interacting within society at large. The difficult question is how to define these cognitive skills. The simplest definition (not given by the authors) is that cognitive skills are mental abilities that help us process external stimuli.

One can come up with more specific cognitive skills, which can be measured via tests and which are widely recognized in the psychology literature. One such skill is how fast the brain processes the data that it receives. Another is the ability to analyze, segment, and blend sounds. A third is the ability to manipulate visual information. Two others relate to the long-term storage and recall of memory, and the effectiveness of short-term memory. Then we add reasoning skills and finally attention skills. Strength in cognitive skills correlates directly with students' ease of learning.

There is no doubt that some of these skills can be learned or improved via the formal educational process. Teachers, for example, emphasize the need to pay close attention to what is being taught, and the teaching of mathematics certainly improves the ability of students to manipulate visual information. However, as the two authors emphasize, schooling can help with cognitive skills, but these also depend on circumstances that are found outside of the schools.

The empirical evidence is quite surprising, at several levels. Most important is that once levels of cognitive skills are introduced into the equations that measure the effect of schooling on economic growth, schooling ceases to have an impact (or has very limited impact) on economic growth. The two authors also demonstrate that these abilities are not necessarily tied to the level of growth that countries have actually achieved; for example, cognitive abilities in China are not very different from those in the United States, yet both are significantly different from those found in Argentina, which is a country far wealthier than China. In other words, other factors are also important in achieving economic growth.

The two major conclusions of the study are worth quoting in full:[10]

1. Cognitive skills have powerful effects on individual earnings, on the distribution of income, and on economic growth; and

2. The current situation in developing countries is much worse than generally pictured on the basis of just school enrollment and attainment.

The United States does quite well in the attainment of cognitive skills, but it is surpassed by both China and India. Japan and the Netherlands are at the top of the list, indicating that these skills do not correlate well with race; in this context, it should also be noted that Argentina is a country whose population is almost entirely of European origin. Cognitive skills can both be learned or be suppressed—with Brazil, Peru, and Saudi Arabia at the bottom of the many countries studied by the authors.

If we take these results seriously, one has to conclude that while the U.S. educational system has not entirely failed as an engine of growth, there is room for improvement in the acquisition of cognitive skills and education.

The elementary school system in the United States is in fact quite successful, for it teaches students reading and the basic rules of arithmetic. Regrettably, the students begin to slide in their academic performance relative to many European and Asian countries at the secondary levels. This occurs in part because these foreign countries are more demanding of their students, an approach that goes against the philosophy of U.S. schools, which are willing to promote students from lower to higher grades despite the students' lack of academic achievement. Hence, if we are going to simultaneously be more demanding of our students and offer them a greater diversity of learning opportunities, we must offer curricula that are also more diversified—and that use skills that are *not* available to the average secondary school teacher. It is for this reason that we encourage and propose the use of machines for the deepening of knowledge.

This does not mean that secondary teachers could not teach a variety of general subjects. The acquisition of language skills, history, general mathematics, and basic science (including medical science) must be taught at the high school level. However, students must be given plenty of time to explore the things they enjoy and would love to explore. The resources are there to make this change, as long as we are willing to sacrifice other types of school expenditures—including expenditures on teachers. Teachers of the future must be able to attend to two, three, or even four times the number of students that they attend to right now: that is what productivity is all about. The evidence exists that this can be done—but only when teachers' unions do not prevent the introduction of machines into routine teaching, a topic covered in the book *Liberating Learning*.[11]

Currently, our high schools have become babysitters for young adults, a significant number of whom are quite unhappy with the environment in which they find themselves. These individuals should be helped to find employment, so that they obtain skills that will allow them to earn a living. If this is done in Japan, which has the highest level of cognitive skills, why can it not be done in the United States? The United States has been perpetuating an educational structure that comes from a past that depended on humans for imparting education; however, machines have the potential of opening new vistas to students, and the sooner the country implements these changes, the better off it shall be.

This chapter may appear to have deviated from our goal of explaining why the U.S. macro economy is in trouble, but efficiencies must be sought everywhere, and educational expenditures make up a significant amount of national, state, and local budgets. Schools have been saddled with outdated personnel who cannot be eliminated because they are members of labor unions, and these unions avoid the substitution of machines for human labor. The United States also spends millions upon millions of dollars on children (who are *not* physically or mentally handicapped) who have low potential of becoming highly productive members of society. The United States has been mandating the teaching of all subjects to all students including students who are not the least bit interested in them. It has been pretending that athletic and artistic success are the most cherished accomplishments of the students, when in fact the vast majority of them do not even have a realistic chance of being successful in those professions. It should instead focus on the specific talents that students have, when they have them. (The special talents of handicapped students must also be discovered, for they, too, can be highly productive members of society.) Furthermore, the technology exists to evaluate the performance of teachers, using test scores and controls for all the variables that might affect student performance. Teacher unions have fought relentlessly against the use of integrated management systems that allow for such evaluations, such as ARIS, whose use was defeated in the New York legislature by the political power of the unions. Most parents, nationwide, are not even aware of the existence of these integrated management systems.[12]

NOTES

1. The result in this example is highly statistically significant, meaning that it would occur by chance alone less than one percent of the time.

2. Gerd Gigerenzer, *Calculated Risks: How to Know When Numbers Deceive You* (New York: Simon & Schuster, 2002), 34.

3. Ibid., 35.

4. These issues are discussed in most textbooks on health economics. See, for example, Charles E. Phelps, *Health Economics*, Chapter 3 (New York: Harper Collins, 1992).

5. Centers for Disease Control and Prevention, *Health, United States, 2008; Updated Trend Tables* (July 2009), Table 27.

6. The information that follows is taken from David M. Cutler and Ellen Meara, "The Technology of Birth: Is It Worth It?," *Frontiers in Health Policy Research 3*, ed. by Alan M. Garber, National Bureau of Economic Research (Cambridge, MA: MIT Press, 2000), 33–67.

7. These numbers are taken from U.S. Bureau of the Census, *The Statistical History of the United States, from Colonial Times to the Present* (New York: Basic Books, 1976).

8. Eric A. Hanushek and Ludger Woessmann, "The Role of Cognitive Skills in Economic Development," *Journal of Economic Literature* 96, no. 3 (2008): 607–68.

9. Ibid., 608.

10. Ibid., 657–8.

11. Terry M. Moe and John E. Chubb, *Liberating Learning: Technology, Politics and the Future of American Education* (San Francisco, CA: Jossey-Bass, a Wiley imprint, 2009).

12. Ibid., 92–93.

Chapter 6

AMERICAN UNIONS: ROBIN HOODS OR WHITE-COLLAR CRIMINALS?

Labor unions have long been a part of American culture. From their inception, however, labor unions have earned the disdain of employers throughout the country. Many dismiss this contempt as capitalist fervor in conflict with the unions' rights to collective bargaining. In many senses, this diagnosis is correct. No one, not even the labor unions, can deny that organized labor increases the costs of labor to firms, thus diminishing their profits. But many people see this impact as necessary, curbing the excesses of greed, and mitigating the profits of shareholders and executives in favor of the common man. Many see labor unions as the competitive market's own Robin Hood, taking some excesses from big business, without ever having a significant impact on the health of those businesses. The press has consistently published opinions favorable to the unions, supporting their efforts to assemble and demonizing the firms that resist their formations.[1]

Unions have also gained incredible backing from politicians country-wide, as union strength in numbers has drawn the grace of vote-hungry candidates. Even in the international community, the ability to unionize is considered a necessary and basic right. It is included in the United Nations' Universal Declaration of Human Rights (Article XXIII.4): "Everyone has the right to form and to join trade unions for the protection of his interests."[2] Until recently, these official positions were supported by public opinion. According to a Gallup Poll from August 2008, approximately 59 percent of Americans approved of unions, while only 31 percent disapproved.[3] In 2009, however, those numbers had slid substantially, with only 48 percent approving and 45 percent disapproving.[4] In general, though, national and international sentiment toward labor unions is clear; organized labor is held in high esteem by the majority.

What we argue in this section is simple: labor unions, at least within the borders of the United States, are not innocent Robin Hoods. Contrary to the position that the popular press and many politicians tend to propagate through the population, unions have a negative effect on the health of the firms with which they interact. While their power may appear to be beneficial and reduce profits only marginally, we contend that the long-term malice of collective bargaining extends far beyond that which the popular press tends to attribute to them. However, this chapter is not focused on the failures of the popular press within this context: misinformation constitutes a societal problem so extensive that we dedicate an entire chapter to it. Rather, this chapter focuses on the long-term ailments that can be attributed to collective bargaining.

DETROIT IN SHAMBLES

Amid the global economic downturn, one major focal point has been Detroit, where Ford, DaimlerChrysler, and General Motors (known as the "Big Three"), lie in shambles. Our human propensity to seek out those at fault brings many to ask, Who or what can we blame? Commentators have explained the decline of the auto industry using, among various possible causes, the decline of the U.S. economy, gross corporate mismanagement, and the shift in consumer preferences away from the large trucks and SUVs that were once the bread and butter of the auto firms. Each of these factors, as well as others, has merits that cannot be ignored. Indeed, it is likely that a broad compilation of these causes contributed to the crisis at hand. And while many of these factors have been sufficiently identified and exposed within the public sphere, many conventional commentators have failed in one significant manner: They have neglected to consider the production process itself within their analyses.

A comprehensive analysis of the barriers to efficient production inevitably leads us to two common denominators among all three major automakers: suffocating government regulation and the United Auto Workers Union (UAW). Government regulation is considered separately in Chapter 3, while this chapter focuses on the impact of the UAW on production. The union has a hold, indeed a monopoly on the supply of labor to all three firms in Detroit. With each new contract negotiation, the union has pushed for more benefits on behalf of its workers at the expense of the companies and their balance sheets. As much as the media tries to ignore it, there is a budget constraint in this employer-employee relationship. Whatever the union negotiates must be paid for out of the profits of the corporations. And as we have observed more recently, if there are no profits to pay for benefits, then the negotiated gains are paid through a loss of capital. For years the UAW negotiated increasingly absurd benefits for its employees, driving labor costs through the roof and ultimately destroying the competitive edge of U.S. automakers. The result of these developments is clear to see. General Motors (GM) and DaimlerChrysler both filed for bankruptcy, while the financial health of Ford has been severely undermined.

UNREASONABLE DEMANDS

We shall first explain why we consider the negotiated benefits of the UAW to be absurd and so dangerous and detrimental to the companies that use union labor. One major "accomplishment" of the UAW has been to protect job security to an extreme. The benefits that the UAW extracted from the automakers created an environment where labor-cost competitiveness was not possible unless the companies faced indefinitely increasing demands for their products—something that was quite doubtful.

One of the most controversial aspects of job security that resulted from collective bargaining was resistance to layoffs. Under the UAW-negotiated Supplemental Unemployment Benefits (SUB) program, laid-off workers were entitled to an almost unaltered stream of income and benefits from the corporations for a period of two years. They received weekly income of 95 percent of their original post-tax income minus $30, plus guaranteed health insurance throughout the two-year period. While some of this was covered by limited state unemployment benefits, the brunt of benefit payments, as well as substantial portions of wage maintenance, fell upon the auto companies. The UAW summarizes the program best by writing "the programs help maintain workers' income during extended periods of layoff. Workers continue to receive a paycheck while performing nontraditional work or community service and taking advantage of opportunities to increase their skills and education."[5] Of course, none of these employee opportunities contributed directly to the automakers' bottom lines, while their paychecks certainly detracted from them.

The UAW also boasted that, according to their 2003 contract, "no worker can be laid off for more than 48 weeks for volume-related reasons . . . "[6] In other words, workers could not be laid off for more than 48 weeks in an automaker's attempt to cut production. Of course, in those 48 weeks, the workers were protected by the above-mentioned SUB program, earning roughly 95 percent of their pre-layoff salaries. After the 48 weeks were completed the employees had to be brought back to work regardless of their usefulness to the company. In the face of this, the SUB program, and all other "job and income security" assurances that the union won through collective bargaining, the UAW effectively eliminated layoffs as a potential tool for the automakers in times of economic distress. Indeed, the UAW boasted on its Web site that "in the face of corporate restructurings at DaimlerChrysler, Ford and General Motors . . . [n]o one was laid off or involuntarily separated."[7] While Robin Hood is glorified in these terms, the underlying detriments are clear through a balance sheet approach: the power to lay off, an effective measure in the toolbox of most corporate executives in a dynamic economy, was removed from the realm of possibility for the Detroit automakers.

The UAW went even further to limit the Big Three's abilities to cut costs in tough times. One example of this is under Chrysler's contract, which limited the rights of the company to close, sell, idle, or otherwise stop production in plants other than those that the union gave explicit permission to do so. If a plant's productive capability was no longer useful, and became a liability to the company, the company was still required to operate the plant under the collective bargaining agreement.[8] In GM's contract, there was a similar clause, which forced GM to produce certain vehicles at certain plants.[9] Ford had similar stipulations within its 2007 contract as well.[10] That is, auto companies were required to maintain their specific production locations for the duration of the labor contracts. In essence, the automakers were obligated to continue to operate plants with large overhead even when those plants became useless to the functioning of the companies. The forced maintenance of potentially unproductive plants represented a major financial drain that was reflected on the balance sheets of the companies—whether in good times or in bad times. Additionally, those displaced by the limited closures agreed to by the UAW and company were protected by the SUB program and various other job and income security programs won by the unions. In short, while downsizing was not completely eliminated from the Big Three's box of business moves, it was severely restricted by union influence.

Outsourcing was also radically limited within the union contracts. Ford's contract provided for an outright moratorium on outsourcing.[11] GM and Chrysler's contract language was a bit less definitive, but they still provided for moratoriums "on outsourcing for core manufacturing jobs and non-core operations."[12] Even when Japanese competitors moved their operations into the United States, one effective option for cutting costs and remaining competitive within the auto industry would have been to outsource some production processes. Yet again, however, the UAW's mission to protect and enhance its constituents at all costs limited, and in many cases removed, the competitive edge of Detroit's executives.

In the face of the collapses of two of the Big Three, it is important to note that the union has granted a number of concessions relaxing many of the aforementioned benefits. Though these concessions may (or ultimately may not) alter the hand that the union has in the restructuring of the Big Three, they do not eliminate the culpability that the union holds with regard to the failure of Detroit. In fact, the necessity of concessions in the face of political and economic pressures only corroborates our argument that union-negotiated contracts directly contributed to the downfall of the auto companies.

A few skeptics, however, may not be convinced by the arguments we have presented against the UAW. They might argue that although the practices of the UAW hindered the health of the balance sheets of the Big Three, the UAW is still a valiant Robin Hood character, simply limiting the profits of executives and shareholders in favor of blue-collar Americans. For years leading up to the recent economic meltdown, many held that opinion, as the companies seemed to function effectively even as the union made the companies less profitable. Recent events, however, have thrown the long-term consequences of union power into the spotlight. Though proponents of the unions in the media and the political system have tried to limit the blame for the recent deterioration of the Big Three, we must now discuss how the long-term negative pressures have contributed substantially to the decline of the automakers.

THE PROOF IS IN THE NUMBERS

To get a better look at the large negative effects of union power, we must analyze the aggregate effects of these negotiated benefits. Many difficulties lie in this approach, for no two groups agree on a single figure for aggregate labor costs of unionized workers. The source of this controversy is obvious, for each commentator has his or her own agenda in presenting the cost of labor. Those siding with the unions tend to try to drive down the reported costs of labor, so as to minimize the apparent discrepancies between union labor wages and competitive manufacturing wages. Those who oppose union power and propose the restructuring of contracts, on the other hand, might tend to inflate labor cost figures so as to legitimize their qualms with the current structure. Amid these conflicting agendas, it is indeed difficult to find a reliable source of labor cost information. Union figures are difficult to find, and even if readily available they would be extremely biased. Most of the information the UAW presents quantitatively reflects straight wages only, and ignores fringe benefits to employees, thus presenting deceivingly low numbers. Secondary analysts on either side of the fence also prove to be unreliable sources, as their numbers are often shaped to match their commentary. These difficulties must be overcome for the sake of objective analysis.

Our solution to this problem is to derive the numbers from original sources; when it comes to quantitative data there is no better provider than the primary supplier. Thus, we turn to the auto companies themselves in search of a quantitative aggregate of labor costs. It appears, through secondary citation of their Web site, that GM once placed a definite quantitative value on hourly labor. However, upon further investigation we find that GM removed this information. The other two companies, DaimlerChrysler and Ford, do provide comprehensive quantitative reports of labor costs.

First, we look to the growth in the cost of union labor in recent years. We discover that the costs of labor for the unionized auto firms have increased at alarming rates. Ford most accurately presents this in its 2007 Negotiations Fact Book, showing the progression of the hourly cost of labor from 1997 to 2006. According to Ford's publications, their U.S. hourly labor costs increased in nominal terms from $43.55 in 1997 to $70.51 in 2006. These figures include gross average hourly earnings, and benefits and fringe costs of workers. The change in Ford's hourly cost of labor represents a 61.91 percent increase in the cost of labor over the 10-year period, in nominal terms.[13]

To determine the real growth of labor costs per hour, however, we must account for inflation. Using the Consumer Price Index, one broad measure of inflation, we find that this increase is less in real terms, as $43.55 in nominal terms in 1997 is equal to $54.70 in 2006 dollars. Thus, the real increase in labor costs per hour between 1997 and 2006 was $15.81 in 2006 dollars, representing a real percentage increase of 28.90 percent per hour over the 10-year period. This real term, of course, represents increases above and beyond compensation for inflation.

These high rates of labor cost escalation are not unique to Ford, but rather they apply similarly to all employees represented by the UAW. Chrysler estimates that the nominal annual escalation of the cost of labor for UAW-represented autoworkers has been 9.7 percent annually since the year 2000. In contrast, Chrysler estimates that the cost of labor for Japanese transplants has increased only 3.3 percent annually over the same time period.[14] For the sake of clarity, one should note that the term *Japanese transplants* does not represent employees in foreign plants, but rather American plants that produce or assemble products of the Japanese companies, abiding by similar American labor legislation as the Big Three.

Interestingly enough, the Japanese transplants have had some limited experience with union representation. Toyota, for example, had a single plant that was represented by the UAW, the "Nummi" plant located in Fremont, California. Amid the global downturn, however, Toyota turned to this plant in its cost-cutting measures, and voted to close it.[15] The increased labor costs associated with the plant's unionized labor surely played a role in the executives' decision to close that particular plant, and the case only bolsters our arguments against the UAW in this chapter.

As we have discussed already in this chapter, the UAW succeeded in many respects as it has strived continuously to enhance the benefits of its constituents. The result has been higher growth rates (by a factor of three annually in recent years) of the cost of labor to unionized firms relative to those of non-unionized firms. The UAW continually escalated the cost of labor for firms at a rate much higher than the rate of labor costs for non-unionized firms.

This progression of labor costs brings us to an estimate of the flow of payments to labor. We want to present the aggregate effects of the growth rates reported above in a single quantitative figure: the cost of labor per hour for the firms in the period preceding the collapse of the companies. In order to maintain a consistent approach with our data, we will focus on the year 2006. Both the auto companies and the union have published an abundance of data regarding this particular year, it being the most recent prior to the contract negotiations of 2007. According to the primary sources, DaimlerChrysler's labor cost per hour worked was $75.86. Ford's labor cost per hour was a comparable $70.51.[16] Chrysler reported GM's hourly labor costs to be in the same range at $73.26.[17] A non-weighted average of these three figures produces an hourly cost of labor for the three unionized firms of approximately $73.21. In comparison, Chrysler reported the hourly cost of Japanese transplants to be $46. Thus, under the same U.S. government regulations and employing similar American workers, the Big Three had a 59.15 percent higher cost of labor than their non-unionized counterparts.

To put these hourly figures in more concrete terms, we turn to total increased expenditures as a result of unionization (see Table 6.1). For example, DaimlerChrysler, according to the figures presented above, had a higher average hourly cost of labor than the non-unionized transplants by approximately $29.86. The company reported that in the year 2006 it employed 46,276 UAW hourly workers.[18] Based on a 40-hour work week at 43.6 weeks per year (Chrysler estimates that the average UAW-represented employee received 42 paid days off per year), the increased cost because of unionized labor to Chrysler alone was $2.4 billion annually.[19] Ford reported that in 2006, it had 77,453 UAW-represented hourly employees.[20] According to the figures above, Ford's hourly additional cost of labor versus the non-unionized Japanese transplants was approximately $24.51. Using the same hourly and weekly assumptions as before, the additional labor costs to Ford totaled approximately $3.3 billion annually. GM employed 80,758 hourly employees at a cost markup of $27.26 per hour versus the Japanese transplants.[21] Again using the same hourly and weekly assumptions, the additional cost to GM totaled approximately $3.8 billion. Using these rough estimates, the total labor cost markup was approximately $9.5 billion annually to the Detroit Big Three auto manufacturers as of 2006.

Not even the most vehement skeptic of the argument at hand can dispute the clear results of the data analysis: The collective bargaining power of the United Auto Workers Union has produced significantly inflated labor costs for the firms whose labor supply they monopolize. The resulting losses—$9.5 billion annually as of 2006—detract from the profitability of the Big Three automakers. In the past, this may not have been visible, for even with the downward pressure on profitability, the firms were able to maintain a positive cash flow and satisfy their investors. This structural liability, however, lurked in the shadows, eating away at the sustainability of the companies that many once thought were unsinkable. Then, as the world economy spiraled downward, the crisis at hand became apparent, and the consequences of unionization, among other factors, was revealed. The severe economic downturn revealed the structural shortcomings of the companies. As Warren Buffett most accurately put it, "It's only when

Table 6.1
Estimated Cost Markup of Unionized Labor—2006

Company	Hourly Unionization Markup	Annual Unionization Markup
DaimlerChrysler	$29.86	$2.4 Billion
Ford	$24.51	$3.3 Billion
General Motors	$27.26	$3.8 Billion

Source: Calculations by the authors

the tide goes out that you learn who's been swimming naked." The structural liabilities of the UAW have contributed to the "lack of clothing," and as the tide retreated to the sea, we realized just how naked the Detroit firms are.

UNIONS ACROSS THE UNITED STATES

There remains one more task to complete, and that is to connect the situation of Detroit to the U.S. economy in general. The burden presented by the United Auto Workers Union upon the Detroit Big Three should be obvious at this point; its influence has inflated the cost of labor for the American automakers and restricted their ability to conduct business competitively. Still, one opposed to our position against strong labor unions might try to dismiss this case study as an isolated incidence of irresponsible and damaging labor conduct. Therefore it is now incumbent upon us to prove a relationship between the UAW and U.S. unions as a whole, thus validating the claim that the union structure within the United States presents itself as a burden to our aggregate economy. To do so, we turn to the empirical effects of unionization at the national level.

In our attempts to remain objective, we turn again to a neutral source of data, this time the U.S. government. At this juncture, we find data presented by the Bureau of Labor Statistics (BLS) most relevant. In a September 2009 survey entitled "Employer Costs for Employee Compensation," the BLS dedicated portions of its publication to the breakdown of compensation to unionized workers and non-unionized workers.

The differences are large, and they prove to be similar to those in our ailing automobile manufacturing sector. For example, in goods-producing industries, unionized workers received a total average hourly rate of compensation of $39.66. Non-unionized workers earned a substantially lower figure, at $30.52 hourly. This represents a $9.14, or 29.95 percent, unionization markup. In service-producing industries, unionized workers earned a total average hourly rate of compensation of $35.64. Non-unionized workers in the service-producing industries, by contrast, earned total compensation of $25.57 hourly. The differences in the service-producing industries produce a markup figure of $10.07, or 39.38 percent, between unionized and non-unionized workers. In total, unionized workers in all private industries earned an average total hourly rate of compensation of $37.02, in comparison to $26.38 for non-unionized private-industry workers. This represents a $10.64, or 40.33 percent, markup for unionization within all private industries.

Like the UAW, the difference in payments to labor is much more pronounced in benefits than in straight wages. For unionized private workers, the average wages totaled $23.00 hourly, in comparison to $19.03 hourly to non-unionized private workers. This represents a markup of $3.97, or 20.86 percent. While significant, it pales in comparison to the differences in benefits. Unionized workers in private industries earned an average of $14.02 hourly in benefits, while the average non-unionized worker earned only $7.34. A $6.68 difference, the unionization markup in payments to employee benefits is 91.01 percent. Like the UAW, the most pronounced markup persists in the benefits payments to employees, though there is a significant markup in straight wage payments to unionized workers as well.[22]

The total percentage union markup for all private industry of 40.33 percent is not far from that of the UAW, suggesting that the case of Detroit is not an isolated incidence of extreme compensation differentials. The findings within the aggregate economy present a significant markup which embodies the claim that the powers of collective bargaining represent a societal liability. A 40.33 percent markup in total payments to labor in the private sector is huge, representing a major drain on the balance sheets of unionized private firms across the country.

Like those arguing in favor of the UAW, some may claim that these payment differentials simply curb profits and do not present fatal obstacles for U.S. firms. In some cases this may be correct, for some firms are strong enough to withstand such an enormous burden. However, in most cases, such as the case of Detroit, many of these liabilities do indeed undermine the fiscal integrity and sustainability of the corporations in the long run. Though all the companies currently in the grip of collective bargaining may not be in immediate peril, Detroit has taught us that long-term liabilities can eventually come to fruition under certain circumstances. When the tide goes out for other American industries, one can be certain that the liabilities produced by collective bargaining will prove to be detrimental to the companies' efforts to appear clothed.

POTENTIAL SOLUTIONS

The main solution, according to the data presented in this chapter, is clear. In order to remove this liability we must reduce, restrict, or eliminate the coercive powers of collective bargaining. There are a number of ways to produce such an outcome, including the limitation of union size, imposition of restrictions on collective bargaining, or, most radically, the prohibition of unions altogether. Each of these potential measures, however, is sure to draw heated criticism from unions, politicians, and a variety of other sources. Realistically, many radical changes will not happen, simply because the opposition would be too great and from too many sources. We look, then, to more feasible measures that might improve our economy by reducing the burden of union power.

One way to diminish the popular support of unions would be to take measures restricting (but not eliminating) their ability to participate in the political process. Much of union strength comes from their support from politicians, especially from candidates and representatives from the left. The relationship, of course, is not one way, as the unions often provide services to the politicians in return for their support. Many unions routinely endorse candidates, making unions a very appealing target for ambitious aspiring politicians. For a more detailed example of union political action, we turn again to our case study of the UAW.

On the UAW Web site, a separate section is designated for the UAW's political action and positions, entitled the Community Action Program. Within it, the union endorses specific pro-labor candidates and attempts to educate and mobilize its constituents in favor of those endorsed. The UAW even has a program that aids in the collection of campaign fund donations from union members. The UAW performs this function in order to dodge legislation prohibiting the union from directly donating to campaigns. The Community Action Program serves a multitude of similar political functions, but this cursory overview provides ample evidence of the political activity of the UAW and unions in general. In turn, the unions often receive support from the political figures whom they help get elected. For example, while Republican President George Bush stipulated within his December 2008 bailout of the auto industry that autoworkers would need to become competitive, many Democrats immediately came to the union's defense. Such political strength only solidifies the monopolistic hold of unions. Any measure that reduces the politicization of unions would in turn reduce the power of those unions, at least in the long run. For example, legislation that prohibits the collection of campaign funds by unions from its constituents would diminish the fiscal connection between politicians and the unions. Of course, the challenge of implementing such legislation is huge, because many politicians benefit from their relationships with organized labor. Regardless of the inherent challenges, however, we find it necessary and beneficial to encourage anyone with such capability to diminish the political powers of the unions. While constitutional rights should be maintained, such as the right to free speech, the more significant ties between unions and their political supporters should be severed. An alternative approach is to enhance the free speech rights of employers, as the Supreme Court recently granted in *Citizens United v. Federal Election Commission (2010)*.

Our discussion highlights the negative impacts of the politicization of unions, but some readers may find it too abstract. In our final and most promising discussion of solutions, we turn to a measure that has already had some limited success in areas of the nation. In doing so, we come across quantitative data that supports our position and gives promise for the possibility of future progress in this area.

Some individual states have already taken measures to limit union influence in attempts to boost employment and productive growth within the states. These measures are called "Right to Work" (RTW) laws, which prohibit companies and unions from entering into agreements that require union membership as a prerequisite for employment. According to the Wage and Hour Division of the U.S. Department of Labor, such laws were in effect in some form in 23 states as of January 1, 2009.[23] While the effects may be debatable, and sometimes inconclusive owing to inaccurate data from the periods before the enactment of the laws, many scholars believe that Right to Work legislation does in fact promote growth in the regions where they are implemented. Research published by Emin M. Dinlersoz and Rubén Hernández-Murillo about the relatively recent switch to RTW in Idaho presents evidence that Right to Work legislation promoted significant employment growth, as well as an expansion in the number of establishments in the state. The two are more hesitant to give definitive statements on patterns of unionization rates as a result of RTW legislation; they claim that it is too difficult to isolate the effects of the law from the changing labor environment within which the application of the law took place. The evidence they present affirms that "Idaho's unionization rate exhibits a significantly faster decline [in comparison to that of its geographic neighbors]."[24]

While Dinlersoz and Hernández-Murillo refrain from making concrete statements on whether the RTW legislation caused the decline in unionization, they do positively assert that a decline in unionization produces definite, distinct manufacturing growth. The growth of the manufacturing sectors of neighboring states that did not experience the decline in unionization also exhibited similar lags in comparison to the growth of Idaho. Aside from discussing the benefits of Right to Work legislation, these findings support the basic assertion within this chapter: that unionization is a burden that is hindering our economic growth and well-being.

What Dinlersoz and Hernández-Murillo avoid in their study of Idaho, other economists have explored through more extensive and inclusive studies of RTW legislation. One such study is published by Ellwood and Fine (1987) entitled *The Impact of Right to Work Laws on Union Organizing*. Following a complicated, precise study of numerous states that have implemented RTW legislation, the two authors find data that "suggest that membership in unions is reduced between 5 and 10 percent after passage."[25] In summary, the two find that RTW laws "have real and significant effects."[26]

Thus, Ellwood and Fine determine that the implementation of RTW legislation has a negative impact on the rate of unionization and subsequently leads to the decline in the overall stock of union membership. When applied to our assertions in this chapter, as well as the concrete findings of Dinlersoz and Hernández-Murillo, the profound impact of RTW legislation provides a compelling incentive toward the national implementation of RTW laws. Right to Work legislation appears to be a moderate and effective means for diminishing the powers of collective bargaining. As such, we encourage an open dialogue at the national level about how such legislation might be passed. We believe rational discussion will produce a national awareness of the dangers of union power that might promote the passage of a federal RTW law.

While we can in no way identify all of the possible specific solutions to union power, or for that matter any structural liability exposed in this book, we do encourage active efforts to diminish the coercive powers of unions. We feel that attempts to limit the politicization of collective bargaining, as well as the implementation of Right to Work legislation at the federal level, are two very effective means to combat the economic liability at hand.

This debate is not exclusive to this work, as many public commentators have offered their opinions about the subject. While each presents his or her own argument, we feel that the data at hand compels the objective individual to consider seriously our position. To many, the reality of this burden is far from desirable. Many individuals, from union organizers to politicians to union employees, reap enormous personal gains from the current structure. We ask, though, that they put their personal benefits aside and consider the economic health of the nation. The coercive powers of collective bargaining affect the firms within the U.S. economy negatively, as evinced by the current state of affairs in Detroit. While other firms may not yet be in similar peril, the fiscal integrity of those firms is undermined by union influence, and it will continue to be until measures are taken to limit the impact of unions.

NOTES

1. For one specific example of a biased account, see one *New York Times* journalist's account of Starbucks employees attempts to organize: http://www.nytimes.com/2005/11/26/nyregion/26starbucks.html?_r=1&scp=5&sq=starbucks%20union&st=cse.

2. United Nations Department of Public Education, "Universal Declaration of Human Rights," 1948, http://www.un.org/events/humanrights/udhr60/hrphotos/declaration%20_eng.pdf.

3. Gallup Poll, "Do you approve or disapprove of labor unions?," cited in Jeffrey Jones, "Americans Remain Broadly Supportive of Labor Unions," Gallup Inc., December 1, 2008, http://www.gallup.com/poll/112717/Americans-Remain-Broadly-Supportive-Labor-Unions.aspx.

4. Gallup Poll, "Do you approve or disapprove of labor unions?," cited in Lydia Said, "Labor Unions See Sharp Slide in U.S. Public Support," Gallup, Inc., September 3, 2009, http://www.gallup.com/poll/122744/Labor-Unions-Sharp-Slide-Public-Support.aspx.

5. United Auto Workers Union, "2007 Media Fact Book," http://www.uaw.org/barg/072/barg072_complete.pdf (accessed January 2009).

6. Ibid., 9.

7. Ibid., 9.

8. United Auto Workers Union, "UAW Chrysler Salary Workers: Major Gains on Job Security," 2007, http://www.uaw.org/contracts/07/chrysler/sal/chry_sal09.php%3E (accessed January 2009).

9. United Auto Workers Union, "UAW GM Report: Product Commitments at GM Assembly Facilities," 2007, http://www.uaw.org/contracts/07/gm/gm08b.php (accessed January 2009).

10. United Auto Workers Union, "UAW Ford Report Hourly Workers: Product and Investment Commitments," 2007, http://www.uaw.org/contracts/07/ford/hrly/ford_hr04.php (accessed January 2009).

11. United Auto Workers Union, "UAW Ford Report Hourly Workers: New Sourcing Language Designed to Bring Work Into Plants," 2007, http://www.uaw.org/contracts/07/ford/hrly/ford_hr06.php (accessed January 2009).

12. United Auto Workers Union, "UAW Chrysler Hourly Workers: Major Job Security Gains," 2007, http://www.uaw.org/contracts/07/chrysler/hrly/chry_hr10.php (accessed January 2009).

13. Evans Marcey, "2007 UAW-Ford National Negotiations Media Fact Book," Ford Motor Company, 8, http://media.ford.com/pdf/07_UAW_Negotiations.pdf.

14. *Chrysler Labor Talks 2007*, "Labor Cost," Jan. 25, 2009, http://chryslerlabortalks07.com/laborcost.html.

15. *New York Times*, "Toyota Says It Will Close Its Only Unionized Plant in the U.S. After Its Partner G.M. Dropped Out," August 28, 2009, B3.

16. *2007 UAW-Ford National Negotiations Media Fact Book*, 8, http://media.ford.com/pdf/07_UAW_Negotiations.pdf.

17. DaimlerChrysler, DaimlerChrysler Public Relations, "Media Briefing Book," 37, http://chryslerlabortalks07.com/Media_Briefing_Book.pdf.

18. Ibid., 5.

19. *Chrysler Labor Talks 2007*.

20. *2007 UAW-Ford National Negotiations Media Fact Book*, 5.

21. GM Manufacturing & Labor Resources, General Motors, "GM Negotiations Handbook," 46, http://media.gm.com/manufacturing/handbook/index.html.

22. U.S. Bureau of Labor Statistics, "Employer Costs for Employee Compensation—September 2009," December 9, 2009, http://www.bls.gov/news.release/pdf/ecec.pdf.

23. U.S. Department of Labor: Employment Standards Administration, Wage and Hour Division, "State Right-to-Work Laws and Constitutional Amendments in Effect as of January 1, 2009 With Year of Passage," Jan. 28, 2009, http://www.dol.gov/whd/state/righttowork.htm.

24. Emin M. Dinlersoz and Rubén Hernández-Murillo, "Did 'Right-to-Work' Work for Idaho?," *Federal Reserve Bank of St. Louis Review* 84.3 (2002): 30.

25. David T. Elwood and Glenn Fine, "The Impact of Right-to-Work Laws on Union Organizing," *Journal of Political Economy* 95.2 (1987): 271.

26. Ibid., 271.

Chapter 7

HOUSING WITHOUT FOUNDATIONS: HOW IDEOLOGY LED TO CRISIS

In the fall of 2008 the world witnessed the worst meltdown of the financial system since the Great Depression. This climactic event was largely the result of a speculative bubble in the housing market that reached its apex in late 2005 and subsequently began to deflate because of rising subprime mortgage defaults. The bursting of the housing bubble led to a freeze in credit markets around the world. This sent shockwaves through the world's financial institutions, bringing down many storied financial titans such as Lehman Brothers, Merrill Lynch, and Bear Stearns. Commentators have been quick to point fingers at capitalism and the free market, citing greedy Wall Street executives and a profiteering corporate culture as the chief causes of the financial crisis. Undeniably, the captains of the financial industry had a hand in it, but few in the media have acknowledged the role of the U.S. government as a major culprit in the subprime debacle. It is evident that the government used its powers to distort incentives and to promote home ownership though increased lending to individuals who would otherwise not qualify for a conventional residential mortgage. Such actions helped to drive up housing prices as crowds of first-time buyers entered the market. Unfortunately, the economics and politics of housing are two divergent realities. However, under crony capitalism the two converged, as government officials and Wall Street financiers actively colluded to distort the housing market for political and personal economic gain. By encouraging irresponsible lending as a means to a political end, the government effectively set the stage for a catastrophe of unprecedented proportions.

THE ORIGINS OF GOVERNMENT HOUSING PROGRAMS

The politics of housing stretch back as far as the Great Depression. Leading up to the Great Depression, the United States was in the midst of a housing crisis. This came at a time when about 40 percent of Americans owned their homes, and financing was difficult by modern standards. Incredibly, between 1925 and 1933 home prices fell 30 percent and between 1932 and 1933 there were nearly 500,000 foreclosures.[1] In order to deal with the housing crisis the government enacted various reforms including the creation of the Federal Home Loan Bank System in 1932. The mission statement of this institution, which still exists today (albeit in a modified form) says, "The mission of the Federal Home Loan Bank System is to provide access to housing for all Americans and to improve the quality of their communities by extending credit through its 8,100 member financial institutions."[2] Further intervention came in the form of increased bankruptcy protection enacted by Congress in 1933, and the passage of the Home Owners' Loan Corporation (HOLC) in 1933. A bold measure instituted by President Roosevelt in 1934 called the Federal Housing Administration (FHA) extended many of the provisions of the HOLC and was instrumental in allowing homeowners to refinance their mortgages over longer time periods. In addition, the FHA provided federally backed insurance for mortgage lenders.[3]

Fannie Mae, or more formally the Federal National Mortgage Association, was born in 1938. Fannie Mae functions in the secondary market for home mortgages by issuing bonds, and then using the funds generated by the sale of those bonds to buy mortgages from participating institutions.[4] It owes its origins to the FHA, which federally backed and provided longer terms of payment for mortgages. This effectively standardized the mortgage market and removed the risk of default. Hence, a secondary market in which bonds were sold to acquire capital was born. This capital was then used to issue additional mortgages and, thereby, increased liquidity in the mortgage market. The purpose of this secondary market was to provide a constant stream of liquidity into the mortgage market. This had the overall effect of reducing average monthly mortgage costs, and opening up home ownership to the masses.

By acting as the backer of new mortgages, the government effectively spurred a generation of increased home ownership. Following World War II, home ownership rose dramatically and the American suburban culture was born. Yet, the spoils of increased home ownership were not shared equally. Minorities were blockaded from engaging in this process through the implicit guise of credit. This had the damaging effect of creating increased levels of racial and ethnic segregation. The amplified government-sponsored lending provided the white population with increased mobility, which it used to migrate to the suburbs. This had unintended demographic consequences because while the whites moved to the suburbs, minorities and ethnic groups remained in the cities and the levels of segregation increased. Segregation and social barriers proved to be pervasive headwinds for minorities attempting to acquire a mortgage. The new housing democracy had failed in its representation of minorities and, in fact, helped fuel the racial segregation the government claimed to be fighting. Hence, once again, the political winds shifted and the government intervened. The motives of their intervention are clear given the racial tensions that characterized the 1960s.

In 1968 the government undertook extensive efforts to increase minorities' access to home ownership. The Civil Rights Act of 1968 was one measure designed to achieve this goal. The Housing Act of 1968 was a logical extension of the Civil Rights Act, and it explicitly forbade discrimination in the sale, rental, or financing of a house.[5] In addition, in 1968 Fannie Mae was restructured into two parts. On one hand, the Government National Mortgage Association, or Ginnie Mae, was designed to increase home ownership among low-income borrowers. On the other hand, a modified Fannie Mae became part government and part private institution. Although it was a publicly traded company, it is technically classified as a government-sponsored enterprise. Such classification is important because Fannie Mae maintains its exclusive federal charter. This gives the company special privileges such as exemption from state and local taxes, the ability to issue government securities, exemptions from many registration and reporting requirements, and exemption from paying certain fees to the Securities and Exchange Commission.[6] This is significant because until its collapse and subsequent bailout in 2008, Fannie Mae had told the media and the politicians that the government was not on the hook for any losses the corporation sustained. At the same time, the firm's executives promised Wall Street investors that if they did fail, the government would pick up the tab. History shows that the latter was, in fact, their strategy.

The Federal Home Loan Mortgage Corporation, or Freddie Mac, was created by legislation passed by Congress in 1970. Its original goal was to provide competition and support in the mortgage market through the securitization process and thereby achieve lower mortgage rates.[7] Securitization in this context refers to a process whereby mortgages are pooled together and then resold as high-yielding mortgage-backed securities to the public. These mortgage-backed securities provided a constant stream of fresh liquidity to finance the purchase of additional mortgages.

As government-sponsored enterprises, both Fannie Mae and Freddie Mac faced a number of constraints. For example, they were restricted to purchasing mostly "conforming loans" with a maximum value in 2005 of \$359,650.[8] In addition, Fannie Mae and Freddie Mac were allowed to purchase only mortgages that had been granted to borrowers who placed a 20 percent down payment on the loan. However, there was a crucial exception to this stipulation—granted to loans that were insured by either the government or the private sectors. Furthermore, both institutions were subject to mission oversight by Department of Housing and Urban Development. At the height of the real estate bubble in 2005, "50% of Fannie Mae's and Freddie Mac's business had to benefit low and moderate income families, 31% had to benefit underserved areas, and 20% had to serve special affordable needs."[9]

In 1977 Congress passed the Community Reinvestment Act, the mission of which is "to encourage depository institutions to help meet the credit needs of the communities in which they operate, including low- and moderate-income neighborhoods, consistent with safe and sound banking operations."[10] Institutions were also subject to periodic evaluations to ensure that their lending practices were in keeping with this legislation. Jimmy Carter, a fierce advocate for the Community Reinvestment Act, hoped that this would help ensure that low-income earners would have greater access to home mortgages. In reality, the Community Reinvestment Act placed legal constraints on banks to extend credit to low-income areas. This entire policy catered to the idea that pumping credit into underserved markets would induce economic growth. However, the policy prevented market forces from directing scarce credit to people who valued it the most. This created disequilibrium in the market and prevented an efficient outcome. Thus, the policy necessarily made some better off at the expense of others who valued the credit more than the actual recipients; the process was equivalent to telling some farmers that they had to allocate a certain amount of apples to people who would pay them less than the market price—thereby preventing others who value the apples more from acquiring them. Surely, the farmers would object to such ill-found logic.

THE EMERGENCE OF COLLATERALIZED DEBT OBLIGATIONS

The 1970s and early 1980s was a period of volatile inflation and fiscal mayhem. This inflation was beneficial to borrowers whose mortgages were locked in at low rates. In effect, borrowers were being paid by the bank to borrow money. Inflation is a debtor's heaven and a lender's worst nightmare because the value of debt decreases in real terms during inflationary periods. Savings and loan (S&L) associations became victims to the times as interest rates spiked under Federal Reserve Chairman Paul Volcker, who aggressively fought to moderate inflation using higher interest rates. This forced S&L institutions into a situation where they were taking substantial losses on the mortgages they had previously issued, as well as hits on the higher interest rates they had to pay depositors.

The politicians responded to the crisis by deregulating the industry. This gave S&Ls greater ability to invest in a wider pool of assets. Suddenly, the S&Ls had full access to federally insured deposits to fuel their "growth" out of the mess. The S&Ls, with their new funds in hand and relaxed lending restrictions, began to engage in extremely risky transactions, especially in real estate, which collapsed and led to numerous failures.[11] This crisis is an excellent example of moral hazard (which is discussed at length in Chapter 11) considering that the funds that S&L executives were gambling with were government-insured deposits and their industry was on the verge of collapse. In effect, "betting the farm" was their best option given the warped incentive structure they faced. In fact, between 1986 and 1995, there were 1,043 S&Ls (holding over $519 billion in assets) that failed or received government assistance. The Resolution Trust Company was set up to untangle the mess, and the total cost of the S&L crisis to taxpayers has been estimated by the Federal Deposit Insurance Corporation to be $153 billion.[12] This is a significant historical point because the government set a precedent that it would use taxpayer funds to bail out lending institutions that had made wildly speculative loans.

While hundreds of S&Ls were imploding, bond traders on Wall Street were making a killing by selling collateralized mortgage obligations (CMOs). CMOs were a new type of financial derivative that converted bundles of mortgages into bonds sold to individual investors or financial institutions.[13] Because these new securities derived their value from the mortgages that backed them, and because these mortgages received the government's implicit backing, they were sold with high credit ratings. Economists hailed the creation of collateralized debt obligations that made the securitization of subprime mortgages possible as a good thing because they helped to diversify risk. In principle, derivatives of prime mortgages were seen as very safe assets and many were given AAA credit ratings. Consequently, government-sponsored mortgage-backed securities grew in value from $200 million in 1980 to over $4 trillion in 2007.[14]

HOUSING FOR EVERYONE

In 1994, under the direction of President Clinton, the National Homeownership Strategy kicked off another campaign aimed at increasing home ownership in America. Clinton commissioned Housing and Urban Development Secretary Henry Cisneros with the task of implementing this goal. His proposal called for increasing home ownership to 67.5 percent by the year 2000. Clinton delivered remarks on the National Homeownership Strategy, proclaiming that many Americans "[m]ay scrape to save, but a down payment is still out of reach. They are locked out by rigid restrictions or by a home-buying system just, as Jean said, too difficult or too frightening."[15] Clinton advocated creative solutions to the problem at hand that could work if the public and private sectors collaborated to break down the barriers to owning a home. By openly encouraging home ownership for people who were unable to save for a down payment, Clinton endorsed a reduction in lending standards. In effect, the Clinton administration actively encouraged bankers to increase the number of individuals that qualified for a mortgage.

These policies were largely continued and in many cases strengthened by President George W. Bush, who proclaimed: "We want everybody in America to own their own home."[16] The Clinton-Bush push for increased housing, especially for minorities, resulted in increased ownership rates between 1997 and 2005 for all regions, all age groups, all racial groups, and all income groups. During this period the total home ownership rate climbed from 65.7 percent to 68.9 percent.[17] Bush provided a substantial boost to campaign for home ownership through the American Dream Downpayment Act, which he signed in 2003. This bill authorized up to $200 million per year in subsidies to low-income and minority households purchasing a single-family home. Under this legislation, individuals could receive up to $10,000 of assistance as long as their income was 80 percent or less of the median income in the area where they were purchasing the home.[18] These efforts led to many new homeowners, especially minorities and low-income earners. Most people hailed the government's actions as a heroic extension of the American dream. Regrettably, many failed to realize that the real estate market was an overblown bubble that was ready to explode.

THE BRITISH HOUSING EXAMPLE

The passionate ideology that drove both Republicans and Democrats to advocate increased levels of home ownership was not conceived in a vacuum; rather, a confluence of events buttressed support for their home ownership programs. One such measure was Margaret Thatcher's success in the 1980s in increasing home ownership in Great Britain. She accomplished this mission by introducing the Mortgage Interest Relief Act at Source (MIRAS), which was Britain's own version of the mortgage deduction.[19] This legislation provided homeowners with tax relief for interest payments on their mortgages. The Housing Act of 1980, or the "right to buy" legislation, was another measure employed by Thatcher to expedite home ownership. The "right to buy" legislation gave Council tenants the statutory right to buy their Council's home at a deeply discounted rate. Council homes are a form of public housing provided by the British government for its citizens. This legislation gave tenants who had lived in such houses for at least three years the right to purchase them for a discount of one-third off the market price. Discounts of up to 50 percent were extended to Council tenants who had lived in their homes for 20 years or more.[20] These measures led the overall home ownership rate in Great Britain to soar from 54 percent in 1981 to 67 percent in 1991,[21] success that proved to be a key catalyst for the U.S.'s push to increase home ownership.

SUBPRIME AMERICA

Much of the spectacular growth in the housing market between 2001 and 2006 contributed to the then booming subprime mortgage market. Subprime mortgages are an altogether different breed of lending. Conventional mortgages typically spanned a 30-year period, required a solid down payment (usually upwards of 20% of the purchase price of the home), and subsequent monthly payments of approximately 25 percent of a household's monthly income or less. These mortgages then appeared as assets on the banks' balance sheets. Given that lenders were profit seeking, they were very careful about choosing to whom they lent their money. A thorough background check and proper collateral were prerequisites for securing a mortgage. The down payment also served an important purpose because it gave the homeowner something to lose if he or she failed to make his or her payments. The process of securitization, however, separated this crucial link between the mortgage originator and the subsequent collector. Mortgages were issued by lenders, and through the process of securitization they were pooled, repackaged, and then sold as high-yielding mortgage-backed securities to third-party investors.

The disconnect between lenders and borrowers created the perverse incentives that led mortgage originators to relax their lending standards, because they were no longer on the hook for defaults. Hence, the 20 percent down payments were reduced to fractional amounts, and a positional arms race among mortgage originators ensued. Originators provided the marketing tools and then completed the transactions, collecting hefty commissions by quickly pooling these mortgages and selling them in the secondary market. Collusion between mortgage originators and appraisers ensued. This led to inflated appraisals, scant background and credit checks, and a total collapse of lending standards. According to financial historian Niall Ferguson, "Those who knew the flakiness of the subprime loans—the people who dealt directly with the borrowers and knew their economic circumstances—bore the least risk. They could make a 100 percent loan-to-value 'NINJA' loan (to someone with No Income No Job or Assets) and sell it on the same day to one of the big banks in the CDO business."[22]

Many subprime mortgages were adjustable rate mortgages (ARMs) that differed from conventional home mortgages in a number of critical ways. An adjustable rate mortgage has a variable interest rate that periodically changes in response to fluctuations in short-term lending rates. Conversely, conventional residential mortgage loans offer a fixed interest rate for the duration of the loan. In addition, ARMs often had a "teaser period" in which borrowers paid "interest only," and these interest rates were often lower than those offered on conventional fixed-rate mortgages. This had the effect of making mortgages accessible to a wider number of individuals. Yet, many borrowers failed to comprehend fully the financial impact that would occur when these "teaser rates" reset after a specified time period to the longer-term lending rates, usually indexed to the London Interbank Offered Rate (LIBOR), plus an additional margin added by the lender. This had the effect of drastically increasing the monthly cost of servicing the debt. However, many borrowers took advantage of the favorable "teaser rate" period hoping to "flip" a property, resell it, and collect a hefty commission before the rates reset.

ARMs are particularly troublesome in that the default rates associated with them are much higher than the defaults rates associated with conventional mortgages, because the rates reset a few years into the loan. This fact, coupled with low interest rates at the time of purchase, set borrowers up for a financial disaster. Considering that mortgage interest rates were near historic lows they had nowhere to go but up. Thus, when interest rates subsequently rose, many borrowers found their monthly payments unaffordable and began to default on their ARMs. Many accusations of predatory lending have been levied against the banking industry as a result of these complex debt instruments. Such accusations are grounded in the belief that mortgage originators deceived borrowers by luring them with artificially low initial interest rates, which made housing *seem* affordable, when in reality, future interest rate hikes were bound to make ARMs more costly for borrowers in the long run.

Throughout the course of the intervening time, Washington's power brokers watched idly, encouraging the speculative mania. Beginning in 1996, the Department of Housing and Urban Development gave Fannie Mae and Freddie Mac explicit target rates, stating that a certain percentage of their mortgage financing had to be allocated to borrowers with incomes below the median in the location where the loans originated. This target rate increased from 42 percent in 1996 to 52 percent in 2005. Another provision stated that Fannie Mae and Freddie Mac had to issue "special affordable" loans. These "special affordable" loans were typically issued to borrowers whose incomes were 60 percent less than the median income in the location where the loan originated. Fannie Mae and Freddie Mac's target rates for these loans increased from 12 percent in 1996 to 22 percent in 2005. It should be noted that the projected goal for 2008, prior to the crash, was 28 percent.[23] Thus, Fannie Mae and Freddie Mac, two publicly traded government-sponsored entities, acted as agents of the government by carrying out their housing goals with private investment capital.

The increased demands placed upon these firms, coupled with additional federal subsidies and insurance guarantees designed to back the mortgages of low-income earners, played a significant role in the rampant proliferation of non-conventional mortgages. Without the implicit backing of the government to bail out investors it is doubtful investors would have taken such risks. In essence, these policies generated excessive moral hazard because investors believed that if trouble came, the government would bail them out. Investors saw it as a one-way bet; for them there was no downside to the investment. Thus, profit-seeking investors flocked to Government Sponsored Enterprise (GSE) supported mortgage-backed securities because they offered high yields and the implicit backing of the government as insurance against potential future losses.

Wall Street began securitizing loans at a record pace in the midst of what many thought was a sustainable rally in the housing market. Private banks were experiencing record short-term profits as a result of subprime mortgages extended to literally anyone who applied, even if their applications were incomplete. Numerous loans that failed to meet the standards of Fannie Mae and Freddie Mac were securitized and resold to investors on Wall Street. In fact, the percentage of subprime borrowers who failed to document fully their income and assets grew from about 17 percent in early 2000 to 44 percent in 2006.[24] Meanwhile, the government's regulatory bodies negligently watched and cheered on the developments, completely oblivious to the catastrophe that was about to happen. Such practices were fueled by the belief that housing prices would continue their upward trek. Under this presumption, even if a small percentage of borrowers did default, the effects would be small and contained.

RISK MISMANAGEMENT

The introduction of the credit default swap added further fuel to the already raging housing market. Credit default swaps were a new type of financial derivative cooked up by the growing legions of "quants" on Wall Street. Quants refer to the growing number of financial engineers who use complex mathematics and statistical analysis to design exotic financial instruments. Credit default swaps allowed banks to reduce their exposure to bad loans by effectively paying a premium for insurance on their investments. Financial engineers believed that they could appropriately model risk and collect the profitable premiums investors paid for the protection offered by credit default swaps—ignoring the fact that an extremely unusual event could result in massive payouts. Absent a catastrophe, the premiums collected on credit defaults swaps amounted to free money that buoyed the profits of financial firms—especially AIG, which had insured more that $500 billion dollars in subprime mortgages by January 2008.[25] Investors and institutions that bought and sold credit default swaps believed that in the event that subprime borrowers defaulted they would be protected by their credit default swaps. Thus, investors and institutions alike filled their books with high-yielding risky assets bought with excessive leverage. Many institutions were tethered together by these credit default swaps, which had ballooned from a $100 billion market in 2000 to a $62 trillion market in September 2008.[26] To demonstrate the interconnectedness of financial firms one only needs to look at Lehman Brothers, which had entered into more than $700 billion of swaps—many of which were backed by AIG.[27] Thus, when the subprime mortgage market turned sour, many of Wall Street's leading firms were forced to take massive write-downs. As firms began to fail and payouts had to be made, a chain reaction was initiated that culminated in the "Panic of 2008."

A ONE-WAY BET

The ideology that drove the bubble in the housing market is complex and was predicated on the idea that housing was a one-way bet. Solid empirical evidence counters this ideology. The Case-Shiller Home Price Indices showed that the trend for housing prices, prior to the bubble, was for the value of homes to increase annually at a rate that closely matched the U.S. long-term trend for growth in GDP. Once prices are indexed for annual inflation it becomes evident that home prices grew at a modest pace prior to the new millennium. In fact, prior to the Dow's decline in 2008, investors who had placed their money in the S&P 500 20 years ago would have seen the value of their investment grow to be worth nearly 2.5 time greater than a similar investment in housing.[28] This empirical evidence suggests that housing is only a modest store of wealth, and that a rational profit-seeking investor would invest in stocks. Why, then, did investors rush to housing?

An analysis of the fundamental factors that drove the housing boom reveals that both population and real per capita income (in 2006 constant dollars) rose from 1997 to 2006. These factors coupled with cheap credit helped to increase demand during this time period. Table 7.1 depicts these trends.

On the supply side, housing starts rose steadily, peaking in 2006 (see Figure 7.1). The cost of building materials also rose during this time period, driving up the price of new homes. Yet, the summation of these two factors provides a weak case for the overall real increase in home prices of 85 percent between 1997 and 2006.[29]

It is evident that a classic speculative bubble had formed in the housing market. This bubble was built on the cheap and easily accessible credit,

Table 7.1
Population and Real Per Capita Income

	Population (in thousands)	Real Per Capita Income (U.S. Dollars)
1997	269094	24100
1998	271743	24854
1999	276804	25700
2000	279517	26163
2001	282082	26024
2002	285933	25546
2003	288280	25517
2004	291166	25465
2005	293834	25857
2006	296824	26352

Source: U.S. Census Bureau

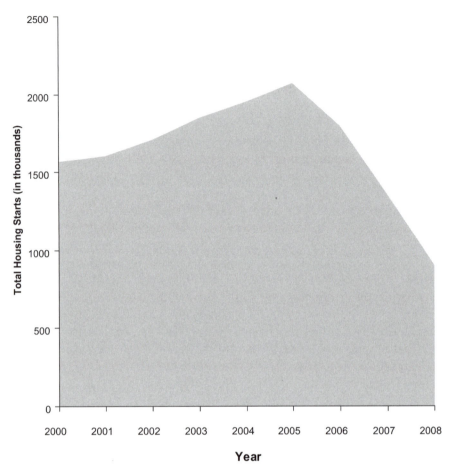

Figure 7.1
New Housing Units Started in the U.S. 2000–2008.
Source: U.S. Census Bureau

and an ideology that held that the extension of home ownership to so many Americans was a giant leap forward. In the view of many, the United States was experiencing a housing renaissance that was reshaping and democratizing the financial system. This catharsis was reinforcing because the politicians, the bankers, and the American people all thought that they had something to gain by perpetuating it.

The government effectively subsidized the entire bubble through direct grant payments to homeowners, and by acting as an implicit insurer of last resort for residential mortgages. A subsidy essentially drives up demand for a particular good by partially offsetting the cost of attaining that good. By offsetting the cost of ownership through subsidies, especially for low-income earners and minorities, the government directly stimulated an increase in the quantity of housing demanded. This increase in demand had the direct effect of driving up housing values.

THE BUBBLE BEGINS TO DEFLATE

The real estate bubble reached its peak in 2005, and subsequently it began to deflate. Analysts attributed this to the plateau effect, stating that housing prices were stabilizing but likely to maintain their values. Yet by September 2006 housing prices began to drop substantially, −9.7 percent from the year before.[30] Many areas in Florida, Arizona, California, Washington, D.C., Boston, and other major metropolitan areas were hit especially hard. As housing prices began to deflate, mortgage defaults began to rise. Suddenly, the entire foundation of the speculative bubble began disintegrating with disastrous consequences.

It quickly became apparent that banks were in trouble as default rates soared past their projected levels. As default rates continued to rise, rating agencies rushed to downgrade shares in collateralized debt obligations. These were the same shares that had been given solid ratings in the years leading up to the crisis, when originators were handing out NINJA loans. As it turns out, the default rates had been seriously miscalculated. Hence, the collateralized debt obligations that financial firms and investors held in their portfolios had been purchased at artificially inflated prices. Investors, realizing that they were going to lose their shirts on shares in collateralized debt obligations, stopped buying them altogether. Subsequently prices plummeted, and without buyers for securitized subprime loans, the subprime market essentially vanished overnight.[31] However, the damage had already been done. Trillions of dollars in toxic assets had polluted the balance sheets of several nations' financial institutions.

Like a pendulum, the upward swing in housing prices was quickly followed by a counter movement. As prices fell many borrowers were left holding the deed to properties that were worth less than the price they had purchased them for. This negative equity helped set off another round of defaults. According to economist Martin Feldstein, by the end of 2008, "More than 12 million homeowners now have mortgage debt that exceeds the value of their homes. These negative-equity homeowners have an incentive to default because mortgages are generally 'no recourse' loans. That means creditors can take the property if the individual defaults, but cannot take other assets or income to make up the difference between the unpaid loan balance and the lower value of the house."[32] For many home-owners their best option was simply to walk away from their obligations. Regrettably, this left banks holding the bag on waves of homes that were worth less than the value of the loan. The sheer scale of the housing bubble, and the risky leverage that dominated many of the banking firm's financial positions, vastly magnified the consequences of mortgage defaults and ulti-mately forced many firms into insolvency.

Further compounding the crisis was the fact that many of the mortgage-backed securities had been acquired by structured investment vehicles (SIVs). An SIV is a type of off-balance-sheet instrument owned by a bank-ing firm and operates by borrowing money using commercial paper and then using that money to buy higher-yielding assets. Thus, when subprime borrowers began to default on their loans because of higher interest rates and a decline in housing prices, investors became wary of SIVs. This led investors in the commercial paper market to cease lending to the SIVs. Because SIVs are an integral supplier of funds to the credit markets, their collapse led to a global credit drought.[33] The asset-backed commercial paper market went from supplying $1.2 trillion of credit before the collapse to $700 billion after the collapse.[34]

In August 2007 the tremors in the financial markets were further aug-mented when American Home Mortgage filed for bankruptcy and BNP Paribas suspended three mortgage investment funds.[35] In the year that followed numerous financial firms began to buckle under the stress of highly leveraged subprime debt. The world was shocked when Bear Stearns was sold to J.P. Morgan in a deal that was underwritten by the Federal Reserve. The list of victims that fell prey to the subprime debacle was extensive, and it included such notable financial firms as Merrill Lynch, Lehman Brothers, Wachovia, AIG, Citigroup, and Bank of America. Many of these firms received government bailouts as the stock market collapsed amid a fury of de-leveraging. As the economic funda-mentals went from bad to worse, the government engaged in a series of unprecedented efforts to calm markets and restore pre-subprime liquidity.

THE AFTERMATH

Under the guidance of Treasury Secretary Henry Paulson, Congress passed the Emergency Economic Stabilization Act of 2008, which was intended "to provide authority for the Federal Government to purchase and insure certain types of troubled assets for the purposes of providing stability to and preventing disruption in the economy and financial system and protecting taxpayers."[36] The bulk of the initial $350 billion installment of the $700 billion plan went to recapitalizing banks and bailing out insurer AIG, as well as the automakers General Motors and Chrysler.[37] The remaining $350 billion has been deployed to continue recapitalizing banks and to buy up toxic assets held on the balance sheets of banks. The goal of this initiative was to get banks lending again and to restore liquidity to the market.

In February 2009, President Obama signed a $787 billion economic stimulus package into law. The American Recovery and Reinvestment Act of 2009 was intended to spur the creation of 3.5 million jobs. About $282 billion of the bill was allocated toward tax cuts for both individuals and businesses. The spending includes, among other things, expanded unemployment benefits, food stamps, and health care subsidies for unemployed workers and aid to states. Another provision of the bill was intended to increase spending for construction of highways and bridges, school renovations, and incentives for health care facilities to replace paper records with electronic systems.[38] The authors of this book believe for reasons discussed in Chapter 12 that the Keynesian economic stimulus plan will not work. Empirical evidence collected by Harvard economics professor Robert Barro demonstrates that government spending fails to stimulate growth in real GDP in any significant way.[39]

In March 2009 the Obama administration attempted to combat the housing crisis by launching a new plan that provided over $75 billion dollars in incentives and subsidies to homeowners. Although the plan originally targeted 3 to 4 million borrowers, as of December 2009 only 759,000 mortgages had been modified, with only 31,000 homeowners receiving a permanent loan modification.[40] The plan was designed to buoy the housing market by stabilizing prices, which would, theoretically, stall the further evaporation of homeowner equity. Administration officials believe that the policy is vital to stave off another wave of foreclosures, which would further exacerbate the already dim housing market.

The Federal Reserve also supported the housing market by buying mortgages in an unprecedented effort to keep mortgage rates suppressed. As of January 2010 the Fed held $909 billion of mortgage-backed securities, and it had purchased a staggering 73 percent of the mortgages that government-backed Fannie Mae, Freddie Mac, and Ginnie Mae had turned into securities.[41] This effort, coupled with the actions of the Treasury, has vaulted government purchases above $1 trillion. The Fed's program ended in March 2010 with an estimated total cost of $1.25 trillion.[42] However, because of pervasive weakness in the housing market it is possible that a similar program will be reinstituted in the future.

In January 2010, as an estimated 15 million Americans owed more on their homes than their homes were worth, the Obama administration's housing strategy was widely criticized for being sluggish and ineffective.[43] Therefore, amid a fury over bank bailouts and double-digit unemployment, the administration accelerated its goals under the Making Home Affordable program, which was designed to hasten the refinancing procedures for homeowners facing foreclosure. The plan was designed to support low mortgage rates by strengthening confidence in Fannie Mae and Freddie Mac, provide up to 5 million homeowners with new access to refinancing, and create a comprehensive stability initiative to offer reduced monthly payments for up to 4 million at-risk homeowners.[44]

MOVING FORWARD

The government has long championed for increased home ownership and the political process has turned the idea of home ownership into a political right. In order to empower this idea, the government has intervened extensively in the housing market by providing subsidies to homeowners, and by using Fannie Mae, Freddie Mac, and Ginnie Mae to carry out its political motives. Unfortunately, the political and economic realities of housing offer divergent paths. The sensible path offered by economics involves requiring a reasonable down payment, proper income validation, and mortgages that are designed to ensure stability. On the contrary, the politicians chose a plan that was designed for expediency and popularity. This plan necessitated a reduction in lending standards and increased access to capital for those who were least capable of following through on their financial obligations. Such objectives were carried out through increased government funding for home ownership programs and stricter mandates on loan allocations for GSE-sponsored mortgage-backed securities. However the old mantra "if it seems too good to be true it probably is" rings loud and clear. As mortgage originators made NINJA loans, the government remained cheering on the sidelines.

The historical evidence presented in this chapter shows that, without a doubt, the government was an accomplice in the subprime debacle. Power brokers in Washington used their influence to distort incentives to favor the short run. They accomplished this goal by encouraging subprime lending and turning a blind eye to the gross negligence practiced by mortgage originators. As long as people were able to purchase homes and voted for the politicians' causes it did not matter to the power brokers. Ultimately, reality set in, as the short term expired and the long-term consequences set in. As a result today's financial system is in peril. Americans have lost confidence in the banking system, their retirement funds have been sharply diminished, and the overall standard of living has fallen.

It may be easier to build a house without a secure foundation. Less time and effort are initially needed. The house may look the same from the outside; it appears strong, sturdy, and like all of the other houses on the street. Yet, when a storm comes rolling through, the structural deficiencies of the house are revealed as it collapses like a house of cards. Similarly, Americans had been living in houses without financial foundations. When the storm arrived it showed the foolishness of building the"American dream" without a solid foundation, which has to be based on productive capacity. Thus, as we look to the future we must be cognizant of our past, remembering that it is best to build on a sturdy base that will stand the test of time.

NOTES

1. Niall Ferguson, *The Ascent of Money: A Financial History of the World* (New York: Penguin, 2008), 242.

2. Federal Home Loan Bank System, "System Mission and Overview," April 19, 2009, http://www.fhlb-of.com/mission/aboutusframe.html.

3. Robert J. Shiller, *Subprime Solution: How Today's Global Financial Crisis Happened and What to Do about It* (Princeton: Princeton University Press, 2008), 15.

4. Ferguson, *The Ascent of Money*, 249.

5. Kevin Fox Gotham, "Separate and Unequal: The Housing Act of 1968," *Sociological Forum* 15, no. 1 (2000): 13–16.

6. Scott W. Frame and Lawrence J. White, "Fussing and Fuming over Fannie and Freddie: How Much Smoke, How Much Fire?," *Journal of Economic Perspectives* 19, no. 2 (2005): 161–3.

7. Ferguson, *The Ascent of Money*, 253.

8. Frame W. Scott and Lawrence J. White, 163.

9. Ibid.

10. Federal Financial Institution Examination Council, *Home Page*, March 17, 2009, http://www.ffiec.gov/.

11. Office of Thrift Supervision, "Office of Thrift Supervision—History," March 18, 2009, http://www.ots.treas.gov/?p=History.

12. Federal Deposit Insurance Corporation, April 19, 2009, http://www.fdic.gov/bank/analytical/banking/2000dec/brv13n2_2.pdf.

13. Ferguson, *The Ascent of Money*, 260.

14. Ibid.

15. "William J. Clinton: Remarks on the National Homeownership Strategy," *The American Presidency Project*, http://www.presidency.ucsb.edu/ws/?pid=51448.

16. Greg Ip, James Hagerty, and Jonathan Karp, "Housing Bust Fuels Blame Game," *Wall Street Journal*, March 20, 2008.

17. Shiller, *The Subprime Solution*, 5.

18. U.S. Department of Housing and Urban Development (HUD), "American Dream Downpayment Initiative—Affordable Housing—CPD—HUD," *Homes and Communities*, April 19, 2009, http://www.hud.gov/offices/cpd/affordablehousing/programs/home/addi/.

19. Amity Shlaes, "Pain Now, Gain Later—November 28, 2005," *CNNMoney.com*, CNN, April 19, 2009, http://money.cnn.com/magazines/fortune/fortune_archive/2005/11/28/8361956/index.htm.

20. Paul Balchin, *Housing Policy: An Introduction* (London: Routledge, 1985), 182–183.

21. U.K. National Statistics Publication Hub, *"National Statistics Online,"* April 19, 2009, http://www.statistics.gov.uk/cci/nugget.asp?id=821.

22. Ferguson, *The Ascent of Money*, 269.

23. Russell Roberts, "How Government Stoked the Mania: Housing prices would never have risen so high without multiple Washington mistakes," *Wall Street Journal*, October 3, 2008.

24. Ip, Hagerty, Karp, "Housing Bust Fuels Blame Game."

25. Andrew Ross Sorkin, *Too Big to Fail* (New York: Viking, 2009), 156–158.

26. Matthew Philips, "The Monster That Ate Wall Street: How 'credit default swaps'—an insurance against bad loans—turned from a smart bet into a killer," *Newsweek*, September 27, 2008, http://www.newsweek.com/id/161199/page/1.

27. Ibid.

28. Ferguson, *The Ascent of Money*, 262.

29. Shiller, *The Subprime Solution*, 32.

30. *New York Times*, "Home Price Drop Is Largest in 35 Years," October 26, 2006.

31. Paul Krugman, *The Return of Depression Economics and the Crisis of 2008* (New York: W.W. Norton, 2008).

32. Martin Feldstein, "How to Help People Whose Home Values Are Underwater," *Wall Street Journal*, November 18, 2008.

33. Gillian Tett, Gillian, Paul J. Davies, and Norma Cohen, "Structured Investment Vehicles' Role in Crisis," *Financial Times*, August 13, 2007.

34. Krugman, *The Return of Depression Economics*, 171.

35. Ferguson, *The Ascent of Money*, 272.

36. H.R. 1424, 110 Cong. (2008) (enacted).

37. Glen Hubbard, Hal Scott, and Luigi Zingales, "From Awful to Merely Bad: Reviewing the Bank Rescue Options," *Wall Street Journal*, February 7, 2009.

38. Laura Meckler, "Obama Signs Stimulus Into Law," *Wall Street Journal*, February 18, 2009.

39. Robert J. Barro, *Macroeconomics* (New York: Wiley, 1990), Chapter 12.

40. "Obama Housing Plan," *New York Times*, Jan 22, 2010.

41. Liz Rappaport and Jon Hilsenrath, "Fed Plan to Stop Buying Mortgages Feeds Recovery Worries," *Wall Street Journal*, January 8, 2010.

42. Ibid.

43. Ibid.

44. *Road to Stability*, U.S. Government, http://www.financialstability.gov/roadtostability/homeowner.html.

Chapter 8

FOREIGN POLICY, FOREIGN FAILURE

The foreign policy of the United States is constantly changing. Though the human ramifications of political actions in the international sphere are the topic of public discourse, the associated economic ramifications are profound as well. While we in no way intend to minimize the human costs which the media and politicians so often focus on, we find it necessary to bring to light just how much modern foreign policy costs in economic terms to the government, and more broadly to society as a whole.

The origins of U.S. foreign policy were very different from the current order of the nation's international relations. Following the conclusion of the Revolutionary War, U.S. officials felt it prudent to avoid conflict with any foreign powers outside of the immediate vicinity of the new nation, especially as domestic affairs were still being organized. Official foreign policy followed this line of thought, for example, in 1793 when President Washington issued the Proclamation of Neutrality.

This is not to say, however, that a young United States of America did not find itself in military conflicts. For a long period after the founding, the United States had its hands full with domestic military conflict, as disputed borders, expansionary aspirations, and discontent neighbors created substantial strife. The United States found itself in what seemed to be a perpetual war with a number of tribes of Native Americans, as well as a significant conflict with Britain as the recently defeated imperialists encroached on U.S. sovereignty. Westward expansion involved conflict and war with territorial claimants such as Mexico, Texas, and Spain. The founding period and long thereafter, however, is notable for the "hands off" approach that the United States pursued with regard to foreign powers other than nations within the immediate vicinity. Consumed by domestic and regional issues, the U.S. government felt no need to meddle in conflict which did not directly affect national security or significant national interests.

As time progressed, however, and the United States gained respect in the international community, the attitude of the federal government slowly shifted toward taking a more involved role in international matters. Vital national interests began to be more broadly defined, for example, as the United States took an active military interest in Cuban liberation in the Spanish-American War of 1898. Upon the onset of the twentieth century, the United States had become an active participant in world affairs and conflict, having just annexed the Republic of Hawaii and setting to colonize the Philippines for the next 35 years.

The common reader doesn't need an overview of twentieth-century U.S. history to confirm this fact, for anyone with a high school education is well aware of the numerous conflicts in which the United States has been involved. Beyond conflict, the country has become increasingly occupied in nonviolent international intervention. Humanitarian efforts have skyrocketed, as government officials employ moral and tactical arguments for extending financial aid to foreigners in need of assistance. The United States continues to find it necessary to involve itself in foreign diplomatic relations, peace talks, and financial assistance for military endeavors among third-party nations. As much as many try to deny it, it seems that the United States has built itself a global empire, and assigned itself the role of "world police."

THE ECONOMIC COSTS OF MILITARY FORCE

The decision to use military force abroad is one that no leader should take lightly. Often, the discourse preceding an invasion or other military action focuses on the human costs of such an action, both to U.S. forces and to others in the area of the military engagement. This is, of course, appropriate, as such decisions have drastic ramifications in this arena. However, while the human costs of war are discussed extensively, before and during an engagement little focus is placed on the economic costs of such action. Perhaps the emotions surrounding lives lost take precedence over a rational discussion of the financial obligations that come with military activity. It is the job of economists, then, to bring these issues to light, not to diminish the enormous sacrifices of the U.S. military or the civilian costs to an affected area, but rather to expound fully on the national dialogue surrounding U.S. military positions in the foreign arena.

In President Obama's 2010 federal budget, the government slated $663.7 billion for discretionary budget authority by the Department of Defense. This request includes a base budget of $533.7 billion, and $130 billion for military engagements in Iraq and Afghanistan.[1] In relation to the Congressional Budget Office's projection for nominal GDP in 2010, these projected expenditures represent 4.55 percent of U.S. total production in 2010.[2]

While viewed alone, these numbers should appear, to the common reader, astounding. Essentially, it means that the United States commits 4.55 percent of its theoretical production to defense spending. We use the word *theoretical* because, while the amount spent is equal to 4.55 percent of projected GDP, the U.S. government has been willing (in some recent administrations) to shirk fiscal responsibility for future debts; the Obama administration being a part of that tradition. Thus, defense spending may not be funded through current taxation and production, but rather through the issuance of bonds to foreign and domestic investors.

However, when this proposal by the Obama administration is viewed in the context of recent defense spending patterns, it actually appears quite normal. In 2007 under the Bush administration, for example, the federal government spent approximately $662 billion on national defense.[3] Based on statistics from the U.S. Bureau of Economic Analysis, these expenditures represented approximately 4.8 percent of U.S. GDP in 2007. Even further back in recent history, defense expenditures equaled approximately 7.4 percent of GDP in 1965 (amid the expansion of the Vietnam War), and 6.1 percent of GDP in 1985 (during the Cold War).[4] Thus, in the twentieth and into the twenty-first century, defense spending has represented significant portions of U.S. domestic production.

Of course, few would negate the claim that the U.S. government has the responsibility and necessity to provide for national defense. National defense is among a limited number of goods considered "public" in nature, the production of which is actually more efficiently achieved by government than by private entities. Broadly defined, a "public good" is a good "for which rivalry among consumers is absent and exclusion of nonpaying customers is difficult."[5] That is, the consumption of "national defense" by one citizen does not reduce the availability of "national defense" to another citizen, and, without taxation, it is very difficult to keep people from enjoying the benefits of defense without paying their share. Thus, it makes economic sense for the federal government to tax the people and provide for national defense. The issue at hand, however, is not *whether* to spend for national defense at the federal level, but *how much* to spend.

Contrary to popular belief, the levels of federal defense spending in the middle to late twentieth century and beginning of the twenty-first century do not represent a consistent pattern of expenditures from the founding forward. In 1830, for example, the federal government spent approximately $8 million on defense.[6] When compared to a GDP of $1.1 billion for that year, the percentage of GDP spent on defense was a mere 7/10 of 1 percent.[7] Similarly, in 1890 the federal government spent approximately $67 million on defense-related expenditures.[8] When compared against production for the same year, the federal government spent approximately 4/10 of 1 percent of GDP on national defense.[9] Until the twentieth century, defense spending was consistently limited to a small percentage of overall GDP.

Wars themselves have become much more costly, even as their necessity to the security of the United States has diminished. Adjusted for inflation to the year 2008, the Civil War cost the Union approximately $45 billion. In contrast, the United States spent about $686 billion on the conflict in Vietnam.[10] Consider the threats to national security in both of these cases. In the former, Confederate rebels had taken arms directly against the United States, on U.S. soil, in a real, formidable threat to national security. In the latter, North Vietnamese communists threatened to spread their ideology to a small state on the opposite side of the world. Yet in Vietnam we spent, in real terms, more than 15 times what the Union did in the Civil War.

Post-9/11, these patterns of increase have continued unabated. Under President Bush, and subsequently President Obama, the war on terror has proven to be an enormous source of expenditures. By the end of 2009, according to budget estimates, the cost of the Iraq War to date totaled approximately $683 billion, roughly equal to the total economic costs of the war in Vietnam. Though plans are in place to scale back operations in Iraq, it now appears inevitable that the total costs of the conflict will far surpass the real expenditures in Vietnam. Expenditures on the conflict in Afghanistan, according to estimates by the Congressional Research Service, totaled approximately $227 billion by the end of fiscal year 2009. With tactical plans in place to escalate military operations in that theater of operation, total economic costs of the Afghani conflict are, by all accounts, expected to rise drastically in the coming years. In total, between September 11, 2001, and the close of fiscal year 2009, the federal government appropriated approximately $944 billion in supplemental funding to the Department of Defense for ongoing operations in the war on terror.[11]

The pattern of increases in expenditures on war has followed fairly consistently throughout the twentieth century and into the twenty-first, with a few exceptions. Few would deny the necessity of U.S. participation in the Second World War, and the United States spent more than $4 trillion (adjusted to 2008) on the conflict, the nation's costliest conflict to date. Additionally, the first Persian Gulf War cost the United States an adjusted $96 billion for the entire conflict—though high in comparison to the earliest conflicts, a lower outlier when contrasted against other military engagements in the late twentieth and early twenty-first centuries. Furthermore, Saudi Arabia and Kuwait paid for a significant amount of that war. In general, though, U.S. expenditures on conflicts have risen consistently throughout its history.

Of course, there are a number of contributing factors to the increase in defense expenditures. At the forefront, as many proponents of sustained defense spending would argue, are changes in technology that have severely altered the landscape of international relations. Changes in weapons technology have increased the threat of mass destruction, in turn requiring the creation of new technologies that are effective in preventing an attack with such a weapon. Transportation technology has evolved to the point where large numbers of combatants can be relocated to anywhere in the world in a matter of days. New, more advanced equipment for soldiers on the ground is more effective at preventing fatal injury, but in turn it is more expensive to purchase. It is true that changes in technology have increased the costs of defending the nation, in nominal terms. However, as defense (and offense) technology has spurred greater nominal costs, similar ingenuity has propelled the nation's overall output at an astonishing rate. Thus, while it makes perfect sense for defense expenditures to grow in nominal terms, claims of technological advances hold little weight when discussing defense spending as a percentage of GDP.

Something else, then, must be behind the fluctuating levels of defense spending with relation to gross domestic product (GDP). In this case, rational thought and common sense point us in the right direction. If one examines progressive federal defense expenditures as a percentage of GDP, a fairly straightforward pattern emerges—real federal defense outlays closely correspond with the foreign policy pursued during that time period. That is, aside from technological changes altering both the equipment with which wars are fought and the manners and venues in which they are carried out, defense expenditures are deeply affected by the prevailing doctrine that the federal government elects to pursue at that time.

While this clarification may seem unnecessary to the reader, its presence serves a specific point—to take the emphasis off of the changing nature of foreign affairs, and back onto decision making at the federal level. Technological changes do alter the costs of war and defense, but such changes are generally followed with similar advances in general technology, which is incorporated in the GDP of the time. What matters most are the specific decisions and doctrines of the federal government at each point in time.

Thus, relatively recent policy developments in the foreign relations arena have had real, correlated effects on U.S. expenditures on defense. In this context, we define *recent* as the period starting at the close of the Second World War. After two costly, devastating wars, U.S. authorities deemed it necessary to maintain a giant standing army, in order to preserve their new position as a world superpower, and to prevent ambitious aggression by foreign militants. Hitler's resilience and short-term successes had instigated a worldwide fear, which in turn prompted a complete alteration in U.S. foreign conduct.

With a standing army, and a freshly assumed role as the police of the world, the United States quickly set out to protect what it perceived as U.S. interests around the world. As the USSR developed into America's most formidable rival, containment of the communist ideology took charge as the most pressing interest of U.S. politicians and military leaders. Containment brought a new type of warfare—no longer was the objective to defeat the opposition, but rather to stop the spread of its influence.

With that idea in mind, the United States engaged in two of its least popular military endeavors to that point, the Korean and Vietnamese wars. Because of the geographic location of the conflicts, the heavy human losses sustained, and the protraction of the fighting, each was largely protested by the population. The new type of warfare that emerged, centered on a theory of containment rather than domination, did not allow for clear-cut long-term ambitions for the military endeavor. Instead, leaders focused on short-run goals, and they used other less-popular gauges to measure success, such as the "body count ratio" measurements of the Vietnamese conflict.

Aside from the enormous human and military costs of these conflicts, they had further ramifications on later U.S. maneuvers in the foreign policy arena. U.S. leaders have been unwilling to shed the role of "world police," or to define more narrowly what national interests merit military commitment. However, leaders have lost the fortitude to fully commit to U.S. victory following an engagement. From Vietnam on, the American public lost the stomach for war, preferring protracted, partial conflicts with limited victories over full-out war in pursuit of a single, definable goal. The result has been more costly, politically waged conflicts, with limited scopes of engagement that prevent the military from achieving sustainable goals.

The only recent conflict that might be considered an exception to this pattern was the First Gulf War under George H. W. Bush in the early 1990s. Though full military domination was again not the goal, Bush successfully shed most semblances of political warfare in order to achieve quickly effectively the campaign's mission. In one sense or another, every other conflict since the Second World War, and especially from Vietnam on, has been limited politically, creating confusing, costly conflicts with limited successes.

To be sure, U.S. military policy has changed since its humble beginnings. The interests of the United States have become much more broadly defined, as it has solidified its position as a world superpower. As a result, the theoretical connection between conflict and domestic security has become much more abstract, especially following the Second World War. The ways in which wars are fought have changed, too, as the public and politicians shed military victory for limited, prolonged, and political engagements. Through these developments, the costs of defense have risen steadily in real terms, while the security of the nation, debatably, has dipped.

FAILED FOREIGN AID

Also integral to U.S. foreign policy are programs of foreign aid to nations in need around the world. The concept of foreign aid—along with related annual national expenditures—is difficult to analyze objectively while dodging personal attacks from staunch supporters. Risking these dangers, however, we move forward in search of a rational, logical investigation into the patterns and effectiveness of federal expenditures on foreign humanitarian efforts.

A heavy presence in the international sphere inherently requires expanded participation in foreign aid. As it is for individuals, if one attends charity dinners each night, one can surely expect a daily request for funds. As the United States has consistently expanded its presence in the international sphere, by intervening in most third-party conflicts, and creating or running a plethora of large-scale international organizations, it has found itself being asked for money regularly. Politically, such requests are most easily handled with an open mind and an open wallet for any proposal that sounds humanitarian in nature. When it comes to starving people with inadequate shelter, it is always better to look like the hero.

The complaint that economists have with this approach is that politicians tend to ignore the difference between looking like the hero and actually being the hero. Many believe that as a privileged nation, we have an obligation to help others in need. We do not contest this notion, but rather stress that people, and unfortunately government especially, approach this topic only superficially. By throwing money at the world's most depressing, inhumane conditions, people tend to assume that they are somehow effectively combating the problems the individuals in those conditions face. It is in this assumption that economics and politics diverge, and rational thought at the policy level disappears.

Federal expenditures on foreign aid have followed a strict upward trend in recent history. From 1980 to 2006, federal aid outlays increased from about $23.7 billion to $39.0 billion, in constant 2006 dollars (adjusted for inflation).[12] That is, in a 26-year period, *real* foreign aid increased over 64 percent. Broken down more specifically, the United States spent approximately $5.2 billion (in 2006 constant dollars) on military assistance in 1980, and $12.1 billion on military assistance in 2006, a 136 percent increase over the 26-year period. Economic aid in 1980 was roughly $18.5 billion (2006 constant dollars), and almost $27.0 billion in 2006, a 46 percent increase over the same time span.[13] In short, the real budget for federal aid is consistently following a steep pattern of increase, as requests for aid grow, and politicians take the most attractive route for their careers.

The question to ask, which politicians and proponents seem to avoid on a regular basis, is whether these increased expenditures are effective at combating the inhumanity and poverty that drives people to write such astronomical checks. Before approaching this question at the international level, a similar situation on a much smaller scale might serve as an enlightening example.

Consider a homeless man on the street, begging for change. Most Americans see such people and, if they do not successfully block their existence from their consciousness, feel pity for their condition. Some take the time to give them some spare change, realizing their own fortune when faced with such a polar opposite from their conditions. If politician comes by, they too find it prudent to give some donation, lest they be branded "heartless" or "greedy" by their opponents.

Assume now that over the course of an hour of begging, that man collects $15 in change, enough money to purchase food for the day. If he has a substance abuse problem, some of that money might go toward sustaining that addiction, and avoiding a painful withdrawal reaction. But, at the end of the day, he is still homeless, with no idea where his next meal will come from or how long he will survive in his present condition. Those who have problems with alcohol or drugs do not shake their habits, and their physical condition deteriorates as they neglect their bodies.

Now, assume an economist with an open heart and a large amount of free time approaches the same homeless individual the next day. Rather than giving him one dollar (or a hundred, for that matter), this economist thinks rationally and realizes that what this homeless man needs isn't loose change, but rather a lifestyle change. The economist invests time in helping him get cleaned up and presentable, finds him an affordable apartment, aids him in a job search, and coaches him on living techniques to make him a productive member of society. Ultimately, by changing the individual's living habits and removing him from the cycle of day-to-day begging, the economist may help him become a productive member of society with a stable way of life.

Though this example may appear idealistic—many cases of poverty and homelessness are much more difficult to remedy, and they may be caused by addictions that cannot be broken, or by mental health issues—it nevertheless serves a valuable point: Handouts are not the answer. Certainly, homeless people will accept loose change to sustain them in the short run, but as long as they live on day-to-day handouts, their routine will never be altered to improve their standard of living. Sustained improvement requires a change in structure, and not simply a buck to get by.

This example can easily be translated into a lesson for international aid. Certainly, the problems that struggling regions of the world face are much more complex than those an individual homeless person might face, but the basic premise of the situation holds true. While handouts sustain an individual or a group's immediate needs, their situations are rarely remedied simply by throwing money at them.

Economists have long challenged the notion that free handouts are beneficial in the long run to people in need. Within the profession, commonly accepted keys to economic success include secure property rights, sound monetary policy, and substantial opportunities for capitalist profits. Economists have found that short-term funding boosts from external sources have little positive effect on growth, and in many cases they are ultimately counterproductive.[14] Though a federal handout grants relief in the short run, it does nothing to remedy the long-term structural situation which third-world citizens face. Whereas compassion drives people to help to save individuals in immediate peril, cold rationality indicates that much of the aid funding would better serve humanitarian goals when devoted toward systemic remedies.

While we are critical of the federal government's role in international aid in this chapter, we do not deny that some federal relief programs do indeed work when it comes to combating poverty. The highest-funded federal economic relief organization, the U.S. Agency for International Development (USAID), devotes substantial portions of its budget toward productive benevolent endeavors, such as developing markets, making productive assets more accessible, and strengthening the rule of law.[15] However, while the organization appears to understand the benefits of sound aid policies, the rhetoric it employs fails to incorporate the consensus that free handouts do not provide sustainable relief. In the same section in which USAID discusses productive, sustainable ideas of aid, it also discusses its ongoing programs to "support government and private sector partners . . . to improve the levels of income their citizens enjoy."[16] Additional federal programs included in the budget for foreign aid, such as U.S. Department of Agriculture Food Grant Programs, ignore this economic logic as well and channel billions of dollars of foreign aid into handout programs. As the U.S. Department of State and USAID Joint Strategic Plan for 2007-2012 states, U.S. development officials still consider food aid to be a key element of American humanitarian programs.[17] It should also be noted in this discussion that money is fungible, meaning that the aid provided may be used for a worthwhile project that would have been funded internally anyway; if that is true, domestic funds may be switched to other projects that the donor might consider worthless.

At the international level, officials seem to follow a similar pattern of understanding and partial defiance of economic rationality. The United Nations, whose humanitarian activities are more than 25 percent funded by the United States, has both development programs and handout programs. Other transnational humanitarian initiatives, such as the Jubilee 2000 campaign, transgress against economic logic even more blatantly. The Jubilee program is an excellent example of economic ignorance, as its main purpose was to petition the cancellation of the debts of impoverished nations around the globe. Without rationally considering this program, many might consider it a noble, generous move. But debt cancellation, like other handout programs, is a short-term solution to a long-term problem. If a nation has developed large amounts of debt to foreign investors because the economy is not self-sufficient, it is unlikely debt forgiveness will magically make the countries economically independent.

Furthermore, debt cancellation reduces investor's confidence in a nation's ability to repay future issuances of debt, making financing much harder for the nation in the long run.

At this juncture in our argument, critics may assert that because of our calculated, economic analysis of aid programs, we the authors lack human compassion in our considerations. Oftentimes, people mistake rational, scientific considerations for materialism or inhumanity. What these people fail to realize is that behind this economic analysis is a specific goal: enhanced efficiency for the benefit of all mankind. Though in the short-run, those who discuss the failures of handout programs may be demonized, the long-term ramifications of their policy suggestions might actually have enormous benefits for the world's poor.

Another interesting discussion, in which rational cynicism is more widely accepted, is the dialogue surrounding federal expenditures on military aid. As noted previously, from 1980 to 2006 the federal government increased its expenditures on military aid by 136 percent. Often, the federal government has used foreign military funding to advance military agendas without committing U.S. troops, avoiding politically costly maneuvers. Many politicians, though, not well known for their fiscal responsibility, do not properly weigh the long-term ramifications of foreign military funding. Similar to positions on combating poverty, many individuals in power find it easier, at least in the short run, simply to throw money at the problem, hoping that a check will miraculously fix it.

A widely cited example of failed military funding in the long-run surfaced after September 11, 2001, when weapons and tactics granted to Afghani militants in the Soviet War in Afghanistan in the 1980s were used against invading U.S. forces. Not only were valuable material resources used by the federal government during that period to equip and train these fighters, but in the end U.S. funds contributed directly to the later loss of U.S. life. Perhaps, at the time, containment of the Soviets seemed a valid goal, and funding of third-party militants the most politically viable option for achieving that mission, but ultimately the costs of such decisions were enormous.

Military aid expenditures allow politicians to further their international interests without risking the political stigma associated with committing U.S. troops to a conflict. Generally, politicians view it as a very versatile tool, and they often apply it to achieve short-term goals. Unfortunately, the changing nature of the international political landscape is such that those we fund in one instance can easily become enemies a short time later, as happened in Afghanistan.

WHAT CAN WE DO?

Unlike other structural issues within this book, foreign policy is not something that can be responsibly addressed with immediate, drastic change. The United States has developed into the world superpower it has been for decades, and it has created a system of dependency, both on its patterns of military involvement and on its policies of foreign aid. Proper resolution of these issues require calculated, gradual changes in U.S. policies, to allow dependent nations around the world time to adjust accordingly.

With specific reference to military policy, the United States must begin to define narrowly what it considers to be "vital interests." Democracy, though a noble cause, should not be pursued if the only way to do so is through military intervention. When it comes to uses of force, the United States should focus on its own interests, and begin to shed its role as the "world police." Dangerous ideologies, such as the communism the United States viewed as a formidable threat for most of the second half of the twentieth century, should be opposed, but military force should be avoided at all costs. The United States should maintain an advisory role in the international sphere, but military intervention should be reserved largely for immediate threats to its own security.

Once leaders make the decision to engage in military combat, wars should be fought to completion. The political, indecisive nature of current military strategy has doomed the long-run success of a number of recent campaigns, such as the war in Vietnam. Citizens and leaders of the United States must realize that military force incurs both human and economic costs, and they must understand that in many situations, once the decision to enter combat has been made, total costs are minimized by fully engaging the target to the completion of the mission. Failure to realize or act upon this notion may, in fact, doom the Iraqi nation to a long-term failure similar to that of South Vietnam after U.S. troops are withdrawn.

The subject of foreign aid is a bit more complicated. As a fortunate, prosperous nation, the United States, most would agree, is obliged to assist those in less fortunate situations around the globe. However, acting on pure emotion rather than calculated analysis generates enormous costs to the United States, while avoiding any real long-term gains in the fight against worldwide poverty. Economists have gathered a wealth of information regarding foreign development, but national and transnational leaders have been extremely slow in processing and implementing the lessons learned by those scholars. Handouts must be kept to situations where imminent crisis has destroyed the productive capacity of a nation in need (e.g., the 2010 earthquake in Haiti) and expenditures on foreign aid should be focused on endeavors with the potential of producing enduring solutions. At the forefront of humanitarian missions should be the development of markets, property rights, capitalist structures, openness to trade, and other goals clearly laid out by economists in the field of international development.

Of course, these changes too cannot be immediate, but must rather be pursued gradually. Patterns of increasing U.S. aid to foreign nations have developed dependency in recipient nations. American officials must begin gradually reducing the magnitude of handouts they grant to needy nations and begin shifting focus toward sustaining, long-term development. Using objective economic facts rather than emotions to grant humanitarian aid will ultimately result in a more sustainable fight against poverty.

If these gradual changes are implemented, both in the military and humanitarian spheres, the excessive human and economic costs borne by the United States might be mitigated in the long run. With a more efficient allocation of resources in both of these arenas, long-term goals such as reduced poverty and conflict might become attainable. The key to success is, in these cases, the shedding of emotion and sentiment in favor of calculated, analytic application of economic reason.

NOTES

1. Office of Management and Budget, "A New Era of Responsibility: Renewing America's Promise (Federal Budget FY2010)," February 26, 2009, 54–55, http://www.gpoaccess.gov/usbudget/fy10/pdf/fy10-newera.pdf.

2. Ibid., 132.

3. U.S. Department of Commerce, Bureau of Economic Analysis, "Survey of Current Business: National Data," June 2009, D-3, http://www.bea.gov/national/pdf/dpga.pdf.

4. Office of Management and Budget, "Historical Tables: Budget of the United States Government, Fiscal Year 2005," 2005, 110–7, http://www.whitehouse.gov/omb/budget/fy2005/pdf/hist.pdf.

5. James D. Gwartney, Richard L. Stroup, Russell S. Sobel, and David A. Macpherson, *Macroeconomics: Private & Public Choice*, 116.

6. Susan B. Carter, ed., *Historical Statistics of the United States, Earliest Times to the Present*, Millennial Edition, Volume 5, "Table Ea636-643—Federal Government Expenditure, by Major Function:1789–1970," (New York: Cambridge University Press, 2006).

7. Ibid., "Table Ca9-19—Gross Domestic Product: 1790–2002 [Continuous Annual Series]."

8. Ibid., "Table Ea636-643—Federal Government Expenditure, by Major Function:1789–1970."

9. Ibid., "Table Ca9-19—Gross Domestic Product: 1790–2002 [Continuous Annual Series]."

10. Stephen Dagett, "CRS Report for Congress: Costs of Major U.S. Wars," *Congressional Research Service*, Library of Congress, July 24, 2008, http://digital.library.unt.edu/govdocs/crs/permalink/meta-crs-10777:1.

11. Amy Belasco, "The Cost of Iraq, Afghanistan, and Other Global War on Terror Operations Since 9/11," *Congressional Research Service* Library of Congress, September 28, 2009, 8, 15, accessed from Federation of American Scientists: http://www.fas.org/sgp/crs/natsec/RL33110.pdf.

12. U.S. Census Bureau, "Table 1258. U.S. Foreign Economic and Military Aid Programs: 1980 to 2006," http://www.census.gov/compendia/statab/tables/09s1258.pdf.

13. Ibid.

14. Robert J. Barro, *Macroeconomics: A Modern Approach*, 99.

15. U.S. Agency for International Development, "Economic Growth and Trade," February 25, 2009, http://www.usaid.gov/our_work/economic_growth_and_trade/.

16. U.S. Agency for International Development, "Our Work: A Better Future for All," May 19, 2009, http://www.usaid.gov/our_work/.

17. U.S. Agency for International Development, "Strategic Plan: Fiscal Years 2007–2012," May 7, 2007, 31, http://www.state.gov/documents/organization/86291.pdf.

Chapter 9

POLLUTING THE ECONOMY WITH ENVIRONMENTAL REGULATION

Pollution is unquestionably an economic "bad." Economic "bads" (a technical term used in economics) possess negative value to consumers, and a consumption behavior that creates economic bads lowers the consumers' overall utility or happiness. Thus, too much smog makes consumers worse off when all other variables are held constant. In the aggregate, smoke billowing out of a factory, or waste flowing down a river, imposes a negative cost on society—which must be weighed relative to the benefits that consumers gain from the output that consumers desire. In other words, firms can produce economic goods that are desirable but that may also generate economic bads. Firms that generate excessive amounts of pollution do so because they are not bearing the full cost of production. Economists call the negative costs that are imposed on uninvolved third parties negative externalities. Negative externalities distort market incentives and lead to a level of production that exceeds the "socially optimal" level—a level that takes place only when the extra benefits from output exceed the extra costs that society bears.

Policy makers have tended to emphasize the incentive problems inherent in markets with negative externalities, but they have largely failed to analyze them within the context of the political process. This view has led to the proliferation of a myriad of environmental regulations that have imposed many arbitrary and largely ineffective measures on firms. We intend to demonstrate that this approach is flawed, and that the real problem lies in distorted information that leads to high transaction costs and poorly defined property rights. Hence, by redefining property rights and providing better channels of communications and information, the full power of the free market can be harnessed to provide enduring environmental stewardship.

PROPERTY RIGHTS, INCENTIVES, AND EXTERNALITIES

Property rights are the cornerstone of free-market environmentalism. They are essential because they determine who has a valid claim to scarce resources.[1] In addition, when scarce resources are owned by a profit-seeking party, a necessary discipline is imposed on the resource owner because the wealth of that party is bound with the productivity of that resource. Thus, if the resource is well managed the owner reaps financial rewards. On the contrary, if the resource is squandered the property owner will suffer economic losses and a reduction in wealth. This incentive structure encourages resource owners to take into account the various opportunity costs of the resource—in other words, the value of the resource in an alternative productive activity.

As differences in opportunity costs arise in a market-based economy, rational economizing individuals can engage in mutually beneficial trade. Consider the example of a farmer who owns the property rights to his farm and a developer who wishes to acquire the farmland in order to build a new housing development. If the farmer is willing to accept $100,000 for the property and the developer is willing to pay the sum, then both parties can be made better off if they engage in the transaction. Therefore, when property rights are easily transferable between parties, the value of the resource rises.[2]

Property rights must also be well defined and enforceable. This is an area in which the government plays a critical role. A government that maintains a well-functioning legal system and the rule of law will encourage property owners to manage their resources in an effective and efficient manner. In areas where these conditions are not well satisfied, property owners will not manage their resources effectively for fear of plunder. This explains why areas characterized by high crime rates tend to have lower property values than areas that are generally considered safe. Similarly if property rights are arbitrary or poorly defined, then conflicts inevitably arise. This brings us to the case of the firm that pollutes but does not bear the cost of the pollution. Instead, the cost of the pollution is borne by the people who live downwind or downstream from the firm's factory. In this case, the firm's private extra cost of production is less than the additional social cost. Hence, the firm's cost structure does not reflect the structure of costs borne by society. This leads to disequilibrium in the market where the quantity produced by the firm is higher than the socially optimal quantity. In this context it is important to note that the "socially optimal quantity" does not refer to a level of production where pollution is non-existent; rather, it refers to a level of production where the extra benefit of production is equal to or exceeds the extra cost.

The consumption of fossil fuels, such as coal and oil, produces both electricity (an economic good) and pollution (an economic bad). No sensible individual would argue that in the absence of a viable energy alternative we should cease to use coal or oil. What we need to do is use fossil fuels up to the point where their extra benefit equals their extra costs. In order to achieve this outcome all of the costs associated with the consumption of fossil fuels, including the external pollution costs, need to be built in to the firm's cost function. Excluding costs such as pollution will lead to an economically inefficient level of production.

In economics, inefficiency implies that a situation can be reconfigured in some way that would make at least one party better off without making anyone else worse off.[3] If a factory owner dumps toxins into a river and the toxins kill all of the fish, then all the people who fish in that river are adversely affected. The inefficiencies created by this externality create incentives for remedial action. A professor at the University of Chicago Law School, Ronald Coase was the first to notice that if people can negotiate with one another at no cost over the right to perform activities that cause externalities, they will always arrive at an efficient solution.

THE COASE THEOREM

The Coase Theorem revolutionized the way economists think about transaction costs and the way rights are assigned to various parties. Coase pointed out that externalities have a reciprocal nature.[4] Take again the case of the polluter who dumps toxic waste into a river and thereby harms the fisherman. The initial reaction many people would have to this situation is that the firm generating the pollution should be forced to shut down. Coase pointed out that this is not always the best option, because shutting down the factory harms the firm as well as the consumers who enjoy the goods produced by the firm. This potentially leaves "money on the table."[5] The better solution, argued Coase, is achieved when the involved parties can negotiate the purchase and sale of the right to perform activities that cause externalities.[6]

Suppose the rights are assigned in such a way that the polluting firm is not allowed to dump waste into the river unless it has the permission of

Table 9.1
Coase Theorem Example

	Filter Toxins	Do Not Filter Toxins
Gains to firm	$500/day	$1,000/day
Gain to fisherman	$500/day	$300/day

Source: Authors' example

the fishermen. Table 9.1 shows the potentially relevant monetary costs and benefits associated with filtering the toxins out of the water. Given this particular cost structure, it is evident that the most efficient outcome is achieved when the firm operates without filtering the toxins. In this case the daily surplus would be $1,300 compared to $1,000 if the filter were used. Yet we would expect that the fishermen would use the power of the law to force the firm to filter the toxins because, in its absence, their daily surplus decreases from $500 to $300. This outcome, however, is inefficient and a better outcome is achievable through negotiation.

If both parties are able to negotiate freely, we would expect some sort of mutually beneficial agreement to be reached. In this case, the polluting firm could offer the fishermen $400 per day in exchange for not filtering the toxins. In this case, both the fishermen and the firm would be better off and the total daily surplus would be maximized. Analyzed within the framework of the Coase Theorem, it becomes apparent that the cost of not polluting in this case is greater than the costs of polluting. "The Coase Theorem tells us that regardless of whether the law holds polluters liable for damages, the affected parties will achieve efficient solutions to externalities if they can negotiate costlessly with one another."[7] The nature of the rights held by persons and entities are important because they determine who will have to pay out and who will have to be compensated. If the rights favored the polluter then the fishermen would have to try to compensate the polluters to decrease the level of pollution.

The Coase Theorem provides an important analytical framework that helps generate efficient solutions to complex problems. It does not, though, provide a workable solution for every environmental problem we face. In many cases, probably the majority, high transaction costs involving the negotiations among affected parties prohibits effective negotiations from taking place. In these cases, well-defined legal restrictions that take into account the external costs relative to the benefits of production are the best mode of achieving a workable solution to problems posed by externalities. For example, laws against littering can be presumed to be beneficial to society because they force people properly to dispose of waste products. In the absence of effective laws, people would litter more and society would be worse off. Negotiating with each and every person who litters is generally impossible. Therefore, the transaction costs for solving this problem are prohibitively high, and a more effective solution to the problem can be achieved through the use of well-defined and enforceable laws against littering. Similarly, smog control devices on automobiles should provide another case in which a legal mandate may be the most effective method of maximizing net benefit. Cars that fail to comply with state and federal regulations may not be driven. Taken on a case-by-case basis, the externalities problem would be impractical to solve through individual negotiations. However, this example presumes that the state and federal regulations do in fact take into account the extra costs of pollution relative to the extra costs associated with implementing the regulations themselves.

We believe that the majority of the external costs generated by polluters arise from situations where property rights are poorly defined and are not enforceable. It has been demonstrated that the manner in which rights are defined has a tremendous impact on the production decisions of polluting firms. Therefore, the effective solution is to redefine the rights so that firms produce where the extra cost to society matches the extra benefit. If property rights favor the polluter rather than the many private property owners who are affected by the pollution, then it is reasonable to expect that production will exceed the socially optimal point. Similarly, if bureaucrats impose excessive regulation that fails to account for the benefits of production, then production will be less than the socially optimal amount.

The difficulty of finding the optimal solution is sometimes overcome by the institutional arrangements that individuals develop on their own. This can be illustrated with the problem of littering. People go to sports events and engage in substantial amount of littering—but it is littering within a closed space that is privately owned. The same can be said by littering within theaters or musical venues that are privately owned. Yet the owners of these closed spaces can estimate the amount of littering that will take place—and therefore charge a high enough price for disposing of the waste that is produced.

Similarly, it could be argued that determining the cost of regulation also fails to account for the externalities that are created by the goods that may replace those which are generating externalities in the first place. Ethanol is a case in point. When ethanol was introduced as a partial substitute for gasoline (and used as an additive), regulators failed to take into account the externalities that the production of ethanol itself created, to the point that it is not clear now that this partial substitute for gasoline is able to reduce externalities taken in the aggregate.

THE TRAGEDY OF THE COMMONS

Property rights are also essential because in their absence resources are over-exploited. Private property links the owner's wealth with the management of the resource; thus the resource is managed to maximize profits in the long run. In their absence, people will exploit the resource for short-term gain. In effect, resource users compete to use as much as possible a resource that is not privately owned, in order to maximize their profits. This leads to a situation where the unpriced resource is used until its extra benefit falls to zero.[8] Economists refer to this scenario as the tragedy of the commons.

The Pacific halibut fishery fell victim to the tragedy of the commons in the 1980s and 1990s; this occurred because technological improvements reduced the amount of time it took the 3,000-member Pacific-Northwestern halibut fleet to catch the annual 50-million-pound stock, from several months to less than one week.[9] With few restrictions placed on fishing, and a wide disparity between the private and social extra costs of fishing, there was no incentive for fishermen to act in the long-term collective interest of the fishery. Consequently, over-fishing threatened the future of the Alaskan halibut. In response to the situation, government managers dramatically shortened the fishing season from almost nine months to just two or three 24-hour periods in the spring.[10] In addition, the government placed a strict quota on the number of halibut that could be caught. This led to derbystyle fishing that encouraged crews to take excessive risks and generate unnecessary waste, as they struggled to maximize profits in such a limited amount of time. As a result, numerous deaths and a plethora of horrific injuries followed the imposition of these regulations. Furthermore, the reduction in the length of the fishing season forced crews to unload the halibut catch for fire-sale prices in an overcrowded market.[11] The overall economic effect was devastating on Alaskan fishing communities dependent on the revenue provided by the annual halibut catch.

The devastation that followed the regulation quickly became apparent. In 1995, the ineffective command-style system was replaced with a more market-based regulation system that issued individual fishing quotas. The individual fishing quotas granted each fishing crew the right to a pre-determined portion of the total allowable catch. The quotas could be bought and sold on the market and have been effective in ending the wasteful and dangerous derby-style fishing.[12]

Following the imposition of the individual fishing quotas, waste decreased drastically, prices were more stable, and the season was lengthened from a few days to about eight months.[13] Fishing quotas altered the incentive structure of the fishing industry. Halibut are no longer subject to the exploitation that is characteristic of unpriced goods that have fallen victim to the tragedy of the commons; rather, the halibut are now viewed as a long-term asset that must be sustained and protected for future use. The policy has been successful in preventing over-fishing and is now used to protect more than 100 marine species in areas all around the world.[14]

A similar tragedy of the commons situation was faced not long ago by bottom-trawling fishermen off the coast of California. The fishermen's bottom-trawling techniques had resulted in the rapid depletion of six ground fish species. Initial efforts by conservationist groups tried to ban fishing for these species altogether. Competing interest generated animosity and prevented an effective solution. In 2006, environmentalists, marine scientists, and the fishermen teamed up and formed a plan that established fishing permits and prevented bottom trawling in at-risk areas. Environmental groups ended up purchasing five out of the six permits in Morro Bay.[15] This had the effect of driving up the price of the permit for permit holders. According to free-market environmentalist Terry Anderson, "using markets, environmentalists and fishers have preserved 3.8 million acres of the ocean off of the coast of central California—an area roughly the size of Connecticut."[16] Ownership of the permit ties the fishermen to the resource for the duration of ownership. If they overexploit the resource then, in the future, they will face declining incomes as the aquatic populations dwindle.

This is an example where free-market environmentalism provides a workable solution to a complex problem. Market-based solutions, such as the fishing permits and individual fishing quotas, are proving to be the most effective solution to maintaining sustainable fish stocks and marine biodiversity. Such solutions are more effective than arbitrary regulations, like those initially used by the government regulators of the northern Pacific fishery, and those still in use by U.S. scallop fishermen.

MANAGEMENT OF PUBLIC LANDS

Energy development on public land is a wildly contentious issue in the United States. The Arctic National Wildlife Refuge (ANWR) has occupied the center stage of this conflict since the late 1970s. Proponents of drilling for oil in ANWR state that the move would provide the United States with a reliable source of oil and reduce its dependence on foreign oil. On the other hand, critics of the plan argue that ANWR's oil will satisfy less than 5 percent of U.S. oil demand—benefits they believe to fall short of the costs produced by ANWR.[17] In reality, both sides use exaggerated claims to further their own agenda. The central issue posed by the U.S. government's ownership of vast tracks of land lies in the absence of a true incentive structure. If a private individual owned ANWR, he or she would have to weigh the benefits of drilling against the costs of drilling. Instead, government bureaucracy politicizes the issue, and this detracts from cost-benefit analysis. In this narrow-minded approach, it is not difficult to see that environmentalists oppose drilling even if the benefits of drilling far outweigh the costs. Similarly, the oil companies back drilling efforts with little concern for the environment. The behavior of each party is individually rational because each party seeks to maximize its profits and influence. In order to further their efforts, both parties engage in extensive rent-seeking activities, where the gains to one party are equivalent to the losses to the other party. In an attempt to manipulate the political process to further their respective agendas, special interest groups have turned a simple cost-benefit analysis into a zero-sum game. Thus, under government ownership there is little or even no incentive to consider the relevant trade-offs associated with drilling for oil in ANWR. If the lands were to be auctioned off then oil companies and environmental groups could bid against each other. In this approach, whichever group places a higher value on the land will bid the highest and obtain the right to use it as they see fit. When making the decision to bid all parties will be forced to use cost-benefit analysis. Hence, the land will be used for its highest valued purpose.

Actions undertaken by the Audubon Society demonstrate how private ownership changes the situation. Since the 1950s the Audubon's Paul J. Rainey Sanctuary, a 26,000-acre preserve at the edge of the Intracoastal Waterway and Vermillion Bay in Louisiana, has allowed an oil company to operate natural gas wells located on the sanctuary's grounds. The site has generated more than $25 million in revenue that has been used to purchase additional lands for the Audubon Society.[18]

Similarly, the Audubon's Bernard Baker Sanctuary in Michigan provides additional evidence that privately held resources are managed more effectively than publicly held resources. Since the 1960s the site has allowed oil companies to drill underneath the preserve in exchange for a share of the oil revenues generated. The society was able to ensure that the drilling platform was located on an adjacent site, and that the wells provided a minimal impact on the environment.[19] The Audubon Society, a non-profit environmental organization dedicated to conservancy, allowed the oil companies to use the resources on their lands because they recognized that the marginal benefit of the revenues exceeded the costs. They used their position to ensure that the energy was harnessed in an environmentally friendly fashion, while at the same time earning revenue to fund future conservancy efforts. This approach shows that under private ownership, the relevant trade-offs are considered and the outcome is economically efficient.

The federal government annually spends billions of dollars managing 614 million acres of resource-rich public lands from coast to coast,[20] but the available evidence indicates that the government has been a less-than-competent steward. Compared to the generally well-managed state lands, the federal lands tend to have higher operating costs and lower revenues.[21] The poor management of federal lands is highly correlated with their inflated operating budgets.[22] These budgets are inflated because the entire budget that remains unspent at the end of the fiscal year is returned to the U.S. Treasury; hence, resource managers spend every last penny to ensure that their budgets are not cut in subsequent years. This warped incentive structure has led to the gross mismanagement of federal resources.

Chronic deficits are made worse by that fact that the ecological conditions of federally managed lands have not improved.[23] Hope Babcock, an expert on environmental issues, professor of law at Georgetown University, and former official of the National Audubon Society, stated, "Few would assert that the historical institutional paradigm for managing the nation's public lands has protected the natural resource values of those lands or provided a harmonious framework for resolving conflicts over their use."[24] Perverse institutional arrangements have led to ballooning budgets and diminishing returns on investment. The ecological health of the national parks has taken a back seat to less pressing measures such as the installment of $3.3 million self-composting solar-powered toilets located in remote chalets in Glacier National Park. Wasteful projects are routinely authorized in spite of the $9.7 billion backlog of maintenance projects for the national parks.[25] It should also be noted that despite the $3.3 million price tag, the toilets failed to work.[26] Such mismanagement of federal resources further accentuates the warped incentive structure that drives spending decisions for federally managed lands.

In order to resolve the issues posed by the perverse institutional arrangements, a majority of the federal government's land holdings should be privatized. Private ownership would allow the lands to be managed by people who had a vested interest in their long-run use. Furthermore, privatization of federal lands would lift the financial burden the current arrangements impose on the federal budget. This would create lands that generate self-sustaining revenue for their owners, and it would ensure that the relevant costs and benefits of the land are fully considered. In order to achieve this goal, the federal lands would have to be split up into parcels that would be sold to the highest bidder. The plan should also foster low transaction costs, which would encourage broad participation.[27] By divesting the government of the responsibility to manage public lands, resources would be more efficiently allocated and society would be made better off.

ENVIRONMENTAL REGULATION AND FARMING

In December 2008, the U.S. Fish and Wildlife Service issued the "biological opinion" that imposed stringent water restrictions on the farming residents of California's premier San Joaquin Valley. The restrictions are the result of a bungled effort to use the Endangered Species Act in order to defend the dwindling population of the federally protected *hypomesus transpacificus*, a 3-inch fish that is more commonly referred to as the delta smelt.[28] The San Joaquin Valley is a bastion of fertile lands known for its bountiful harvests and quaint farming communities. However, as a result of a court ruling on a 2006 case filed by the Natural Resource Defense Council and other environmental groups, billions of gallons of water desperately needed in the drought-stricken San Joaquin Valley are being diverted from the mountains east and north of Sacramento into the ocean.[29]

The economic consequences of the water restrictions have devastated the valley's residents whose livelihoods' depend on the harvest. Without the ability to pump water, the valley's farmland has been fallowed and scorched. A 14.3 percent unemployment rate has accompanied the imposition of the water rights restrictions, and in some areas such as the farming town of Mendota the unemployment rate has reached as high as 40 percent.[30] The federal regulations curtailing the use of water pumps in the San Joaquin Valley will be expanded in 2010 as the result of the National Marine Fisheries Service's recent conclusion that local salmon and steelhead populations need to be defended from the valley's water pumps.

The public outcry over the imposition of the water restrictions has been tremendous. In June 2009 the Obama administration refused Governor Schwarzenegger's request to designate California a disaster area because of the severe drought, despite the fact that the U.S. Drought Monitor currently lists 43 percent of the state in a condition of severe drought.

In addition, numerous advocacy groups have filed over 30 legal challenges to the "biological opinion," citing that the regulations violate the U.S. Constitution's commerce clause and that the Fish and Wildlife Service failed to weigh properly the economic costs and benefits of the water restrictions.[31]

The "biological opinion" has threatened the political futures of California's incumbent politicians, who are being pressured to abolish the draconian regulations. Yet, such efforts face strong headwinds from the entrenched government bureaucracies responsible for implementing the regulations, and from the environmental lobbies who are unwilling to "admit failure" and compromise.[32]

The delta-smelt case demonstrates the inefficiency that occurs when society surrenders itself to command-style regulations that are founded on an abstract and elitist vision of what ought to be. Policies founded on this logic have perverse consequences that far outweigh the benefits associated with them. The federal government's regulations have devastated the livelihoods of tens of thousands, and transformed one of the most productive U.S. agricultural regions into a drought-stricken and desolate tract.

Unexpectedly, in March of 2010, the water began flowing again into the San Joaquin Valley in order to induce two undecided members of Congress to vote for health care reform, yet another example of crony capitalism. It is yet unclear whether this policy reversal will be sustained.

ENVIRONMENTAL REGULATION AND HOUSING

The erosion of property rights is also to blame for California's high median home price, which averaged three times the national average, at least prior to the current recession.[33] In an effort to promote "open" or "green" spaces, judicial and political forces began backing planning boards and environmental agencies after the landmark *Petaluma* decision in 1975. The *Petaluma* case led to the explosion of new building restrictions that promoted the "public good."[34] Many of the zoning limitations imposed took the form of land use restrictions. The land use restrictions had the effect of dramatically driving up home prices in areas where they were imposed. Empirical evidence collected and examined by the National Bureau of Economic Research found that zoning laws were highly correlated with high housing prices.[35] Hence, the zoning laws were highly favorable for individuals who owned property in areas where the laws were implemented. Building proposals were shot down, and in many areas the stock of housing failed to increase as quickly as the surrounding areas.

This explains why housing in California was roughly on par with the national average before beginning to diverge sharply in the 1970s.[36] Therefore, it was not the cost of the home that was high; rather it was the cost of land on which the home sat.

Arbitrary restrictions imposed by building commissions and environmental groups are often sold to the public as actions that promote "sustainable development." However, their economic impact effectively limits the housing stock and drives up housing prices for newcomers. Such policies inhibit economic growth because people are unable to obtain affordable housing in areas where these restrictions are in place. The high home prices contribute to a higher cost of living, which has a detrimental impact on people with low or moderate incomes. Zoning laws effectively impose an arbitrary monopoly on the development of land because development can only take place if the board or agency approves it. This is problematic because boards and agencies are unlikely to analyze the costs and benefits associated with the proposed development. In the context of the political process, boards and agencies have an incentive to thwart future development because such actions would decrease land values and thus anger voters. Elected officials are unlikely to grant permits to unpopular development projects, even if they are economically productive. Zoning laws handicap property owners because the use of the land is subject to the whims of the planning board or environmental agency. As a result, land is allocated not by its price and the forces of competition, but by third parties who are influenced by their own prejudices and competing political agendas.

Land restrictions artificially drive up home prices and prevent low- and moderate-income earners from obtaining affordable housing. Zoning laws also allow affluent communities to create arbitrary barriers to development and thus preserve the status quo of their communities. Such policies have taken a toll on minorities. In San Francisco the black population has declined from 96,000 people in 1970 to 47,000 people in 2005. A similar trend has been seen in other areas with pervasive land restrictions including Los Angeles, Marin County, and Monterey.[37]

GLOBAL WARMING AND FREE-MARKET ENVIRONMENTALISM

Global warming is an extremely contentious political issue. Many competing theories about its causes have emerged and gained the political backing of interested parties. Republicans tend to attribute global warming to the geological and astronomical cycles of the earth and Democrats tend to blame global warming on human activity. Concerns over global warming have evoked a strong call for the regulation of greenhouse gases. Such calls have been amplified in recent years by celebrities and politicians who have brought the issue to the center stage of the media. Examples of such efforts include Al Gore's movie, *An Inconvenient Truth*, and the *Live Earth* show sponsored by a plethora of famous musicians. Although the debate remains far from over, a myriad of proposals for regulation have emerged—most notably the Kyoto Protocol.

The Kyoto Protocol imposes a legally binding constraint on the emission of greenhouse gases by industrialized nations. In the environmental community the Kyoto Protocol is hailed as a milestone in the effort to save the planet from harmful greenhouse gases that many scientists credit as the chief source of the "climate crisis." However, economists are skeptical of the Kyoto Protocol and many believe that the costs far outweigh the benefits. In the 1998 Geophysical Research Letters a renowned climatologist with the National Center for Atmospheric Research, T. M. L. Wigley concludes that even if the measure achieved its objective of reducing carbon emissions to 5 percent below the 1990 levels, the results would be barely discernible for decades. In fact the Kyoto Protocol would only slow the projected rate of global warming of 2.5 degrees centigrade over the next 100 years by a maximum of 0.28 degrees centigrade.[38]

Climate protection is best characterized as a public good, economically. The marginal benefits generated by climate protection are greater for society than for individual firms. This leads firms to under-produce the public good. In addition, the largely unknown benefits that may arise would only be discernable in the distant future, and the short-run adjustment costs would be enormous. Consequently, the incentive structure of the Kyoto Protocol does not encourage heavily industrialized countries like the United States to adopt its policies. Furthermore, the Kyoto Protocol exempts developing countries from binding emission targets.[39] This further undermines the use of the Kyoto Protocol as an effective tool to combat greenhouse gases.

To comply with the Kyoto Protocol the United States would have to cut its greenhouse gas emissions by 40 percent.[40] This is an impossible goal because such a reduction, even over a prolonged period, would cause significant and adverse impacts on the U.S. economy. Several economic analyses have demonstrated that the law of diminishing returns holds true for greenhouse gas reduction. In fact, the additional cost of controlling emissions increases from $10 per ton to $80 per ton as greenhouse gas emission targets are increased from 5 to 25 percent.[41] Meanwhile, the benefit of the reduction would be a maximum reduction of the predicted temperature rise by one-tenth of one degree centigrade by 2050.[42] Such a minimal decrease will hardly abate the effects of global warming. In this case, simple cost-benefit analysis demonstrates that the costs for the Kyoto Protocol far outweigh its possible benefits.

Problems in the global commons can be solved by removing the perverse incentives that exacerbate environmental problems by encouraging resource managers to squander scarce resources. In order to achieve this objective, strong property rights backed by the rule of law must be implemented on a global scale. The empirical evidence leaves no room for doubt that property rights are instrumental in ensuring that scarce resources be used by those who value them most. Mutually beneficial trade facilitates such an outcome; property rights encourage economically efficient outcomes. In fact, an index of property rights formulated by Gwartney, Lawson, and Block found that per capita growth rates average 2.4 percent annually for countries with secure property rights and −1.3 for countries that did not have secure property rights.[43]

The relationship between economic growth and pollution is important because for industrialized nations rising incomes afford greater environmental quality.[44] The Kuznet curve, developed by Nobel Laureate Simon Kuznet demonstrates this relationship. In the early stages of economic development people are willing to accept more pollution, an economic bad, in exchange for increased economic development, which yields economic goods. However, as income levels rise the desire for environmental quality correspondingly increases. Thus, at different levels of economic development the relevant trade-offs differ. This assertion is supported by empirical evidence showing that, as income increased, the terrestrial, aquatic, and atmospheric conditions in the United States have all improved significantly.[45] Per capita carbon output in the United States has remained constant over the last 25 years, and emissions per unit of output have been steadily declining.[46]

If environmental conditions are generally improving in the aggregate, then one has to wonder: Why do environmentalists often speak about doomsday scenarios? One plausible answer is that sometimes the government misjudges risk. It has been reported, for example, that "[t]he Interior Department exempted BP's calamitous Gulf of Mexico drilling operation from a detailed environmental impact analysis last year, according to government documents, after three reviews of the area concluded that a massive oil spill was unlikely."[47]

The general answer to the question above is that environmental regulations often cater to special interest groups. Green business has become big business and numerous players are competing for tougher regulations so they can cash in on selling products geared toward shifting mandates. Thus, the political process serves to promote concentrated benefits and spread the cost widely among the taxpayers. This is not to say that all environmental regulation is useless and unnecessary. Rather, it demonstrates how the warped incentive structure inherent in bureaucratic entities is not the most efficient mode of fostering enduring environmental stewardship.

Protecting the environment is best accomplished by ensuring people who manage or own resources have a vested interest in them. Such interest will compel individuals to weigh the economic costs and benefits of using resources. Owners who manage resources well will be rewarded with economic profits and those who plunder resources or mismanage them will fail in the long run. To ensure that market forces direct consumers and firms to efficient outcomes, owners must possess secure property rights that are readily transferable and enforceable. Government plays an important role in ensuring that these conditions are satisfied. Such conditions will achieve what arbitrary quotas and other forms of regulation cannot—namely allowing markets to use prices and the forces of competition to allocate scarce resources in a manner that maximizes the productive potential of the resource.

Owners who possess secure property rights will ensure that the tragedy of the commons is avoided and seek compensation for any damages imposed by others on their property through the court system. Free-market environmentalism harnesses the awesome and unbeaten power of markets to allocate goods and resources efficiently. Furthermore, it structures incentives so that they cater to self-interest—not special interests. By reforming the numerous regulatory bodies to adopt the principles laid out in this chapter, the United States' precious natural resources will be more effectively and efficiently managed. This will benefit the economy and the environment. The market has been effective in supplying the nation with bread, televisions, and cars. Command-style principles are ill-founded and lead to tragic results, as in the case of the fisheries. Thus, being green is not about creating a sea of arbitrary regulations that cost a fortune and provide little protection; rather it is about having a vested interest in the future. Only a vested interest in the future, fostered by secure property rights, will provide us with the tools to create enduring environmental stewardship.

NOTES

1. Terry L. Anderson and Donald R. Leal, *Free Market Environmentalism* (New York: Palgrave Macmillan, 2001), 4.

2. Ibid.

3. Ben Bernanke and Robert H. Frank, *Principles of Microeconomics*, 3rd ed. (New York: McGraw-Hill, 2007), 351.

4. Ibid., 352.

5. Ibid.

6. Ibid.

7. Ibid., 353.

8. Ibid., 361–362.

9. Donald R. Leal, "Saving Fisheries with Free-Markets," *Milken Institute Review* 57, no. 1 (2006).

10. Terry Lee Anderson, *Greener Than Thou: Are You Really an Environmentalist?* (Stanford, CA: Hoover Institution, 2008), 68.

11. Ibid.

12. Leal, "Saving Fisheries with Free-Markets," 59.

13. Ibid.

14. Ibid.

15. Anderson, *Greener Than Thou: Are You Really an Environmentalist?* 85.

16. Ibid., 86.

17. Anderson, *Greener Than Thou: Are You Really an Environmentalist?* 63.

18. Pamela S. Snyder and Jane S. Shaw, "PC Drilling in a Wildlife Refuge, *Wall Street Journal*, September 7, 1995.

19. Anderson, *Greener Than Thou: Are You Really an Environmentalist?* 64.

20. Terry L. Anderson, Vernon L. Smith, and Emily Simmons "How and Why We, Privatize Federal Lands," *Policy Analysis* 363 (1999): 1–4.

21. Ibid., 66.

22. Ibid., 66.

23. Ibid., 5.

24. Ibid.

25. Anderson, *Greener Than Thou: Are You Really an Environmentalist?* 66–67.

26. Ibid.

27. Anderson, Smith, and Simmons, "How and Why We Privatize Federal Lands," 7–9.

28. *Wall Street Journal*, "California's Man-Made Drought," September 2, 2009.

29. Ibid.

30. Ibid.

31. Ibid.

32. Ibid.

33. Thomas Sowell, *Economic Facts and Fallacies* (New York: Basic Books, 2007), 32.

34. Ibid.

35. Ibid., 99.

36. Ibid., 32.

37. Ibid., 36.

38. Anderson, *Greener Than Thou: Are You Really an Environmentalist?* 53.

39. Christoph Böhringer and Carsten Vogt, "Economic and Environmental Impacts of the Kyoto Protocol," *Canadian Journal of Economics/Revue Canadienne d'Economique* 36, no. 2 (2003).

40. Anderson, *Free Market Environmentalism*, 160.

41. Edgar K. Browning and Mark A. Zupan, *Microeconomics Theory Applications*, 9th ed. (Hoboken, NJ: Wiley, 2005), 231.

42. Anderson, *Greener Than Thou: Are You Really an Environmentalist?* 160.

43. Ibid., 165.

44. Ibid., 54.

45. Ibid., 44–49.

46. Ibid., 51.

47. Juliet Eilperin, "U.S. exempted BP's Gulf of Mexico drilling from environmental impact study," *Washington Post* May 5, 2010.

Chapter 10

TAXING MORE
AND PRODUCING LESS

Contrary to popular opinion, taxes are necessary and proper for life in an organized society. In order to reap the benefits of government, a population must inevitably foot the bill for the goods and services that government provides. As discussed in the introduction, a government produces a number of services that benefit the population, specifically those services of a "public good" nature. Included among them are the provisions of security, a sound legal system, and the creation and maintenance of public roads and highways. While we do not intend to legitimize all of the spending by federal, state, and local governments, we find it prudent to recognize that governments indeed produce a number of goods and services that are beneficial to the public.

As we recognize the benefits of certain government spending, we inherently accept and support the government's right and necessity to tax the people. We emphasize that taxation does not, in and of itself, constitute a net liability. What we aim to do in this chapter is to analyze the basic tax structure of the U.S. federal government and its effects upon the economy. In the coming pages we will find a complex and inefficient collection mechanism, one that constitutes a liability within its structure rather than within its function.

Under the current tax code, the federal government has multiple sources of revenues, with the two main sources being the individual income tax and contributions to social-insurance programs such as Social Security and Medicare. While Social Security was originally designed as a form of forced savings, its collection is now a source of funding for a plethora of federal programs. As a result, collection on its behalf has to be treated as government revenue. Other less significant sources of revenue include corporate profits taxes, excise taxes, and the borrowing of funds which is paid for by the printing of money from the Federal Reserve System. The printing of money at the Federal Reserve presents an interesting case, for while the public does not feel the effects directly through a primary collection agency, the printing of money allows the government to capture economic resources directly in the short run and, in the long run, tends to raise the rate of inflation—thus lowering the purchasing power of accumulated wealth and implicitly taxing people. In some less-developed countries, most recently in a number of Latin American countries, the printing of money by the Central Bank has accounted for up to half of all government revenues.

We will first discuss the general structures of the income tax and social-insurance contributions, the largest sources of federal revenue. Then, after gathering up the additional lesser sources of revenue, we will analyze the aggregate effects that the current structure of taxation has on the U.S. economy.

FEDERAL INCOME TAX

The federal income tax is the single largest source of revenue for the federal government. It is most generally characterized by its graduated-rate or progressive structure. Basically, this means that the percentage contribution of an individual's income toward the income tax rises as his or her income rises. For example, in 2009 a head of household earning under $11,950 of taxable income was required to pay an income tax of 10 percent. A head of household earning more than $11,950 but less than $45,500 was required to pay 10 percent of the first $11,950 ($1,195) and 15 percent of taxable income over $11,950. These rate increases continued to the limit of $372,950, at which point a household was required to pay $104,892.50, plus 35 percent of any income above such limit.[1] The intent of this is to shift the overall burden of taxation away from low-income individuals and toward high-income individuals. This goal will be promoted with the coming expiration of the Bush-era tax cuts.

Complicating the graduated or progressive tax is the web of possible itemized deductions and credits that might be employed in order to reduce the overall taxes an individual owes to the federal government. Deductions exist for charitable donations, medical payments, a variety of business expenses, and a host of additional expenditures. These complicated write-offs often leave taxpayers scratching their heads and drive many to seek out costly professional tax advice and assistance.

SOCIAL-INSURANCE CONTRIBUTIONS

Contributions to social-insurance programs have risen fairly consistently since the Great Depression and the New Deal ushered in the modern welfare system. Although originally designed to be a forced saving mechanism, the current structures of the U.S. social-insurance programs are plagued by inefficiencies and impending failure. We focus our attention on the most famous (and most certainly doomed) example, the Social Security system. It is, as defined by the Social Security Administration, "the single largest social program of the federal government."[2] While the causes surrounding the impending demise of the Social Security program are significant, they are too complex and removed from the basic thrust of this chapter to merit detailed description. Indeed, a proper discussion of the history and failures of the various social-insurance programs would easily constitute several volumes of in-depth analysis. For the purposes of this work, it is sufficient to say that payments to social-insurance programs are significant and constitute a large proportion of federal revenue, and, combined with the federal income tax, present a difficult web of code and federal regulations which the common taxpayer must struggle through annually.

A variety of other federal revenue sources complicate the structure of taxation even further. From corporate profits taxes to excise, customs taxes and the printing of money at the Federal Reserve System, the internal revenue structure is an incredibly complex maze.

Given the complicated, confusing structure of revenue collection by the federal government, the implementation of the Internal Revenue Code is costly. Aside from the actual revenue collected by the federal government in order to fund its programs, the costs of resources used by the population to comply with the current system of taxation imposes significant and largely unnecessary burdens on the people. These costs, which will now be enumerated in both qualitative and quantitative terms, reduce the productive capacity of the economy, and they could be diminished through significant reform.

The most immediate and apparent cost of the current tax structure, which most individuals or households experience first-hand on an annual basis, is derived from the difficulty in filing federal income tax returns. Given the complexity of the structure of taxation, most individuals are hesitant or incapable of filing their own taxes. Fear of mistakes, which are often punished through heavy penalty fees, drive individuals to hire personal accountants or tax preparers to file their returns for them. Depending on the complexity and variety of individuals' or households' income, many hire accountants year-round in order to keep proper track of their income and the applicability of various tax mechanisms to each of those incomes. Ever-changing tax incentives, such as new potential deductions, lead uninformed individuals to seek professional help to avoid missing out on tax breaks as well.

In this particular endeavor, combined with potential underhanded tricks known only to professionals well-versed in current tax code, many households face a costly trade-off: Either pay a higher total tax, missing obscure write-offs and professional evasive maneuvers, or reduce their tax payments substantially by hiring costly tax specialists. The incentives often drive individuals toward the latter, hiring tax professionals and thus creating an additional cost of taxation—one that does not reach the coffers of the federal government. And while individuals ultimately decide whether to hire such specialists and absorb the additional costs, the complexity of the tax code offers significant incentives for such behavior. The incentives presented now drive more than 50 percent of families to hire professional firms to prepare their taxes.[3] Additionally, those individuals who prepare their own taxes must spend days collecting the appropriate data and learning complex rules, incurring substantial implicit costs in the form of foregone opportunities.

The incentives for firms to avoid taxes are even greater than those for households. Firms spend billions of dollars annually in attempts to maximize their legitimate write-offs, as well as in more devious manners of evading taxation. Aside from the quantitative ramifications of the complex tax policy, the corporate world is also affected heavily by the incentives for underhanded and dishonest tax conduct. Large firms in general have extensive teams dedicated to the study of taxation and the ways in which the entities can minimize their tax expenditures. Often, the incentives that the complex structure of taxation offers for dishonest or underhanded conduct drive organizations to act questionably in their accounting practices. Subsequent controversy surrounding these questionable practices can reduce the productive capacity of the organizations by the potential loss of executives, or in severe cases through the closure of the firms because of criminal behavior. While we feel the need to stress that we in no way endorse or excuse illicit and subversive tax evasion, it is important to note that the incentives within the current tax structure do lead many firms and individuals to assume enormous costs and risks in their attempts to avoid taxation.

The incentives to use tax professionals are derived in large part from the complexity of the tax structure. Indeed, the historical progression of the

U.S. tax code shows how monstrous the code has become, such that it is nearly impossible for even a professional in the field to become familiar with all aspects of it. Perhaps one of the best measures of this complexity is within the verbiage of the code itself. In 1955, the entire revenue code and IRS regulations consisted of approximately 1,396,000 words. As of 2005, the code and regulations consisted of an astonishing 9,097,000 words.[4] The result is an extensive, wordy system of taxation that a tax professional can navigate with only the most intense dedication, and within which the typical individual is completely lost. These unnecessary complexities require the commitment of vast amounts of time and resources.

When viewed numerically, the total costs of the collection of taxation under the current system to individuals, households, and firms are enormous. The Tax Advocate Service estimates that "taxpayers and businesses spend 7.6 billion hours per year complying with tax-filing requirements."[5] The estimated annual federal income tax compliance cost in 2005 has been stated at over $256 billion.[6] Additionally, the Tax Foundation estimates that federal income tax compliance costs could grow to over $480 billion in nominal terms by the year 2015.[7] These costs, of course, represent expenditures in compliance with tax code, above and beyond the actual income taxes paid to the federal government. Such enormous costs represent a major drain on the balance sheets of households and businesses beyond the initial negative pressure applied by the actual taxes.

Collection at the governmental level also has its undue costs. As of the end of fiscal year 2007, the IRS employed over 86,000 people. The nominal operating costs, as of the same year, were over $10.7 billion annually. Broken down, $7.7 billion of these costs constitute labor compensation and benefits, while $3.0 billion went to other miscellaneous costs.[8] While small in comparison to the private costs of tax compliance, these figures are nevertheless significant sums of money. A more simplified operation, stemming from a less complex tax code, might free up some government funds for use within more productive government functions, or for paying down the national deficit.

The aggregate costs of tax collection and compliance paint a very disturbing picture. It is estimated that "the resources involved amount to between 3 percent and 4 percent of national income (or 12 to 15% of the revenues collected)."[9] These incredible costs of implementation reflect the inefficient structure of the current tax system, and they represent an enormous burden on the balance sheets of almost all individuals, households, firms, and even the government. The inefficiencies create costs that limit society's productive capability drastically.

Some may claim, however, that payments to accountants, tax attorneys, tax preparers, and IRS employees do not hinder the aggregate health of the economy. While some firms and individuals experience increased costs, there is an entire industry employed for the sole purpose of assisting individuals, households, and firms in their compliance with tax code. In fact, the payments to these professionals appear in GDP, and so while individuals and firms must forego some consumption and investment in order to fund their compliance, GDP remains unchanged.

The rationale expressed in this approach is similar to that which was described in the discussion of security expenditures in Chapter 1. Just because it is included in the GDP does not mean it is beneficial to the national economy. If the billions of dollars committed to tax code compliance were allocated to more productive uses, such as research and development, then the future standard of living would undoubtedly improve. Consider also the estimated 7.6 billion hours committed annually to tax preparation and compliance. If the tax code were simpler, then this labor would be available for more productive activities which could produce desirable final goods and services; this time could even be used for leisure activities. Many tax professions also require years of specialized education which could be directed toward other productive professions were the tax code simpler. In short, the resources and time currently allocated to compliance would serve the economy much better if they could be committed to more productive functions.

Another major liability presented by the current tax code is the incentive that it provides for dishonesty and illegal activity. Aside from the monetary costs associated with the specific acts of tax fraud and tax evasion, the risk that individuals and firms assume in order to maneuver successfully and game the complex tax structure has a severe negative impact on the U.S. economy. While each individual is responsible for making honest, legal, and morally sound decisions, it would be naïve to deny that structural incentives toward dishonesty increase such occurrences. That is, a complex, confusing, and easily manipulated tax structure such as this invites transgressions against it. The IRS rightfully investigates and prosecutes those who are guilty of tax evasion or fraud but it cannot possibly reach all of those who have cheated the system; hence justice cannot be applied impartially. If, however, the tax structure were less complex, there might be less opportunity for questionable conduct by both taxpayers and government enforcement agencies.

The specific negative impacts of perverse tax conduct are multifold. First, the government, realizing that the tax structure invites dishonesty, must employ substantial professional resources toward the investigation of complicated cases of potential tax evasion or fraud. As of the year 2008, for example, the IRS employed over 2,600 Special Agents in its Criminal Investigation department.[10] In that year, the Criminal Investigation department initiated 3,749 investigations, and it successfully saw 1,957 investigations to sentencing.[11] Those guilty of tax evasion and fraud deserved the punishment they received as a result of IRS investigation and federal prosecution. However, many of those who are prosecuted and imprisoned in criminal tax investigations are often highly productive individuals within the community. Among the ranks of those investigated for tax fraud are actor Nicolas Cage, singer/songwriter Willie Nelson, and even former IRS commissioner Joseph Nunan. If a less easily manipulated, less complex system of taxation could reduce the opportunity and incentives for dishonest behavior, it is possible that fewer productive individuals would end up under investigation or in prison, instead dedicating their time to making positive contributions to society. Also significant is the tax revenue lost by successful maneuvers through loopholes and complexities within the tax code. A simpler code might discourage such dishonesty and reduce the amount of lost income tax. In short, while individuals are the sole determinants of their own dishonesty, a structure that is simpler would likely provide fewer incentives that encourage individuals to furtively elude their civil responsibilities.

Finally, we must address the societal liability present in the graduated structure of the tax system. In shifting the burden unevenly upon those with higher income, the tax structure essentially reduces the incentives to work at higher levels of income. As individuals' incomes rise they must pay a higher percentage of their earned income to the IRS. Therefore, the incentive to work at higher incomes is weakened because the total take-home wages are a lower percentage than at lower incomes. This reduced incentive structure makes working at higher income levels less attractive.

The current graduated structure of the tax system has also created a distorted arrangement of individual costs and benefits. According to the Tax Foundation, the poorest 20 percent of taxpayers shouldered approximately 2.6 percent of the total federal tax burden in 2004, while receiving the benefits of approximately 33.8 percent of government spending. In contrast, the top quintile carried 52.8 percent of the total federal tax burden in the same year, while receiving the benefits of only 15.0 percent of federal government spending. While one might argue that moderate progressivity in these statistics is desirable, the gross polarity between the two groups is alarming. Although this divergence is caused by the overall tendencies of government spending as well as by the tax structures, revamping the federal collection mechanisms will help to mitigate these vast gaps.[12]

It is important to note in our considerations, however, that the problems with a radically progressive tax structure seem to have been identified within the system and, to an extent, alleviated. As late as 1960, the highest tax bracket had an astounding marginal tax rate of 91 percent. Subsequent tax cuts dropped the top marginal tax rate first to 70 percent, then 50 percent, and later to a low of 30 percent.[13] Thus, the current maximum marginal tax rate, though it still may decrease incentives to work at high income levels, is relatively moderate compared to historical levels. The recent trend implicitly recognizes the flaws of a graduated structure. Current political sentiment, however, threatens to reverse this trend. Such popular opinion is dangerous to the capitalist incentives that drive the economy. Further, it is dangerous because tax rates higher than some maximum level diminish incentives to work so much that total tax revenues actually decrease. This is best exemplified by a common graph in economics, the Laffer Curve, shown in Figure 10.1.

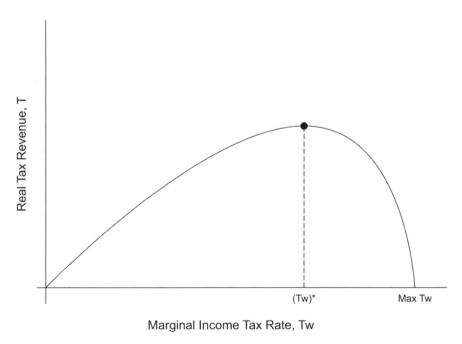

Figure 10.1
Laffer Curve.
Source: Authors' illustration

The Laffer Curve[14] shows that beyond a maximum level of taxation, higher tax rates diminish total government revenue. While lower-income earners under the current structure of taxation may not be at this level, research in the field indicates that those earners in top tax tiers may actually have been beyond this maximum in recent years.[15] Additionally, the Laffer Curve illustrates a point vital to this chapter: Incentives matter. The U.S. tax structure has significant effects on economic incentives. In the efforts to raise revenue for the government, it is imperative to consider the incentives and disincentives posed by various structures and levels of taxation.

The liabilities presented thus far are substantiated by public opinion about the nation's tax code. According to a 2007 survey published by the Tax Foundation, 83 percent of the population believed that the tax policy is "very complex or somewhat complex."[16] Furthermore, "seventy-eight percent [of those surveyed] believe the federal tax system needs 'major changes' or 'a complete overhaul.' "[17] While the public may not be able to enumerate the specific pitfalls that impose undue costs on the economy, the general consensus recognizes the existence of the liabilities we present. With this evidence in mind, we must search for an acceptable approach toward reform.

VIABLE ALTERNATIVES

We turn now to potential measures to mitigate this incredible structural liability within the U.S. economy. Just as the inherent problems with the structure of taxation are not new topics, neither are attempts at reform. In fact, over the years politicians, economists, and a variety of other sources have put forth numerous potential reforms that might address some or all of the liabilities identified within this chapter. While it is impossible to consider every proposed reform, we now strive to identify the most viable and potentially successful alternatives.

Two proposals in particular stand out: the "Fair Tax" and the "Flat Tax." Both of these have gained incredible publicity and popularity in the attempts to combat the increasingly burdensome system of taxation which, according to the preceding analysis, has developed into a significant liability for U.S. productivity and economic prosperity. While both plans have respective merits and shortfalls, we believe that ultimately a combination of the two systems will effectively reduce the liability of the current tax structure.

THE FAIR TAX

The basic premise of the "Fair Tax" is the replacement of most sources of federal revenue with a single retail sales tax. The proposal has gained wide backing in the media and the political sphere; it has even achieved significant popularity among large groups of taxpaying citizens. As a bill in the House of Representatives, it was introduced on January 6th, 2009, by Representative John Linder. This proposal seeks to eliminate income, payroll, estate, and gift taxes and replace them with a 23 percent tax on retail purchases of goods and services. To shift the tax burden away from those living in poverty, it offers households a "prebate" of retail taxes that would be paid up to a certain point of consumption. Proponents claim that this measure will "ensure that each family unit can consume tax free at or beyond the poverty level . . . "[18] In all, the "Fair Tax" proposal would greatly simplify the means of federal revenue, reducing many of the afore-mentioned liabilities.

The specific benefits of such a program are easy to see. Beyond the sim-plification of the federal revenue process, the disincentives toward hard work presented by a gradual income tax system are eliminated. Those in poverty would be granted relief from any taxation—and persons in extreme poverty could actually end out on top if their "prebate" check exceeds their consumption taxes paid over the course of the year. Additionally, a con-sumption tax like this would create incentives for saving and investment—vital for the continued progress and prosperity of the economy.

While there are many benefits associated with the "Fair Tax," and it would successfully mitigate the liabilities posed in the current system of federal revenue, there are a number of issues which would arise if the "Fair Tax" were implemented. First, many state and local governments derive their incomes from retail taxes already in place. The imposition of federal sales taxes of 23 percent, therefore, would not be the only tax on the purchases of goods and services for consumption. In some states, retail taxes could exceed 30 percent. Pressures from retailers could then force some states to diminish or abandon their sales tax programs and revise their own revenue codes. Such revisions could very well drive state revenue systems to more complex methods, which would reinstate many of the very liabilities that are abandoned in the revamping of the current federal tax code.

Undoubtedly, retailers and a variety of other businesses would be wholeheartedly opposed to the plan, as it would most likely decrease the demand for the goods and services they produce. While increased incentives for saving and investment are generally a good thing, such a drastic imposition would certainly alter the current structure of payments within the economy significantly. Because the productive assets within the economy are ideally positioned and employed in such a manner as to facilitate efficiently current patterns of consumption, investment, and savings, a radical alteration of such patterns could throw the U.S. economy into disarray, at least in the short run. This is not to say, however, that the economy would not readjust, but rather that the transition from the current system to a "Fair Tax" would be rocky and costly.

Finally, and perhaps of most concern, are the pernicious incentives that the "Fair Tax" system imposes. Though the proponents of the new tax structure tend to downplay the significance, there would undoubtedly be an incredible surge in the black market. That is, with a sales tax approaching or even exceeding 30 percent when state and local revenues are factored in, the incentives to buy and sell goods and services on the black market would be greatly enhanced. The smuggling of goods from foreign nations and the sale of those goods through undisclosed cash transactions would surely skyrocket. Services provided to consumers would also be increasingly conducted "under the table" so as to avoid significant tax liabilities. Because the retail tax would become the only form of federal taxation, those who could successfully dodge the tax through black market transactions would reap enormous financial rewards.

In order to prevent such actions, the federal government would need to employ more labor and resources toward the enforcement of proper sales techniques. Such expenditures would ultimately be passed on to taxpayers in the form of higher taxes. Additionally, those who found ways to dodge the retail tax would place themselves at risk and employ resources to evade taxation—resources that could be assigned to more productive functions. In short, the incentives produced by the "Fair Tax" proposals present significant motivation for dishonesty, which will ultimately detract from U.S. productivity and prosperity. Thus, while the "Fair Tax" proposal successfully mitigates many of the societal liabilities posed by the current structure of federal taxation, its use as the *sole* source of federal revenue presents serious problems.

THE FLAT TAX

We now look at another proposal, the "Flat Tax." In its simplest form, the flat tax is a source of federal revenue that taxes income at a constant rate. For the purposes of our analysis, we will focus on one particular type of

"Flat Tax" proposed by Robert E. Hall and Alvin Rabushka. In recent years, the tax has gained incredible popularity and has been introduced as legislation in a number of different bills. Henceforth, our discussion of the flat tax will refer to the Hall-Rabushka flat tax, which is, in our opinion, the most complete and realistic flat tax proposal available.

In their book *The Flat Tax*, Hall and Rabushka outline a significantly simpler model of taxation, based on a flat tax rate of 19 percent on individual and business income. There would be two forms for taxation, the Individual Wage-Tax Form and the Business-Tax Form. All income would be taxed at the source. That is, wages would be taxed from individuals, and corporate income would be taxed from businesses. By eliminating individual capital gains taxes, the problem of double taxation that exists within the current system would be eliminated and disincentives toward savings and investment removed. For example, dividends would not be taxed when paid to investors, as they have already been taxed as revenues to the firms. The only deductions allowed at the individual level would be personal allowances to prevent taxation below a specified level of poverty, and write-offs for dependents. Businesses would be granted allowances for capital investments, wage and benefits payments, and the purchases of intermediate goods (goods which are used to later produce final goods and services for sale).

The benefits of the implementation of a flat tax similar to the one Hall and Rabushka propose and promote are multifold. First and foremost, it successfully simplifies the process of federal revenue collection. It consolidates federal revenue sources, thus making both tax administration and compliance much easier and less costly. It also eliminates most deductions, credits, and other lawful methods of reducing one's tax liability. While taxpayers may initially be opposed to such a concept, the benefits that the economy would reap across the board are enormous. No longer would taxpayers face the trade-off between expensive tax services and higher tax liabilities. Tax returns, the two authors boast, could be completed by individuals and businesses alike on a simple postcard-sized form. The enormous amounts of time and resources currently committed to tax compliance could be assigned to more productive functions, enhancing the economy and promoting prosperity.

The simplicity created would remove opportunities for dishonesty present in the current system. That is, with fewer loopholes to navigate and less complexity to obscure dishonest accounting practices, it is hoped that many people would simply file their taxes honestly, realizing that the potential opportunities for gaming the system are minimal. The federal government would more effectively collect a greater percentage of the taxes it is owed, with less emphasis and expenditures on enforcement. The "postcard tax return" that Hall and Rabushka advocate would surely require a much less extensive bureaucracy to manage than the IRS currently employs. The resources saved through this reduction could be applied to more necessary, productive government functions, to lowering future tax rates further, or even to paying down the national debt.

The flat tax would also remove the disincentives toward hard work at high income levels that are currently embodied in the U.S. graduated system of taxation. While it would continue to protect impoverished individuals from being overcome by tax liabilities, it would impose a flat rate of taxation at all levels, thus equalizing the incentives to work at all levels of income. Coupled with a simple flat tax on business revenues, the United States would quickly enhance its status as an attractive location for successful, productive individuals and prosperous firms alike.

As is the case with any proposed radical reform, however, critics have raised a number of issues in opposition to the flat tax, three of which stand out. First is the opposition that professionals within the field of taxation would surely mount against the implementation of such a reform. A plethora of different professions profit greatly from the current structure of federal taxation, as the system encourages the use of expensive professional tax help. One must expect that those who benefit considerably from the current complexity in the IRS code would oppose any significant simplification. Should such reforms pass, there would be a concentrated loss in the tax services industry. However, while many tax professionals would indeed be displaced, they could, over time, shift functions into more productive roles in society. The vast resources expended educating an army of tax specialists could be redirected toward education in more productive fields. While those who have dedicated their careers to the current tax system would indeed suffer a shock, the long-term societal benefits would significantly outweigh these costs.

Another concern raised is that of reduced incentives for certain charitable contributions. That is, with most deductions eliminated, the tax incentive of charitable donations would be removed. Some fear that without these incentives, charitable donations would drop significantly. These concerns are based on the assumption that individuals largely derive their personal incentives for charitable donations from tax breaks. Though empirical evidence does not support this dismal thought, if initially charitable donations decline significantly, some limited deductions for charity could be inserted in the tax code without reversing the positive effects of the simplification of the tax structure.

Finally, while the flat tax does remove some disincentives for saving, the nation's economic development and the modern propensity for Americans to avoid savings may merit calls for additional tax incentives for saving. Most simply, such a system could be implemented by lowering the flat tax rate and introducing a lower-rate variant of the fair tax. While the actual rates are open to statistical analysis and discussion, a lower fair tax may discourage wide use of the black market and create the proper incentives for savings and investment. The implementation of a lower-level retail tax would not significantly diminish the benefits derived from the simple model of taxation, while providing additional incentives to save.

Surely additional issues can be raised, with either of the individual proposals, or with our own combination of the two. While we do not assert that these systems completely eliminate the burdens of the collection of federal revenue, perfection is not necessary to merit change. We find that, in light of all other proposals to date, these are the most viable and realistic. Even if some issues do exist with the proposals, the implementation of a flat tax with an added retail tax to provide additional incentives for savings would do the U.S. economy, and indeed U.S. prosperity, a great service. We encourage active national dialogue regarding the best ways to implement such reform. It is a fact that few will refute: The current federal structure of taxation is a liability to productivity and prosperity, one that must be reformed.

NOTES

1. U.S. Internal Revenue Service, "1040 Instructions Booklet 2009," http://www.irs.gov/pub/irs-pdf/i1040.pdf.

2. U.S. Department of the Treasury, "Social Security Reform: The Nature of the Problem," Issue Brief No. 1, http://www.ustreas.gov/press/releases/reports/post.pdf.

3. James D. Gwartney, Richard L. Stroup, Russell S. Sobel, and David A. Macpherson, *Macroeconomics: Private & Public Choice* (Ohio: Thompson SouthWestern, 2006), 425.

4. J. Scott Moody, Wendy P. Warcholik, and Scott A. Hodge, "The Rising Cost of Complying with the Federal Income Tax," *Special Report 138*, The Tax Foundation, December 2005, 4, http://www.taxfoundation.org/files/sr138.pdf.

5. U.S. Internal Revenue Service, *National Taxpayer Advocate: 2008 Annual Report to Congress*, 1, http://www.irs.gov/pub/irs-utl/08_tas_exec_summ0108v2.pdf.

6. Scott A. Hodge, J. Scott Moody, and Wendy P. Warcholik, "Special Report: The Rising Cost of Complying with the Federal Income Tax," The Tax Foundation, January 10, 2006, http://www.taxfoundation.org/research/show/1281.html.

7. Moody and Others, *Special Report*, 2.

8. Linda E. Stiff and Others, *Data Book 2007*, U.S. Internal Revenue Service, 63, http://www.irs.gov/pub/irs-soi/07dbbudgwork.pdf.

9. Gwartney and Others, *Macroeconomics: Private & Public Choice*, 425.

10. Internal Revenue Service, "Enforcement Statistics—Criminal Investigation (CI) Enforcement Strategy," 2009, http://www.irs.gov/compliance/enforcement/article/0,,id=108792,00.html.

11. Ibid.

12. Andrew Chamberlain and Gerald Prante, "Who Pays Taxes and Who Receives Government Spending? An Analysis of Federal, State, and Local Tax and Spending Distributions, 1991–2004," The Tax Foundation, March 2007, 44–74, http://www.taxfoundation.org/files/wp1.pdf.

13. Gwartney and Others, *Macroeconomics: Private & Public Choice* (Ohio: Thompson SouthWestern, 2006), 425–6.

14. Popularized by Arthur B. Laffer (see any encyclopedia); the concept goes back to the fourteenth century.

15. Robert J. Barro, *Macroeconomics: A Modern Approach* (Ohio: Thompson SouthWestern, 2008), 336.

16. Andrew Chamberlain, "What Does America Think About Taxes? The 2007 Annual Survey of U.S. Attitudes on Taxes and Wealth," *Special Report*, The Tax Foundation, April 2007., 154, 5, http://www.taxfoundation.org/files/sr154.pdf.

17. Ibid., 5.

18. Americans for Fair Taxation, "The Fair Tax Prebate Explained," 2007, 1, http://www.fairtax.org/PDF/FairTaxPrebateExplained2007.pdf.

Chapter 11

ENSURING DISASTER
WITH MORAL HAZARD

Risk is everywhere. Without it, we could hardly be productive. While many people consider the term to have a negative connotation, the concept of *risk* is essential to economic as well as personal success. Taking risks is a necessary, healthy component of a prosperous economy.

The types of risks we face are numerous. Some, we assume upon ourselves as we strive for personal gains. For financial gains, people assume risk in their portfolios by purchasing stocks, bonds, and by placing their savings on the line to start businesses. Most people are aware of the risks associated with each action, and they understand that in order to make substantial and sustained gains, a certain amount of risk is necessary.

Risk exists beyond the pages of the business section as well. When we drive one mile to the supermarket, we face about a .000083 percent risk of injury in a vehicular accident, and when we walk barefoot on the beach we face a risk of stepping on glass.[1] While we often don't consciously acknowledge these risks, we usually know that they exist. Why, then, do we act, knowing that there are potential negative effects of any given action? We already have the answer: Without taking any risk, our society would be paralyzed. If fear of potential negative outcomes persisted, we would hold all of our money in cash beneath our mattresses, wouldn't venture beyond our homes, and even would refrain from interacting with other human beings. Our world is a world where risk is necessary to survive and, further, to thrive.

Beyond our natural propensity to ignore some risks, we have other mechanisms to promote activity in our hazardous world. More specifically, in various functions we take on different forms of insurance, assuming constant costs to hedge risks of larger losses. For example, we take on health insurance, paying a set annual cost, and mitigating potential future costs that might arise from expensive medical procedures. We purchase homeowners insurance in order to alleviate the risk of catastrophic losses from fires or vandalism. Automobile insurance protects us from potentially large losses that might occur in an instantaneous crash.

These insurances allow us to carry out our basic daily routines more confidently. For example, with health insurance we are less wary of riding a bicycle, because we know that if we fall off, our health care costs will be mitigated or eliminated through our insurance coverage. We can more confidently employ appliances—such as clothes dryers—because we know that if they were to spark a fire, insurance would cover the costs. We can drive expensive automobiles at speeds in excess of 70 miles per hour, for we know that if we wreck our vehicle, we alone will not suffer a loss equal in value to the car.

This confidence that insurance grants takes on a specific term in economics: moral hazard. Broadly defined, moral hazard is "the tendency of people to expend less effort protecting those goods that are insured against theft or damage."[2] When people do not face risk of a personal catastrophic loss as a result of their actions, they are much more likely to ignore those risks in their everyday actions. Their tendency to ignore risks gives rise to moral hazard.

Before we proceed, we should make it clear that the concept of moral hazard has many possible definitions. For example, moral hazard occurs when the behavior of the insured party changes in a way that raises costs for the insurer, since the insured party no longer bears the full costs of that behavior. Moral hazard can be tied either to potential or actual behavior. However, in this chapter we use the broader definition given in the previous paragraph because it serves to emphasize the "optimal" amount of risk taken, relative to an insurance scheme. If the insurer is able to predict correctly the behavior of the entity being insured, then moral hazard (in its *broad definition*) is not a problem and we will refer to it as "good" moral hazard. However, when the insurer is either unable to predict the risk correctly, or for other reasons chooses to ignore it, then moral hazard becomes a problem—and we will refer to it simply as "moral hazard"; when this happens, individuals or entities are shielded from the consequences of their own actions and are likely to engage in *too much* risk-taking behavior.

As we stated before, people's tendency to ignore risk can have benefits for society. Without the moral hazard generated from automobile insurance, for example, many would be unwilling to take expensive cars on public roads. Insurance allows them to ignore this risk, for if they do get into an accident, they will not have to shoulder the costs alone. Consequently, individuals are much more willing to travel in their own vehicles. The personal and economic benefits of such effects are obvious, as easy transportation allows for the free movement of individuals and capital. Similarly, with health insurance, we are more willing to get into shape by riding a bicycle, because the costs associated with an accident on the bicycle are limited.

In other cases, however, moral hazard can play a detrimental role. Insurance structures that promote individuals to take risks that produce little or no benefit, for example, only hinder the productive capacity of our economy. In contemporary economic analysis, economists often focus on such negative cases of moral hazard, where risky actions are encouraged by distorted payoff structures. Depending on the specific context, moral hazard can take on a variety of roles within our society.

There can be, then, too little or too much moral hazard, and in order to understand its optimal amount we must again address the costs and benefits that it provides. Just like privacy, economic regulation, and even the number of cocktails in an evening on the town, there is a socially optimal amount of moral hazard. Leading up to the optimal amount of moral hazard, we find each additional increase in the level of the moral hazard to be beneficial, by making us more productive, allowing us to sleep easier at night, or lowering our blood pressure, by reducing the potential costs associated with the risks we face. However, once we pass that theoretical boundary, subsequent increases in moral hazard actually make us worse off, at least in the long run. We take unnecessary risks that, owing to the insurance structure that produces the moral hazard, appear attractive at the time but are in fact too costly. The extra benefits do not outweigh the extra costs. A theoretical analysis will illuminate such an issue.

HYPOTHETICAL CASE

Consider the previous example involving vehicular insurance. To make our example more specific, we will focus on a hypothetical individual, Joe, who owns a moderately expensive car, knows how to drive properly, and has no insurance. Like most Americans, Joe is also much more productive when he can travel long distances freely and quickly. Unfortunately, though his vehicle serves this purpose perfectly, there is a possibility that in any given trip, even if he is following all proper driving techniques and safety precautions, Joe could find himself in a vehicular accident in which he wrecks his car. Without any insurance, Joe would have to absorb the astronomical costs of the accident single-handedly. Facing the possibility of such a catastrophic loss, Joe instead determines that it is better to keep his vehicle garaged and carry out his daily business within walking distance of his home, severely limiting his productivity.

Now, Joe is approached by an insurance agent who offers to assume the costs of any collision, if Joe pays a sum substantially smaller than the costs of an accident upfront each year. Accepting this offer, Joe now no longer faces the chance of an astronomical loss from wrecking his vehicle. Consequently, he decides to drive his new vehicle, allowing him to travel freely and quickly over a large geographic area, and therefore making him significantly more productive. In this hypothetical example, this is what we would consider "good" moral hazard, and there is no financial conflict between Joe's behavior and his insurance company.

However, after a few weeks of operating within the comforts of automobile insurance, Joe realizes the significant benefits that he has received in the form of increased productivity. Seeking to increase his personal benefits, Joe decides to take additional risks that would not be normally contemplated by the average driver: driving much faster than is safe or the law allows, disobeying traffic regulations, and driving under the influence. Joe is making the contingency of a collision more likely because of the comfort his insurance policy grants him. If his insurance agent were aware of Joe's reckless behavior, she would withdraw Joe's insurance.

Later that year, Joe is on the town with friends, and he has somehow slipped beyond an "optimal" amount of alcoholic beverages. As the night winds to a close, Joe is faced with the dilemma of operating his vehicle while impaired by the alcohol, or facing the inconvenience of finding an alternate source of transportation home. Remembering his insurance coverage, Joe decides to drive under the influence. In the course of his travels home, however, he strikes another vehicle, injuring both himself and the other driver, and destroying both vehicles.

This situation represents a case of "moral hazard" in which the payoff structure has encouraged the taking of unnecessary, socially dangerous risks. The excessive risks that Joe took led to incredible costs, both monetary and personal. Furthermore, the risks that moral hazard promoted had dubious benefits; there was no increase in productivity or leisure, as there had been when Joe was encouraged to drive his vehicle properly and legally. While there were some risks involved in Joe's initial behavior, which insurance allowed Joe to ignore, the social and personal benefits derived were significant. When Joe changed his behavior, an incredible risk was undertaken for little to no long-term benefit.

This hypothetical example illustrates the paradox of moral hazard—to a point, it is beneficial and even necessary to a functioning society, but beyond that optimal point, it can generate enormous societal risks and costs. While the example of Joe is hypothetical, there are a number of large-scale instances of moral hazard that harm the U.S. economy, and more broadly, the society as a whole.

REAL CASES

Moral hazard had a large hand to play in the savings and loan crisis of the 1980s, and more recently the housing crisis of 2008. In the former, government insurance programs encouraged speculators to make extremely risky investments, causing hundreds of savings and loan institutions to collapse. In the latter, government backing of subprime mortgages distorted incentive structures to favor irresponsible lending actions, encouraging loans to individuals who, under normal circumstances, would never have been candidates for the mortgage packages they received.

Moral hazard, however, is not limited to Wall Street. As our hypothetical example shows, the scope of moral hazard is virtually boundless, and the implications of each case are profound. One such example of moral hazard took place in the lead-up to Hurricane Katrina, which hit the Gulf Coast in 2005. While moral hazard clearly is not behind the weather patterns that caused the national disaster, risky behavior encouraged by distorted incentive structures assured widespread damages, which might have otherwise been avoided or mitigated.

Hurricane Katrina was by far the costliest hurricane in the history of the United States. According to estimates, the storm caused approximately $81 billion in damages and displaced well over one million individuals, many for extended periods of time.[3] The costs of human lives were also significant, with over 1,800 individuals confirmed dead.[4] Finally, production, transactions, and all semblances of economic function were eliminated in the region for quite some time after the storm hit.

This last point requires a bit of additional elaboration, for when many people consider costs, they think only about what has been directly lost as a result of a disaster. To truly evaluate the full impact of an event, however, one must consider what might have been the case had that event not occurred. Certainly, the direct costs of $81 billion were significant, but to fully assess the costs of the crisis, lost productivity must also be taken into consideration. Unfortunately, it is practically impossible to assign a specific, definitive number to lost productivity as we are able to do to explicit costs.

These figures, however, may not convince many readers of the active role that policies played in the costs of Hurricane Katrina. Moral hazard obviously did not play a role in the physical development of the storm. To understand the role that moral hazard played, then, we must look past the immediate physical event, and assess how and why the costs of the hurricane were so large. In order to do this, an initial distinction is necessary. Our argument is based on the separation of the physical disaster and the costs of the event. Had the hurricane hit a desolate, uninhabited coast in Texas, for example, the human and economic costs of the hurricane would have been exponentially lower than when it hit the New Orleans area. While Mother Nature chooses the location and magnitude for natural disasters, human decisions, such as where to settle and build, largely determine the impact of those disasters on society.

Humans chose to live on the Gulf Coast and in areas notorious for their vulnerability to hurricanes; and in the case of Katrina's most costly victim, New Orleans, below sea level, in addition to all of the other risks of the area. While hurricanes were common by national standards, and the region apparently had learned to cope with regular, lower-scale hurricanes, the threat of a catastrophe was well known. According to a solicitation for private contractors to devise a disaster response plan for an event such as Katrina, the Federal Emergency Management Agency, or FEMA, was well aware of the risks of such an occurrence. In the "Scope of Work" section of a 2004 "Combined Catastrophic Plan for Southeast Louisiana and the New Madrid Seismic Zone," FEMA acknowledged that "the emergency management community has long feared the occurrence of a catastrophic disaster."[5] FEMA further detailed in the section that "Louisiana is highly susceptible to hurricanes because the topography is generally low-lying river delta and some of the most densely populated areas are actually below sea level."[6] Predicted effects of a catastrophe in the area included widespread flooding of urban areas and "severe economic repercussions for the state and region."[7] In this one section, FEMA acknowledged the inherent, long-known threat of a catastrophic hurricane in the region, and the residency patterns that further amplified the costs of any potential disaster. Instead of trying to enact policies that minimized the threat, however, FEMA and other federal and state government agencies instead searched for policies to mitigate the damages following such a disaster. These policies reinforced risk-taking and set up the region for disaster.

In order to make our analysis of the moral hazard leading up to Hurricane Katrina more comprehensible, we now focus on the most affected location on the Gulf Coast, New Orleans. Much of New Orleans is below sea level, making it extremely vulnerable to flooding. This vulnerability was known well before the impact of Katrina. As Mayor Ray Nagin said as he announced a mandatory evacuation, "[w]e are facing a storm that most of us have long feared."[8] Officials and the public understood the inherent dangers of living in New Orleans, in the direct path of some of our nation's worst hurricanes and below sea level, yet they still chose to inhabit the city by the hundreds of thousands. Understanding the risks, then, basic logic drives us to believe there must be some distortion in incentives that encouraged so many individuals to ignore the inherent perils of living in the area.

Herein we find the connection between the natural disaster and moral hazard. Given the known threat to residents of New Orleans, a city directly in the path of some of the nation's worst natural disasters, and mostly below sea level, hundreds of thousands of individuals seemed to think it was a good idea to root themselves in the area, essentially setting themselves up for loss. Within this framework, and simple background research, we find that our theories concerning moral hazard are correct, and distorted incentive structures were behind the catastrophic losses of the storm.

RISK-TAKING BEYOND REASON

Like most cases of moral hazard, at the root of the Katrina disaster is a system of insurance programs. Perhaps most prominent and most responsible for the distorted incentives in this system is that of flood insurance. Because New Orleans sits largely below sea level, the area is prone to flooding. Standard insurance policies normally don't cover for losses in floods for a number of reasons, including "the predictable nature of where floods will occur."[9] Flood coverage supplements available in the private sector are normally limited to properties in areas with low risks of flooding, or carry very low limits and very high deductibles.[10] Since flood risks are widely published by a number of government agencies, and individuals generally have free choice over the location of their residence, the private insurance industry rightly expects them to make sensible decisions regarding the risks of flooding. The limited availability of flood insurance in the private sector reinforces the standard incentive structure regarding the risks of floods, and it encourages individuals to avoid unnecessary risks of flooding by choosing residencies with low flood risks.

Realizing the lack of availability of flood insurance, however, the federal government thought it wise to implement the National Flood Insurance

Program, or NFIP, to provide flood insurance for structures in high-risk flood areas. Furthermore, the program provided (and continues to provide) flood insurance to buildings constructed before the institution of the program at subsidized rates.[11] Buildings constructed after the institution of the program were charged rates consistent with average losses and expenses since the institution of the program.[12] Through the rates it charged more recent buildings and the general structure of the program, the NFIP was actually financially self-supporting from 1986 to 2005, indicating that its fees covered the risks of the insured assets. Because the fees covered the risks, incentives seemed to be largely uninhibited, and the case for moral hazard appeared weak.

What the program and its proponents failed to consider, however, was the less prominent, yet significant risk of a catastrophic event such as Hurricane Katrina. The NFIP managed to get by for an extended period through luck, avoiding the ever-present threat of such a disaster. When Katrina hit, however, that ignored risk became a reality, and the NFIP became indebted to the U.S. Treasury for well over $20 billion.[13] Through these losses, it became clear that in the long run the NFIP was insolvent, and did not accurately reflect the risks faced by its insured properties in the rates that it charged. By diminishing the costs borne by individuals who faced the risks of flood damage, the NFIP reduced the disincentives for living in New Orleans and other risky locations, enhancing the chances of catastrophic losses from a natural disaster.

Beyond the specific case of Katrina, the NFIP has encouraged absurd behavior on a broader scale involving risk-ignorance. The incentives to ignore risk have led to a number of situations that, when viewed through the lens of common sense, seem absurd. For example, a home valued at approximately $114,000 had claims over a 10-year period totaling $806,591 in damages, and another property valued at under $50,000 had claims over an 18-year period totaling over $161,000.[14] It seems unlikely that such instances would persist in a model where costs are borne in the private market. However, under these systems of distorted incentives, such absurdity is a reality.

PRIVATE VERSUS PUBLIC INSURANCE

Given this situation, many might feel it appropriate simply to eliminate the NFIP, thus placing the risks of flood back on those individuals who choose to live in high-risk areas. Subsequently, individuals facing risks of catastrophic losses that the private industry is unwilling to insure will leave these high-risk areas for safer locations within the nation. In turn, this will mitigate the costs of any future hurricane or natural disaster like Katrina.

While such analysis makes sense to the rational observer, the situation is again complicated by the federal government. According to FEMA, the NFIP was instituted because prior to the program the federal government was incurring higher and higher costs of disaster relief. The federal government has a historical record of providing disaster relief and recovery funding to help rebuild an area after it has been struck by a natural disaster. If the NFIP were repealed, moral hazard would likely remain in place, as residents could feel confident that the federal government would not permit them to shoulder all the costs of a natural disaster alone. This applies for damages beyond flooding, and it thus furthers the incentives for risky behavior.

It appears that the solution, then, is not only to repeal the NFIP and other government-subsidized insurance programs related to natural disasters, but also to diminish severely the federal government's role in disaster relief. Once the public is made aware that federal relief is diminished, the hefty disincentives for living in the paths of substantial natural disasters will be placed back on the individuals, and many will change their behavior so as to encounter less risk. Had this been the case prior to Hurricane Katrina, the human and economic costs of the disaster might have been much less, as fewer individuals would have lived in the at-risk areas, and subsequently less property and productive assets would have been in line to be damaged. While reducing moral hazard will never decrease the physical scope of a storm or other natural disaster, it will reduce the potential costs, both human and economic, as a result of that disaster.

With specific focus on the case of New Orleans and Hurricane Katrina, some might argue that our reasoning with regard to risk is flawed, and that the insurance programs are beneficial because the ability to ignore the risks of disasters helps individuals be more productive. Some might argue that, similar to our initial example of general automobile insurance, flood insurance and disaster relief allow individuals to carry out productive or otherwise beneficial activities without fear of shouldering catastrophic losses. In the short run, this may be correct, as the long-standing tradition of moral hazard has created a structure where it is economically beneficial for individuals to operate within New Orleans and other risky areas. However, if moral hazard is reduced, in the long run the productive character of the high-risk areas on the Gulf Coast will be transferred to less-risky areas.

While historically there may have been significant benefits to having such a metropolis near the ocean, changes in transportation technology have diminished those benefits substantially. We should create incentives to transfer physical resources and human capital that currently reside in New Orleans to safer locations; this can be done by reinstating the risks of loss back onto the individual decision maker. This would have little impact on the productivity of those resources or individuals in the long run. To put it simply, how much less productive would a city like New Orleans be if it were located further north on the banks of the Mississippi River? In fact, it would likely be more productive in the long run, avoiding the constant disruption of severe storms and the ever-standing threat of another catastrophe like Katrina.

POLICY IMPLICATIONS

Understandably, some might be taken aback by our proposals. To be clear, we do not advocate abandoning humanitarian missions to save the lives of those individuals threatened by natural disasters, regardless of the irrational decision making that may have led them to their predicament. Instead, we advocate a diminished role in relief efforts within the same location, in order to promote relocation to less risky locations. Another option, perhaps more attractive to politicians seeking to maintain votes in the region, might be actually to redirect disaster relief funds toward relocation. Relief costs, then, would still fall on the federal government, but the future private losses of property, life, and production would be mitigated. It simply makes too much sense, when one realizes that costly storms will hit an area over and over again, to get out of the way rather than face the repeated economic and human costs associated with staying.

In other cases, the negative effects of moral hazard have yet to come to fruition. Take, for example, the economic crisis of 2008, and the role of the federal government in bailing out financial firms in the face of imminent financial collapse. Many of these failed firms engaged in risky behavior, maximizing profits in the short term and ignoring the potential future losses that might result. When those losses came to light, however, the federal government stepped in for a number of cases to prevent bankruptcy and save corporations. Such was the case with American International Group, Citigroup, Bank of America, and a number of other failing financial corporations in 2008 and 2009.

Aside from the public outcry over taxpayer funds' being used to save private corporations, an underlying danger exists in the federal government's bailouts of distressed private financial firms: moral hazard. The federal government set a dangerous precedent in its actions, establishing an insurance system where the full costs are not taken into account. Such an insurance scheme will undoubtedly encourage unnecessarily risky behavior on the part of private firms who believe that they are candidates for federal bailouts, should they fail. Given the public outcry and economic downturn associated with the current economy, the effects of moral hazard have, however, been mitigated in the short run. Following this precedent and the unwavering capitalist incentives for profits, though, financial firms will again find another risky route for quick profits and some will base their decisions, at least in part, on the perceived assurance of government support should their actions lead to disaster.

THE LESSON TO BE LEARNED

A third and final full example of moral hazard in our modern economy is presented in the government's role in the downfall of Detroit's "Big Three." Upon the initial collapse of the automakers, the federal government extended an offer of significant loans to the companies, presenting them with temporary reprieve from their financial woes. Within the structure of this initial bailout, however, the federal government included harsh requirements of those corporations that accepted federal funds. Although some may claim that these stipulations mitigated the effects of moral hazard, the federal government nevertheless set a significant precedent in its initial actions, similar to that which was set in the federal government's dealings with the financial sector. Companies realized that if they employed enough voters, they could turn to the federal government in times of distress for a short-term fix. Such would explain the flood of applications for federal funds from non-financial corporations in distress immediately following the Bush administration's bailout of Chrysler and General Motors.

However, the Obama administration reversed some of these precedents by showing its willingness to allow Chrysler and GM to slip into bankruptcy. Such determination to slow federal involvement in private activities may have mitigated some moral hazard that the government has created in the economic downturn. However, with respect to the automakers, the actions of the Obama administration may have initiated another instance of moral hazard, with regard to labor unions. Prior to bankruptcy and into the filing proceedings, the Obama administration heavily favored the United Auto Workers (UAW) Union. As Chapter 6 regarding unions illustrates, the UAW played a heavy hand in the downfall of the auto giants, and their inability to grant adequate concessions further hindered attempts to avoid bankruptcy. The Obama administration, however, stood strong with labor unions, and it appears to endeavor to prevent the UAW from losing as much as others involved in the auto failures. This grants a sort of insurance to other unions in labor negotiations, encouraging them to remain steadfast in their demands, risking the financial integrity of the companies with whom they work for more attractive wages and benefits. This is because federal precedents set by the Obama administration show that should the companies fail, unions can expect at least moderate support from officials. Such moral hazard will encourage riskier negotiations, with union officials more willing to take their companies to the brink of disaster in order to meet their goals of enhanced compensation.

Of each of these three examples—Hurricane Katrina, the bailouts of financial corporations, and the varied governmental involvement in the failures of the Detroit automakers—the risks encouraged by the cases of moral hazard held little or no productive or positive value. While risky behavior in each sector resulting from moral hazard may provide short-term growth, such growth can be heavily outweighed by the long-term detriments eventually borne by society. More confident unions in negotiations may lead to better compensation for smaller groups of individuals in the short run, but in the long run such tenacity undermines the security of both the company involved and the economy as a whole. While bailouts may delay bankruptcies, incorporating them into business decisions sets corporations up for catastrophic disaster. And while some people may experience individual productivity by living in New Orleans, the stability of the country as a whole would be better off if the population and productive resources of the area were relocated to a place that faces a smaller risk of devastation.

These examples show the detriments of moral hazard. They indicate a transgression beyond the optimal level of risk-taking, to a point where individuals and corporations are induced to place themselves and others in situations where the costs of the risks they face severely outweigh the benefits they receive. Understanding the detriments of these cases of bad moral hazard, then, what can we do?

CONCLUSIONS

In the case of Katrina, as we outlined earlier, the federal government must severely reduce its involvement in disaster relief in high-risk areas. Though it could be a disastrous move politically, there are long-term benefits to such an approach. With regard to the auto companies, the federal government should refrain from bailing out private corporations and should make it clear to the business world that the actions taken in 2008 by the Bush administration will not be repeated in future crises. Further, the government should allow bankruptcy proceedings to move forward without significant interference, abstaining from altering the normal, legal structure of costs and benefits among those involved with the corporation. An unbiased, restrained approach to bankruptcy adjudication will increase the costs of individual actions on those who take those actions, reinstating normal incentive structures and normalizing decision making in the business community.

Some argue that the answer is more complicated when it comes to bailouts of financial corporations by the federal government. While the economy surely would have suffered as a result of the collapse of a major financial institution, the long-term detriments of a federal bailout are very significant. While the use of federal funds in 2008 and 2009 may have postponed major disaster, such action set the stage for extraordinary moral hazard in the future. Those who argue that the bailouts were necessary need ask themselves, Which is the better alternative, temporarily avoiding a major financial meltdown now, or setting the stage for occasions of irresponsible behavior of equal or ever greater magnitude in the future? Though the perils of moral hazard in this case have yet to be exposed, they are nevertheless present.

Interestingly, one pattern of behavior of the federal government in its handling of the financial companies that was widely criticized may have, in fact, diminished some of the negative effects of its actions: the inconsistency with which the government applied federal bailouts. Such inconsistency, though detrimental to the stock market, has kept some corporations on their toes regarding failure. This is because inconsistency makes it impossible for executives to be certain that they are protected from bankruptcy by the federal government.

In analyzing the previous three real-world examples another interesting observation comes to light: In each case, moral hazard encouraging unnecessarily risky behavior by individuals and private corporations was initially instigated by the actions of the federal government. While moral hazard operates at a variety of levels within society, it appears that many instances that pose systemic risks to the economy stem from the federal government. Given this observation, it would seem only prudent to seek out measures to reduce the involvement of the federal government in private matters. Along with a laundry list of other grievances the public rightly has with most federal programs, the excessive moral hazard that it tends to produce often has detrimental effects on our economy.

Moral hazard is not always a bad thing. In order to expand the economy continually, individuals must take risks that offer potential for a positive result. In this sense, insurance coverage and other structures that encourage individuals to look past certain risks are positive, in that they stimulate and sustain production and growth. At some point, however, the optimal amount of moral hazard is reached and, unfortunately in a number of cases, exceeded. In these instances, individuals and corporations are often driven to take unnecessary risks, which do little or nothing for productivity and greatly exacerbate the chances of loss at both personal and systemic levels. Such was the case of moral hazard on the Gulf Coast in the period leading up to Hurricane Katrina, and such is the situation slowly materializing as a result of federal actions in the economic downturn of 2008. To prevent further losses, and to sustain the growth that has propelled our nation to its status as a world superpower, we must seek to identify the optimal level of moral hazard within our society, and then ensure that we do not surpass that level. Failure to moderate moral hazard to its productive bounds will result, as history has proven, in disaster.

NOTES

1. Vehicular estimates derived from 2007 injury data from The National Highway Traffic Safety Administration, "2007 Traffic Safety Annual Assessment—Highlights," NHTSA, August 2008, 1, http://www-nrd.nhtsa.dot.gov/Pubs/811017.PDF.

2. Robert H. Frank and Ben S. Bernanke, *Principles of Microeconomics* (Boston: McGraw-Hill Irwin, 2007), 390.

3. Richard D. Knabb, Jamie R. Rhome, and Daniel P. Brown, "Tropical Cyclone Report: Hurricane Katrina," The National Hurricane Center, NOAA, Updated 10 August 2006, 12–13, http://www.nhc.noaa.gov/ms-word/TCR-AL122005_Katrina.doc.

4. Ibid., 11.

5. "Combined Catastrophic Plan for Southeast Louisiana and the New Madrid Seismic Zone: Scope of Work," Federal Emergency Management Administration, FY 2004, 4, http://waxman.house.gov/uploadedfiles/FEMA_Scope_Of_Work.pdf.

6. Ibid., 5.

7. Ibid., 6.

8. Associated Press, "Katrina Heads for New Orleans," *Fox News Network, LLC*, August 29, 2005, http://www.foxnews.com/story/0,2933,167270,00.html.

9. Chartered Property Casualty Underwriters Society, Connecticut Chapter, "Flood Insurance and Hurricane Katrina," *CPCU eJournal*, September (2006): 2.

10. Ibid., 2.

11. Federal Insurance and Mitigation Administration, "National Flood Insurance Program: Program Description," Federal Emergency Management Administration, August 1, 2002, 2–3.

12. Chartered Property Casualty Underwriters Society, "Flood Insurance and Hurricane Katrina," 9.

13. Ibid., 10.

14. Ibid., 9–10.

Chapter 12

THE BURDEN OF THE KEYNESIAN CROSS

Many college-educated individuals have taken at least one course in economics. Traditionally, the students begin with what is known as a macroeconomic principles course, where students learn basic macroeconomics with the help of what is known as the "Keynesian Cross." Students are warned that the principles course is only an introduction to the subject and that many complications—or even outright contrary views—will follow in advanced courses, but experience has taught the instructors that the course is a good approach to get many students hooked on the subject. The economics major is initially attractive, possibly because the subject is new to the students and relatively easy to grasp; however, the vast majority of students do not continue with economics as a major (possibly because of the math required for advanced courses) and most of them will remember only the Keynesian Cross as a tool for understanding macroeconomic issues.

We shall then begin with the Keynesian Cross, which is depicted in Figure 12.1. While we are trying to limit the amount of formal economics in the text, this simple graph is crucial to understanding where many politicians are coming from.

The basic Keynesian approach[1] begins with a simple identity (a concept that is true by definition). This identity states that "final" expenditures in the economy—made up of Consumption (C), Investment (I), and Government Expenditures (G)—have to equal the Income (or National Product) that is generated within the economy. The idea behind this identity is that when people, firms, or governments buy output, that output generates income to someone; the reason that "final" expenditures need to be used is to avoid double-counting. (Bread is a final good, which already includes the value of wheat. Counting both bread and wheat is an example of

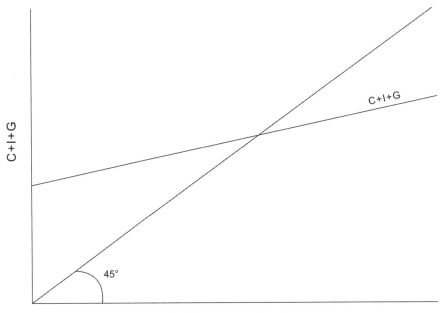

Figure 12.1
Keynesian Cross.
Source: Authors' illustration

double-counting). Because the income that people receive is based on the production of some good or service, the income (when properly measured) will be equal to the output that is produced in an economy over a period of time, usually one year. This identity between expenditures and income (or output) gives rise to the 45° line.

Keynesian economics now moves on to make a theoretical statement, which is captured by the slanted line in Figure 12.1. If government and investment expenditures are "given" (meaning that they are not yet explained), then the great English economist John Maynard Keynes argued that the expenditures of people on consumption (in the aggregate) were highly predictable and based on the disposable income that people received. Keynes also came up with the brilliant concept of a marginal propensity to consume, which states that as aggregate income rises, aggregate consumption expenditure will rise by a constant positive value that would be less than 1. Taking government expenditures and investments initially as given, and now adding the behavior of consumers to it, the result is the slanted line appearing in the graph. The intersection of the slanted line with the 45° line gives what is known as the equilibrium level of income and output in the economy. The Keynesian Cross is then the basic tool that can be used to predict the level of economic activity in a country.

From a macroeconomic point of view, the approach that has been outlined is indeed extremely powerful. If one were to know the marginal propensity to consume plus the behavior of firms and governments, then total output in the economy can be not only predicted but also manipulated. (To make the model fully operational, one needs to add the foreign sector plus some statistical analysis, but that will not be part of this discussion.) The reader should note that the Keynesian Cross suggests that the economy is driven by three factors: investment behavior, government expenditures, and government taxation (which affects investment and disposable income). The consumers normally behave in a passive fashion, simply responding (via the marginal propensity to consume) to the income that they earn.

The model can be made quite complicated, however. For example, consumers may alter their consumption *levels* (without changing their marginal propensity to consume) for some extraneous reasons, such as changes in their wealth. Investment expenditures (which have very little to do with financial investments but rather with the accumulation of physical capital and inventories) can also change due to interest rate movements and the business climate. Government may choose to provide more or fewer services (depending on the needs of the population or the political decisions of the legislators) by increasing or decreasing taxes and borrowing to achieve its goals. But the government also has the ability to create money entirely out of thin air, either directly or indirectly via the financial sector.

The Keynesian Cross, as described so far, leads to the conclusion that if anything goes wrong in the economy—in terms of lack of enough production to achieve the full employment of the population—the government can come in and fix it. If the business firms lack confidence in the future and do not invest enough, the government can always spend money that would substitute for the money the business firms would have otherwise spent. The same holds true for those cases where the consumers lose confidence in the economy and reduce their consumption levels. It should be noted, however, that in Keynesian economics the consumers do not generally drive the economy, despite the fact that consumer expenditures account for the greatest percentage of total expenditures. Consumers *react* to changes in wealth, to changes in interest rates, and to changes in credit conditions; it would take extraordinary circumstances (e.g., wars, crash in asset values) for consumers to alter their predicted behavior. Therefore, the economy is driven by investment and government expenditures.

Keynesian economics had its heyday shortly after the Second World War. Keynes had argued that the Great Depression took place because governments failed to replace the expenditures of consumers and those of firms when they lost their confidence in the economy—as a result of the stock market crash of 1929. His point of view gained credibility because it did appear that the government expenditures that resulted from the Second World War brought the United States and other industrial countries out of the slump associated with the Great Depression. His approach suggested that in times of depression, fiscal deficits and money creation would get countries out of trouble—a view that is again popular under the current economic crisis.

EARLY CHALLENGES TO THE KEYNESIAN THEORY

The early Keynesian theory was expanded to include the determination of nominal interest rates via what is called the IS-LM diagram, which will not be discussed here. However, one important assumption of this extension warrants mentioning, namely that the price level would not be rising. This assumption fit well with the experience of the Great Depression, when prices did not rise but experienced a mild drop. We mention this assumption at this point because it will give rise to a series of complications later in our discussion.

There were several main challenges to the early Keynesian approach. In the 1950s, Milton Friedman[2] and Franco Modigliani[3] argued that the consumption behavior of people was much more complicated than had been presented by Keynes. In their view, people respond not to current income but to long-run income streams that people expect to have over their lifetimes. However, this complication could be incorporated within the Keynesian approach without difficulty. If anything, this modification of Keynesian theory gave greater credibility to the idea that the expectations of people (which would take into account their future income and hence their wealth) could have a serious impact in the economy.

The second theoretical criticism came from the work of Milton Friedman and Anna Schwartz in the 1960s,[4] who argued that the Great Depression was precipitated by the government (and specifically the Federal Reserve Bank, which controls the money supply) reducing by almost one-third the money supply during the depression period. This dramatic fall was felt much more strongly in output than in the price level. While this was not a devastating blow to Keynesian economics, it demonstrated conclusively that the government could act in a perverse fashion and, in fact, contribute to the worsening of economic conditions. On a more general front, these two economists pointed out the importance of the money supply in maintaining a healthy economy. The consensus was reached that an optimal amount of money creation was needed for economic well-being: neither too much nor too little. It was concluded that an actual decrease in the money supply could be devastating for the proper working of an economy. Please note, though, that Keynes was no fan of inflation, attributing to Lenin himself (correctly, according to recent research) that the best way to destroy the capitalist system was to "debauch the currency."[5]

Others, at the theoretical level, also pointed out that the Great Depression was the result of the Smoot-Hawley Tariff Act of 1930,[6] which dramatically increased the ad valorem tax on imports and reduced trade. The taxes jumped from 25 percent in the 1920s to 50 percent in the 1930s. The importance of this addition to our understanding of the Great Depression is twofold: countries cannot assume that other countries will not retaliate against policies that diminish imports and trade; and microeconomic ideas are relevant to the understanding of depressions because if a country engages in policies that lead to less specialization and trade, then that country will face negative consequences. It has been argued that the restrictions on trade affected different countries differently; for example, the United Kingdom was not as severely affected by trade restrictions as the United States, because the United Kingdom had a huge empire at the time that allowed it to make decisions based on comparative advantage and engage in substantial trade.

These theoretical challenges to Keynesian economics did not kill off the basic theory, but the experiences of many countries—especially the less-developed countries—did manage to weaken it significantly. It seemed to the political leaders of poor countries that if Keynesian economics was correct, then expansion of the government sector was the one and only action necessary to achieve prosperity; and given the backwardness of their fiscal system, they chose money creation to stimulate their economies. Many of these countries also neglected the negative role of trade restrictions in achieving efficiency. The leaders of many countries decided to expand the government sector while simultaneously restricting trade, trying to develop so-called infant industries into full-fledged competitors in the world markets.

Most less-developed countries failed in generating sustainable economic growth. The reason was twofold: These countries lacked the technological know-how to expand their industrial bases, and most countries
were too small (in market size) to sustain growth without international
trade. One could argue, of course, that there were exceptions—but these
are not real exceptions. The European countries and Japan, which had
been devastated by the war, did have the technological know-how to bring
back their industrial bases. Some small and poor countries, like Korea and
Taiwan, were willing to absorb technological know-how from foreign
countries and engage in trade expansion, rather than trade contraction.
And even Brazil, which experienced some level of growth, had a very large
internal market that could substitute for international trade. All of these
experiences led to other types of challenges to Keynesian economics,
which we will now discuss.

LATER CHALLENGES TO THE KEYNESIAN THEORY

The experience of less-developed countries, together with the experience
of countries dominated by the communist ideology, paved the way for a
drastic understanding of the process of growth. If one goes back to Adam
Smith and the early classical economists, one learns that the size of the
market, the level of specialization and trade, the use of prices as a mechanism to allocate resources, and the accumulation of physical capital are all
factors that contribute to economic growth. (Many of the early economists
misunderstood the role of population and human capital in promoting
growth.) In the 1950s, however, there was a drastic addition to these factors, when Robert Solow[7] and Trevor Swan[8] developed formal models of
economic growth, and it was found that technological advancement was
in fact the most important factor in achieving economic growth.

The experience of communist regimes demonstrated how the above factors played a role in economic growth. Although Russia had a long history
of technological achievements, and it engaged in very rapid capital accumulation, its growth prospects were compromised because it did not use
the price mechanism to allocate resources and hence it could not achieve
efficiency in production. China had a huge internal market but also did
not use prices to allocate resources, and it did not allow for profits that
would create the incentive to accumulate capital. Let us emphasize for
future reference that the problem in these countries was not lack of
demand for goods or failing companies—the problem was a lack of supply
of goods because of the inherent economic inefficiency of production and

the huge subsidies (which governments never called "bailouts") to firms that were in fact unproductive.

The experience of other less-developed countries was just as daunting. Even when they opened up to trade because of the lack of sufficiently large internal markets, they were still reluctant to accept foreign investments (and the technologies associated with these) and continued to preserve institutional structures that would not be conducive to economic growth. Let us pay attention to some of these.

If prices are going to serve as an allocation mechanism in the economy, that presumes that prices reflect production costs and demand conditions; that means that a competitive mechanism must be allowed to operate in the economy. While it is theoretically possible for government-owned firms to operate as profit-making enterprises, these must make up a small percentage of the whole economy, for otherwise they have an overwhelming control over markets and then distort the allocation of resources. Competitive markets—which serve to generate meaningful prices—then are most likely to flourish when private property is allowed to thrive. This means that the ownership of resources should be in private hands, to stimulate competition and insure the proper allocation of resources.

The above does not mean that government regulations are out of place within a market economy; in fact, government regulations can improve resource efficiency. This can be done, for example, when monopolies are either regulated or banned, when collusion among firms is prohibited, when firms are forced to absorb the externalities that they impose on others (e.g., pollution), and possibly most important when local and national firms are forced to accept competition from international firms. Regrettably, competitive markets are never perfect because they normally require a very large number of firms to participate in those markets, and governments can at most open up countries to international trade to maximize the number of competitors in individual markets. This is, of course, where politics comes to play a large role in the workings of an economy. Even countries that accept the idea of international competition will have institutional arrangements that allow for trade restrictions. Sometimes, restrictions are not even necessary to reduce trade, because subsidies to domestic firms can also be used to choose winners and losers in the marketplace.

The most recent developments in growth theory have been in a field called endogenous growth theory, whose main developers are Paul M. Romer,[9] Robert E. Lucas[10] and Robert J. Barro.[11] Technology appears to be the driving force behind economic growth (when other conditions are met), therefore the next question is how that technology is acquired.

For society to acquire technology, firms must invest in the development of technology and countries must invest in the development of the human capital that will give rise to the creation of that technology and its possible implementation. Because technologies are relatively easy to copy once they are known, governments need to protect their use (to create the profits that will provide the incentive for their developments) and may even need to subsidize private and public enterprises to achieve an optimal amount of investment in technology.

From our perspective, however, the importance of growth theory is that it changes the framework within which macroeconomics is understood—and that is the real challenge that Keynesian economics confronts. Keynesian economics is not based on the microeconomic foundations of economic efficiency; in fact, Keynesian economics pays very little attention to productivity and efficiency gains in the allocation of resources. That is the subject matter of growth theory, and it is for this reason that the authors of this work view Keynesian economics as a burden to understanding what needs to be done to achieve sustainable growth.

People seem to have faith in Keynesian economic theory because it appears to explain how we got out of the Great Depression—namely, by huge expenditures on the war effort that led the country to prosperity. It is then imperative to understand why wars per se are not productive, even if they lead a country to full employment.

WARS AND INEFFICIENCIES

The idea that wars can lead to prosperity is odd indeed. Historically, wars are associated with fiscal catastrophes and the demise of empires.[12] Governments borrow far beyond their means of repayment and countries literally go bankrupt. (This does not mean that wars are not sometimes necessary. If a country is attacked and it faces the possibility of future plunder by an adversary—as Germany, Japan, and Russia plundered the countries that they invaded during World War II—then war becomes necessary as a means of self-defense.)

Wars, however, can lead to full employment and even *measured* output growth, because governments can mobilize their populations for total war. Let us assume that we begin our analysis at a point at which war has not yet taken place—a situation where the country is simply getting ready for a potential war, which will take place far away from the home country. Assume, too, that one-third of the labor force produces guns, bombs, ammunition, ships, and airplanes to deliver the strikes of war.

If that were the case, that means that two-thirds of the labor force must be producing the goods and services that they will consume (and that firms will use for plant and equipment) *plus* the goods and services that the other one-third of the population needs for its own sustenance. In other words, if a country plans to feed the workers producing war-related goods, it has to tax the workers producing other types of goods. If that level of productivity were achievable, then it would also be achievable by the workers in the war-related industries when they transfer to non-war-related industries—meaning that all workers could be much wealthier if there were no war! Wars redistribute the allocation of workers among industries; they do not generate additional output out of nothing. Even when wars generate new technologies, these are incorporated into the civilian economy many years after the wars end.

Because war is destructive of human and physical capital, believing that war is somehow desirable is the equivalent of believing that hurricanes, earthquakes, and tsunamis are desirable. Hurricane Katrina, for example, not only killed people, but it also destroyed houses, infrastructure, buildings, factories, and so on. Can we say that Katrina was desirable because it gave rise to the employment of thousands, who would then restore the houses, infrastructure, buildings, and factories? That does not make any sense, in the same way that wars do not make sense from an economic point of view. Furthermore, the items that are necessary for war—such as fighter planes, bombs, guns, and ammunition, are items that cannot be consumed for pleasure and hence they cannot benefit the population producing those goods (unless the war is necessary to prevent plunder).

What, then, are wars good for? The answer, which has already been given, is that wars can lead to full employment of the labor force. The question, then, is this: Can full employment be achieved in any other way?

The Keynesian approach gives one possible answer: Full employment can be achieved if the government spends enough money. Of course, the money must not come from other people, for that means that the government is taxing Peter to pay Paul and hence there is no "stimulus" of the economy. However, money may come out of thin air, created by the printing presses and the financial sector—more on this approach below. (It is curious to point out that the extraordinary expansion of government debt and the rapid growth of the money supply over the last two years has not led to an expansion of employment and to only a mild expansion in output—but the financial sector is surely thriving. It is as if all the money created is used for the acquisition and accumulation of financial assets, regardless of whether these assets reflect improvements in production.

This suggests that Keynesian policy, as currently implemented, is simply leading to another bubble in the financial sector—which is ultimately likely to collapse.)

Classical economics says that full employment can be achieved if labor markets are allowed to clear—in other words, if supply and demand allow the market to reach a wage rate that will provide jobs to all those who want to find jobs at the market-clearing wage.

Communist regimes argue that full employment can always be achieved because government firms will be provided with sufficient subsidies to hire all the workers who wish to work. It is then granted that because workers will have too much money, rationing of goods will be necessary to allocate those that are being produced. People have a lot of paper money in the few remaining communist countries (North Korea being a good example) but there are few goods to buy because the system is extremely inefficient.

Each solution has a benefit and a cost. The communist-style solution fails to make use of market prices, and resources are not going to be allocated efficiently. The classical approach to full employment implies that in fact there will be many markets where some people will make a lot of money and others will make very little (because of labor scarcities in some markets), leading to income inequalities and possible political conflict within countries. The Keynesian solution (which one could hardly ascribe to Keynes himself!) seems to provide the best of two worlds, for it allows for the existence of markets (and efficiency) while providing everyone with jobs. The problem with this solution is that it fails to take into account potential inflation, when the money supply is increased by leaps and bounds in order to reach full employment. When inflation does not materialize, it may be attributed to the fact that excess money is being used for the creation of another financial bubble, as noted above.

There are several other catches to the Keynesian approach. One is obvious: Inflation does not prevent inequalities in the marketplace. Those whose services are most in demand will demand the highest wages, and will likely get them; those whose services are most likely to be provided by others will get the least reward. The second one is less obvious: Inflation creates its own social and political conflict within the nation. Inflation is a heavy tax on those living with fixed incomes, such as the elderly, and in a democratic society they will exercise their political power, which is generally formidable since they have the time to participate in politics. Furthermore, many people will try to engage in activities that beat the inflationary spiral, thereby separating themselves from more productive activities. Also, once the government gets its hand on money creation, it is bound to favor its supporters and penalize its opponents. The potential for crony capitalism is raised.

There is one additional complication to the Keynesian approach: the possibility of stagflation. When workers learn that the government will create money out of thin air in huge quantities, then they will jack up wages in advance to protect themselves. That will occur in all industries. If that is the case, then full employment is not likely to be achieved, for full employment depends on wages clearing the market, and inflationary expectations will prevent the markets from clearing. Hence the unemployment persists and the inflation proceeds unabated. This situation was experienced during the presidency of Jimmy Carter in the United States, and it could be repeated in the near future.

The authors of this work adopt the classical approach to achieving full employment, with two caveats. The first is that we accept the idea that some level of taxation and income transfer is necessary to maintain the well-being of those most in need for no fault of their own; taxation, however, must be uniform across all sectors of the population, for we cannot simultaneously develop a situation where large sectors of the population do not pay taxes and are maintained by those who are the most productive. Taxation has to cover everyone who is able to work. The second caveat is that the government must create sufficient amounts of money to maintain wage and price stability; the experience of the Great Depression, when the government decreased the money supply significantly and then faulted the private sector for failing to pay enough to the working population, cannot be repeated. Nominal wage decreases of significant amounts are not in anyone's interest.

THE ONE LAST KEYNESIAN DEFENSE OF MACROECONOMIC POLICY

Some Keynesians might object that we have misrepresented their position with regard to fiscal and monetary policy. These Keynesians are likely to state that they are fully aware of the dangers of increasing the money supply to any level that leads to severe inflation (e.g., above 5 percent). From their point of view, fiscal policy can be conducted without drastic changes in the money supply by simply borrowing funds to use for government expenditures.

If that is what Keynesians want to do under the current climate of deep recession, we have objections—but our objections are of a lesser degree than those that have been previously stated. However, this so-called Keynesian policy is not the one followed by the Obama administration, which has proposed government budgets in the trillions of dollars and is simultaneously using the Federal Reserve Bank to purchase government bonds. We want to make it clear that the current administration is monetizing the debt, increasing what is known as high-power money by unprecedented levels. Therefore, the analysis that follows has more of a theoretical import than a practical application. The reason we wish to cover it in this work is to challenge the contention that the Obama administration is "only borrowing funds," when in fact everyone knows that it is monetizing the debt—in essence, creating money out of thin air via the Federal Reserve Bank.

A long time ago a famous classical economist developed an argument that has been resurrected by Robert Barro[13] and it is now known as Ricardian equivalence, in honor of David Ricardo—the originator of the argument. Ricardian equivalence states that there is not much of a difference between borrowing funds and taxing people. Its importance is that if there is such equivalence, then the Keynesian argument for using debt to pay for government expenditures turns out to be similar to taxing Peter to pay Paul— or in other words, its fiscal impact would be either zero or negligible.

The argument for Ricardian equivalence is somewhat complicated and the evidence for its existence is ambiguous. Since we are trying to reach a wide audience with this work, we will try to explain it in a simple way. We first assume that the money supply is constant at all times. The government wants to increase expenditures and it issues bonds, say, for $500 million; the funds are then collected from willing consumers. The government spends the funds and supposedly "stimulates" the economy because consumers (to make the explanation as simple as possible) do not reduce their consumption—in fact they feel wealthier because they are now holding government bonds that show up in their balance sheets as assets. Surprisingly, Ricardian equivalence *denies* this apparently tight and credible argument.

The simplest denial is possible if the government plans on retiring the bonds one year later. If that were true (and the money supply is not changing, by assumption) then the government will have to collect in taxes not just the $500 million to repay the principal on the bonds, but an additional amount (e.g., 5 percent of $500 million). That means that $500 million spent this year has to be fully recovered next year in taxes (in present value terms the two sums of money turn out to be identical); therefore, any "stimulus" to the economy in expenditures taking place today is matched by the "lethargic impact" of taxes one year later. We are back to taxing Peter to pay Paul, even though the argument now extends across time periods.

For Ricardian equivalence to be valid, taxpayers must be aware of the scam that the government is engaging in; and if they are, they must take some action to avoid its consequences. This means that taxpayers must increase their savings in the present day to pay for future taxes, or at worst reduce their consumption next year to pay for the additional taxes (and interest) that must be paid to bondholders one year hence. The argument is mathematically valid whether we are considering paying out the bonds 1 year later, 10 years later, or even never. Modern-day Keynesians argue that taxpayers are not too sophisticated and that they can be fooled by the government; therefore, governments can "stimulate" the economy by borrowing and then spending the funds that have been borrowed.

The literature on Ricardian equivalence is vast and the empirical evidence is inconclusive. The approach that we take in this work is that governments that borrow can stimulate the economy somewhat, but not as much as Keynesians predicted. In an ideal world of full information, Ricardian equivalence should hold, but the world not only has limited and ambiguous information but it has misinformation written all over it (see Chapter 2).

ONE LASTING PROBLEM WITH KEYNESIAN ECONOMICS

Keynes wrote his macroeconomic theory during a period of time when there was no inflation. Under those circumstances, nominal interest rates were one and the same with real interest rates. As it was mentioned before, the IS-LM diagram had nothing to say about inflation but could help determine the prevailing interest rates.

Economists, of course, argue that real interest rates (adjusted for inflation) determine economic behavior. These rates can be understood as reflecting two major considerations: the productivity of capital and the value of time to consumers. Hence the relevant interest rates, to those of us who disagree with the Keynesian approach, must be real variables rather than nominal variables. In the Keynesian approach, the injection of money into the system will lower interest rates; to many of us, the injection of money into the system will increase nominal interest rates and leave real interest rates unchanged. The consensus compromise among economists seems to be that Keynesian economics works better in the short run and the classical approach works better in the long run—when people come to realize the impact of money creation on prices.

Regrettably, students attending a principles class often fail to understand the distinction between real and nominal interest rates—and this serious problem pervades the discussion of economic policy in the population at large. Most people still believe that the Federal Reserve System can control "interest rates"—when in fact all that it can control are the nominal rates. Traditionally, the Federal Reserve Bank has limited itself to controlling short-term rates, although under current conditions our Central Bank is even trying to control long-term rates. This confounds even further the economic policy discussion, for the government is consciously trying to distort the most important prices in the economy (the interest rates).

WHICH MACROECONOMICS SHOULD WE BELIEVE IN?

Traditional Keynesian economics has been greatly changed and modified in the years since its creation. For some of us, Keynesian economics is dead because it failed to take into account the supply side of economic analysis. This does not mean that Keynes did not make substantive contributions to the profession, but that those contributions are now so outdated that they should be buried permanently as tools of economic analysis. Yet so-called Keynesian economics lives on, and this requires an explanation.

The most obvious explanation is that Keynesian economics provides an aura of respectability to those who want to use governmental policy to alter economic outcomes. In a sense, Keynesian economics provides politicians with the type of respectability that the scientific materialism of Marx provided communist parties. The evidence against scientific materialism is so overwhelming that no one dares to use it again to argue in favor or against economic policy. The reason is that the USSR failed and communists in China accepted private property and markets; they have turned out to be capitalists in disguise. Keynesian economics will die out only when Keynesian policies lead to total disaster in the capitalist world. Surprisingly, the failure of Keynesian policies can be observed in modern-day Japan, which has been in a state of inertia over the past two decades, despite the introduction of one stimulus package after another. The United States has now become the last big test for Keynesian economics, and if it fails (as we predict it will) the Keynesian approach will finally pass away.

The alternative to Keynesian economics is modern growth theory, where the supply side of economics returns to have a central role in the workings of an economy. In this approach, technology is king, but the king needs the protection of large markets, competitive prices, profit incentives, rational institutions, free trade, capital accumulation, and non-intrusive govern-ments. Governments have roles to play but only supportive roles. Keynes himself was a great man and a great economist who could understand the failures that occurred during his own times. Those who have read his book *The Economic Consequences of the Peace*, written in 1919, can marvel at his tremendous intellect and foresight. As economists, we can still praise him for his initial understanding of the consumption function—especially since others were able to build better theories on top of his initial insights. Regrettably, the Keynesian approach to macroeconomics should be buried.

One final reminder: Wars do not lead to prosperity. Wars can lead to full employment, but the distortion of production is so great that wars are highly undesirable. Those who believe in war, any war, as a path to prosperity are like people confronting a great illusionist who can convince them that an illusion is in fact true.

NOTES

1. The basic Keynesian approach can be found in practically all elementary textbooks, which will use either graphs or equations. See, for example, Robert H. Frank and Ben S. Bernanke, *Principles of Economics*, 3rd ed. (New York: McGraw-Hill, Irwin 2007), Chapter 26. Bernanke, as of 2010, is still the Chairman of the Federal Reserve Bank.

2. Milton Friedman, *A Theory of the Consumption Function* (Princeton, NJ: Princeton University Press, 1957).

3. Franco Modigliani and Kalman J. Cohen, *The Role of Anticipations and Plans in Economic Behavior and Their Use in Economic Analysis and Forecasting* (Urbana: University of Illinois Press, 1961). The Modigliani articles were pub-lished before this date but we cite this work for easy reference to the reader.

4. Milton Friedman and Anna Schwartz, *A Monetary History of the United States, 1867–1960* (Princeton: Princeton University Press for the National Bureau of Economic Research, 1963).

5. Michael V. White and Kurt Schuler, "Retrospectives: Who Said 'Debauch the Currency': Keynes or Lenin?," *Journal of Economic Perspectives* 23 (2009): 213–22.

6. This legislation is discussed in every standard encyclopedia.

7. Robert M. Solow, "A Contribution to the Theory of Economic Growth," *Quarterly Journal of Economics* 70 (1956): 65–94.

8. Trevor W. Swan, "Economic Growth and Capital Accumulation," *Economic Record* 32 (1956) : 334–61.

9. Paul M. Romer, "Government Spending in a Simple Model of Endogenous Growth," *Journal of Political Economy* 98 (1990) and "Increasing Returns and Long-Term Growth," *Journal of Political Economy*, 94 (1986).

10. Robert E. Lucas, *Studies in Business Cycle Theory* (Cambridge, MA: MIT Press, 1981).

11. Robert J. Barro, *Macroeconomics* (New York: Wiley, 1984).

12. The cost of war is a theme that has been analyzed by Niall Ferguson in *The Cash Nexus: Money and Power in the Modern World, 1700–2000* (New York: Basic Books, 2001) and in *The War of the World: Twentieth-Century Conflict and the Descent of the West* (New York: Penguin, 2006).

13. Robert J. Barro, "Are Government Bonds Net Wealth?," *Journal of Political Economy* 82 (1974): 1095–1117.

Chapter 13

PUTTING IT ALL TOGETHER

One often wonders why it is so difficult to determine the truth; this is the case at the personal, group, or even societal level. The reason is that biases and emotions prevent us from being objective, and sometimes issues are so complex that unraveling their structure simply takes a long time—from years to decades to even centuries. The Germans of the 1930s followed a madman into self-destruction because foreseeing the consequences of Hitler's actions proved emotionally impossible to them. Almost a century after the Great War (now known as the First World War), historians still debate whether the United States' participation in that war was to its collective advantage. The cost of the war "to end all wars" was tremendous loss of human life and political upheaval for years to come; and since the benefits continue to be difficult to quantify, historians wonder if U.S. participation in the war was one of the great debacles in American foreign policy.

The above paragraph should make it clear that while we believe that we have determined the roots of our current economic crisis, it will take years to ascertain whether we are correct. It will also take years to determine whether the crisis is as serious as we make it out to be, or whether simple but drastic macroeconomic policies (as advocated and implemented by the Obama administration) will suffice to get us out of the economic downturn. We have tried to provide the reader with both tools and evidence in favor of our view, which we summarize here as follows: The wealth of a country depends on its productivity, and that productivity is significantly affected by the institutional arrangements that determine the organization of production and consumption. There is no doubt that some macroeconomic policies (controlled by the government) can potentially advance or harm the productive capacity of a country, but we have argued, using economic analysis and case studies, that placing the emphasis on those policies is a misguided approach to solving the current economic problems.

HOW THE CHAPTERS FIT TOGETHER

We began by asserting that the concept of wealth is captured by balance sheets, where we have to measure the productive potential of assets and the negative consequences of liabilities. However, we urged the reader to think of liabilities in two different senses: traditionally, as *debts* that must be paid in the future, and nontraditionally, as *drawbacks* that decrease the earning potential of assets—including people, natural resources, physical capital, or even technology. This unconventional use of liabilities shows that assets may be more or less productive depending upon the circumstances that they face. We made it clear that when we look at the wealth of society as a whole, we must look at the balance sheets of individuals, households, firms, and even governments (at various levels).

Chapter 1, then, provided the tools (balance sheets) that make us aware of how well we are doing in accumulating aggregate wealth. In a recession or depression, wealth is going to be destroyed, either because assets become less productive or because debt is rising, but we must determine the reasons why this is taking place. This approach is much broader than simply taking into account good or bad macroeconomic policies, but it does not exclude them from the analysis. The emphasis of the chapter is on factors of production (land, labor, physical capital, and technical know-how) but we also assert that social capital (which involves trust and other relationships that are incorporated in culture and institutions) is also important.

Furthermore, when people and economic entities make economic decisions, the assumption is made that all economic players are well informed. Note that this assumption precedes the analysis of how well institutions could perform; for even if our institutions were the most productive that we could design, when decision makers do not know what is happening, their decisions fail to address reality.

Chapter 2, then, addressed the issue of lack of information, partial information, and even misinformation, with the media being the main purveyors of misinformation. Economics as a science emphasizes that decision makers must take into account real variables and not nominal variables; for example, discussions about interest rates that do not take into account expected inflation are worthless as tools of economic analysis. The same is true for prices and wages in one industry that do not take into account prices and wages in all other industries. Interest rates are especially important because they tie all future monetary values into a common denominator (called present value) that adjusts for the value of time. The government, of course, can influence nominal interest rates via macroeconomic policies, but the value of time is determined by people's circumstances and preferences. When the government manipulates nominal interest rates, information for decision makers becomes more costly, for they need to figure out the real rates. Some entities may make money as a result of these manipulations, but this does not mean that the economy is better off in the sense of being more productive.

Chapter 2 also addressed informational problems in labor markets, the difficulty of determining the value of money in financial portfolios, and the informational problems in international trade. When we put together all of these informational problems, we realize that they create uncertainly in the value of both assets and liabilities—thereby making it more difficult to calculate the value of wealth for individuals, households, firms, and governments. If these decision makers fail to take into account informational problems, they are bound to make the wrong decisions; and if they do take them into account, their decisions become more costly, for they have to use resources to overcome the existing uncertainty. Either way, lack of information, partial information, or misinformation is bound to make us all poorer.

Chapter 3 began our first case studies. To put it in context, we repeat that misinformation is widely diffused. What, then, is the institutional arrangement that is capable of conveying valuable information to the average participant in the economy? The answer is simple: the market process. It is literally impossible for an egg producer, for example, to know the aggregate demand for eggs in an individual market, but he or she knows that if the price of eggs is rising (in real terms, after adjusting for inflation) then a greater effort should be devoted to the production of eggs; if the real price of eggs is falling, then fewer eggs need to be produced. The free market system is the main purveyor of valuable information.

The importance of this chapter is that it shows how government regulation interferes with the role that markets play. While markets require regulations that set the rules of the game, often enough excessive regulations create incentives that impair the productive behavior of firms, giving rise to the wrong market signals. The chapter takes on the CAFE laws, nuclear power, and privacy laws. The CAFE regulations forced U.S. auto companies to produce vehicles in which they did not have a cost advantage. The U.S. nuclear power industry has been shackled by regulations that do not apply in other developed countries (such as West European countries), thereby distorting the price of energy within the United States. Privacy laws, in turn, undermine the workings of labor markets, as people place less trust in letters of recommendation and individuals with various disorders are allowed to acquire educational levels for which they are unsuited. The negative impact of privacy laws on labor markets is both broad-based and nefarious.

In all of the above cases, the impact on wealth is pervasive. CAFE regulations lower the productivity of the auto industry, thereby reducing wealth. Constraints on nuclear power give rise to risky investments in deep off-shore wells that can have devastating environmental consequences. The excessive regulation of the nuclear industry also has an economy-wide impact, as the prices of alternative sources of energy rise and the price of energy fails to reflect potentially lower production costs. This in itself undermines the informational role of the market for energy. Privacy laws introduce uncertainty in labor markets, raising the cost of obtaining valuable information. Wealth is thereby reduced.

Chapter 4 illustrated how the various markets producing health care are supposed to work. The chapter pinpoints the unfunded liabilities (in the traditional sense) of our current mixed public-private system. It then considers two alternatives to the current system: a government-run universal health care arrangement, and what we call value-based competition among health care providers. The chapter is carefully nuanced in its discussion of costs and benefits of the two approaches, but we conclude that we prefer more rather than less competition in the health care sector. We recognize, however, that no matter which approach is chosen, health care is bound to absorb a significant amount of resources. Because the United States faces a budget constraint, choosing more health care translates into choosing fewer other commodities.

Chapter 5 took a unique approach to health and education. There we argued that if people had a full understanding of the effectiveness of medical treatments, they might possibly choose less health care and more lifestyle changes. Regrettably, the "need" for health care is so entrenched in our group psychology that the writers of this book despair about the possibility of making radical changes to health care. Our analysis suggested that once values are introduced into the discussion of health issues, it may well be impossible to reach a national consensus on the provision of health care. If that is true, health care should be provided at the state or regional level where people could then decide, based upon their personal values, which trade-offs they find acceptable.

The rest of the chapter argues that improvements in cognitive abilities in the population should replace the goal of achieving simply more schooling for people. The chapter makes a distinction between these two goals and explains why the introduction of more machines (including computers) would not only improve the curriculum but also replace teaching staff. These changes would not just improve the productive capacity of our human capital but free people to do work in other areas of the economy—thereby increasing the labor force available for other productive processes. Our productive potential and wealth will diminish in relative terms when other countries adopt modern technologies and do better in the educational field. An important source is cited that demonstrates that teachers' unions are restraining technological advancement and productivity in the classrooms.

Chapter 6 took on the power of labor unions, which ends up creating market distortions. The chapter argues that the power of many labor unions rests on raw political power. Labor unions have been extremely costly to U.S. auto companies and other business enterprises. Fringe benefits that are payable in the future also increase the liabilities of unionized companies, making them poorer; and the union-imposed restrictions on the use of assets reduce the value of assets and the market value of companies. This chapter illustrates *par excellence* the main thrust of this book; namely, that the competitive nature of enterprises can be diminished when both their assets are impaired and their liabilities are increased. Keeping companies afloat via bailouts also has a negative impact on other producers of the same goods, as too much output in the market forces the price of the goods to fall. This is a clear case where macroeconomic policies (in the form of bailouts) end up having a negative impact on the workings of the micro economy, for prices are distorted and too much of the wrong goods are produced.

Chapter 7 explained how political decisions can trump economic decisions, using the housing market for illustrative purposes. While many people would agree that in an ideal world everyone should own a home, government attempts to impose this view on the housing market led, in an inexorable way, to the creation of a housing bubble that was unsustainable and was thoroughly destructive of the financial sector. The chapter tells how the current economic crisis was triggered by the housing bubble, which in turn was caused by political ideology and a financial sector that abandoned any semblance of conservative (risk-averse) economic behavior. Politicians and big-time financiers colluded to make themselves both popular and rich, regardless of the consequences to the nation. What the chapter describes is not the workings of a free market, where competitors expose the risks and malfeasance of their peers, but rather crony capitalism driven to destruction by political ideologues.

Government can flex its muscles when it wants to do so, and Chapter 8 developed this theme in its most destructive scenario: our engagement in war. Both Korea and Vietnam were very costly and very unpopular wars. The same can be said for the current wars in Iraq and Afghanistan. The chapter demonstrates that these wars take up a significant amount of our economic resources. We fail to address the benefits of these wars because they are not truly quantifiable; therefore we argue that our country should not engage in wars unless they are totally necessary, as when an opponent first attacks us—as in the Second World War. The wisdom of our engagement in the First World War is still being questioned by historians. Wars have very limited value as agents of economic change and prosperity, and, like natural catastrophes, they can only make us poorer (even when they reduce unemployment).

Chapters 9 and 10 are different from others in that they covered not only the excesses of regulation and taxation but also provided alternative institutional arrangements. Chapter 9 evaluated solving the pollution problems via regulations, and drew the conclusion that market-based solutions make far more sense than government regulations. If we are right, then U.S. wealth would rise with market-based solutions. Similarly Chapter 10 evaluated the U.S. system of taxation, demonstrating that given its high cost and negative consequences for labor markets, we would be better off with a combination of the "fair" and the "flat" tax. Institutional change has the potential to make us wealthier.

Chapter 11 went beyond criticizing regulations and into the analysis of direct government participation in the economy. It also served to summarize an idea that was central in many previous discussions: the optimal level of any activity. When the private sector refuses to produce a service at below-production costs, the government can flex its muscles and subsidize that activity. This has happened in the case of insurance, where taxpayers as a group (via forced taxation) provide insurance for high-risk activities that the private sector would not provide.

We had noted in the text that no one is against privacy laws, but everyone should be against *excessive* privacy—when the additional costs of privacy exceed the additional benefits that privacy can bring. The same argument holds true for insurance. Those who are insured against certain risks will be willing to ignore them and as a result engage in productive activities; but how far is it worthwhile to insure? When the private sector charges too high a premium (because the risks are excessive) then people and entities will change their behavior and will not seek insurance. However, if the government steps in and subsidizes the insurance premiums, then excessive risk behavior will result—and this is likely to lead to disaster. Chapter 11 covered Hurricane Katrina, flood insurance, and the current bailout of financial institutions. In the first two cases, social wealth has decreased because government interference led to disaster; and the chapter argued that a similar disaster is waiting to happen with the current bailouts of financial institutions.

Chapter 12 will be addressed in the section that follows.

POLICY IMPLICATIONS

It should be obvious to the reader that our approach to the current economic crisis does not involve the use of macroeconomic tools, which are made up of fiscal and monetary policies. These tools are part and parcel of what is known as Keynesian economics, and, while we have a very high regard for John Maynard Keynes as an economist from the past, we believe that his policy instruments do not fit well with our current understanding of why our economy has gone into crisis.

We have argued in this book that long-term growth depends on productivity, and neither fiscal nor monetary policies squarely address this issue. Keynesian economics addresses the demand for goods and services, but few could argue that the Bush administration, which had enormous budget deficits, was facing a lack of demand for domestic output. In fact, domestic demand was so strong that it needed to be supplemented with the purchase of many goods from abroad. The budget deficits have continued unabated during the Obama adminstration, which has proposed in February 2010 a federal budget of $3.8 trillion for fiscal year 2011 while we are currently experiencing a $1.6 trillion deficit for fiscal year 2010.

The theoretical underpinnings of Keynesian economics are the subject matter of Chapter 12, which was written as a response to those who feel that Keynesian tools need to be applied under current conditions. The traditional argument runs to the effect that Keynesian tools are needed because we were able to get out of the Great Depression only after we became involved in the Second World War and spent ourselves out of the depression. However, Chapter 12 made it clear that wars are destructive of assets, and that they cannot provide a solution to the current lack of productivity.

The United States does not lack demand; it lacks an economic foundation that is competitive with the economic base that has been developed abroad in recent years. The U.S. car manufacturers have been unable to compete with foreigners because labor costs have been too high and because of CAFE regulations. Energy costs in the United States are too high because we refuse to introduce nuclear power plants as major providers of energy. Labor markets are performing poorly because of the privacy laws that the country has imposed upon itself. People spend too much on education and health care because they are poorly informed about the realistic outcomes that can be expected via the current provision of educational services and excessive health care. The government permits people to live in areas that are bound to be hit by hurricanes and floods, and everyone pays taxes to cover up these mistakes. The ideologues in government promoted a housing bubble that led to an excessive demand for housing and the near collapse of the financial sector. The U.S. tax system is too complicated and costly; and the list goes on.

All of these examples deal with productivity issues, not with macroeconomic policies. We have pointed out in the text that the increase in debt and the increase in the money supply appear to be benefiting only the financial markets—via the creation of another bubble in asset prices. The way this works is as follows: one branch of government creates money, which it lends to financial institutions at a rate of interest close to zero; and then another branch of government borrows that money through the sale of government bonds at much higher interest rates. No wonder the financial sector is doing well, regardless of the underlying problems of the rest of the real economy (that which produces goods and services other than financial services). The close ties among politicians, government agencies, and the big players in the financial sector have not been severed with the election of President Obama. While the financial sector grew and prospered during the Bush years as a result of government support of the housing industry, the financial sector is now propped up by bailouts and the huge expansion of government debt. The means of sustaining crony capitalism have changed but the usual suspects are still on the loose.

We must remember that some countries are wealthier than others because they are more productive—barring the exceptional cases of the few countries that stand above huge oil reserves. Productivity is attained via specialization, technological change, investment in human and physical capital, institutional development, and political stability (which requires fiscal and monetary restraints). Prices must also reflect production costs and serve as the main conveyor of economic information.

When a government fails to adhere to fiscal and monetary restraints (the Obama administration expects budget deficits in the trillions of dollars for years to come), then the government engages in activities that the private sector could instead produce. The partial takeover by the federal government of the auto industry, educational policies, health care, the financial sector, and some types of insurance will undermine markets and private production and, most importantly, has de facto politicized economic relationships.

It makes sense for the federal government to provide national defense—but not offensive wars. It makes sense for the federal government to provide objective rankings of performance in the educational sector and the health care sector—but it makes no sense for it to get involved in the provision of education or health care. These services should be left to local communities and the states, which would then be in a position to experiment with alternative arrangements.

We the people have given the government the right to tax and redistribute income, but all of this must be done above board and with clear justification. Trade restrictions do tax and redistribute income, but their consequences are not made transparent. Taxes need to be made simple, and there cannot be a *large* segment of the population not paying income taxes while a *small* segment pays the vast share of those taxes. This is bound to create class warfare.

The government can subsidize activities that build up knowledge and infrastructure because these activities have big payoffs for all the people. Also, the government should prosecute monopolies, whether in the business or labor sectors. This means that the U.S. government should attack the OPEC cartel relentlessly and also curtail the power of labor unions.

Americans, as a society, need to respond to behaviors by people, firms, and governments that impair or make costly the productive activities of others by creating new property rights that protect resources and allow for the trading of those rights. Regulations that go beyond setting the rules of the game should only be used when everything else fails. The consequences of regulations are often too difficult to predict and usually too costly to enforce.

The nation stands at the crossroads of its economic life. We can choose to be more productive by making the necessary institutional change, or we can choose to have the government deliver more goods, more regulations, and more restraints upon all of us. Crony capitalism (consisting of collusion among market players and government officials) must be defeated by market competition and a stop to the excessive growth of the money supply and the public debt. Productivity growth is what made the nation rich in the past, and that is what the authors of this book choose for its future. Which, then, is the reader's choice?

INDEX

About the Authors

NICOLÁS SÁNCHEZ has a Ph.D. in economics from the University of Southern California (1972) and has taught at Texas A&M University and at the College of the Holy Cross, where he is currently Professor of Economics. He has published many academic articles for top economic journals, such as *The Review of Economics and Statistics*, *Economic Development and Cultural Change*, *Journal of Economic Behavior and Organization*, *Land Economics*, *The American Journal of Agricultural Economics*, *Weltwirtschaftliches Archiv*, *Cuadernos de Economía*, and many others. He has also published chapters in scholarly books and has written over 150 articles for the popular press. He has been a guest lecturer at several American universities and also at universities in Mexico, Puerto Rico, and Spain. He enjoys city life.

CHRISTOPHER KOPP is an undergraduate majoring in economics and mathematics at the College of the Holy Cross. Chris is a member of the Economics Department and College Honors Programs, and his primary academic interests include the study of macroeconomics and financial markets. Chris has also studied international macroeconomics at the London School of Economics and Political Science. He graduated from Saint Francis High School in his hometown of Hamburg, New York, in 2007. Outside of the classroom Chris is an airplane pilot and enjoys the outdoors.

FRANCIS SANZARI is an undergraduate economics and political science double major at the College of the Holy Cross. A member of the Economics Department and College Honors Programs, his academic interests outside of economics include the study of American public policy. He graduated in 2007 from William Hall High School in his hometown of West Hartford, Connecticut. He spent the summer of 2010 working in international business in Malaysia and Singapore. An Eagle Scout, Francis particularly enjoys hiking, camping, and the outdoors.